The Facts Of M

Murder is the willful killing of one person by another.

It is estimated by the Federal Bureau of Investigation that:
Almost 24,000 Americans
were murdered every year for the last five years.
77% of murder victims are males.
23% of murder victims are females.
91% of murderers are males.
90% of female murder victims are killed by males.
87% of murder victims are eighteen or older,
85% of murderers are eighteen or older.
48% of murder victims are ages 20 to 34.
51% of murder victims are black.
94% of black murder victims are killed by other blacks.
46% of murder victims are white.
84% of white murder victims are killed by other whites.
70% of victims are murdered with firearms.
47% of murder victims knew their murderers.
35% of murder victims were acquainted with their murderers.
12% of murder victims were related to their murderers.
29% of females murder victims
were killed by their husbands or boyfriends.
3% of male murder victims
were killed by their wives or girlfriends.
29% of murders result from arguments.
19% of murders result from robberies.
41% of murders occur in the Southern States.
23% of murders occur in the Western States.
19% of murders occur in the Midwestern States.
17% of murders occur in the Northeastern States.
The most murders occur in December.
The fewest murders occur in February.
The murder rate in metropolitan areas
is more than twice the murder rate in rural areas.
There is one murder in America every twenty-one minutes.

Murder Is A Brutal Fact Of Life.
The Murder Reference Is About The Facts Of Murder.

Warning - Disclaimer

THE MURDER REFERENCE

**Everything You Never Wanted
To Know About Murder In America**

MAUREEN HARRISON & STEVE GILBERT
EDITORS

EXCELLENT BOOKS
SAN DIEGO, CALIFORNIA

EXCELLENT BOOKS
Post Office Box 927105
San Diego, CA 92192-7105

Copyright © 1996 by Excellent Books. Printed in the U.S.A.

"This publication is designed to provide accurate and authoritative information in regard to the subject matter covered. It is sold with the
understanding that the publisher is not engaged in rendering legal or
other professional service. If legal advice or other expert assistance is
required, the services of a competent professional person should be
sought." - From a Declaration of Principles jointly adopted by a Committee of the American Bar Association and a Committee of Publishers.

Publisher's Cataloging in Publication Data
The Murder Reference: Everything You Never Wanted To Know
About Murder In America/
  Maureen Harrison, Steve Gilbert, editors.
     p. cm. -
Bibliography: p.
1. Murder. 2. Murder - United States. 3. Murder - Law and Legisla-
tion - United States. 4. Murder - Bibliography. 5. Murder - Statistics.
6. Murder Victims. 7. Mass Murder. 8. Serial Murder.
I. Title. II. Harrison, Maureen. III. Gilbert, Steve.

HV6524 H24 1995   LC 96-83104
364.1'523'0973-dc20

ISBN 1-880780-12-7

Introduction

Murder most foul, strange and unnatural.
                    - **William Shakespeare's Hamlet**

Murder is a brutal fact of life.

Almost *twenty-four thousand* Americans were murdered in 1995. Every year since 1965 at least ten thousand Americans have been murdered. Almost every year since 1973 at least twenty thousand Americans have been murdered. In only the first five years of this decade more than twice as many Americans were murdered as were killed in the entire ten-year Vietnam War. Murder is now ranked third (after only accidental death and suicide) of all non-disease deaths in America.

The Murder Reference is about the facts of murder.

This book is designed by its editors, a law librarian and a textbook editor, to be the all-in-one comprehensive resource for readers, writers, and researchers studying murder in America. *The Murder Reference* is made up of four complementary elements:

In Chapter I: *America's Murder Laws,* you will find selected excerpts from the criminal murder laws of all fifty states, carefully edited into plain non-legal English for the general reader.

In Chapter II: *Murder Statistics* you will find the real "who, what, when, and where" facts and figures of murder in America, drawn from authoritative federal and state law enforcement sources and offering both a historical and contemporary overview of murder in America.

In Chapter III: *The Chronology Of Headline Murders,* you will find a selection of twentieth century murders that so outraged and traumatized the public, either by their brutality, depravity, or insanity, that they have become a part of our common memory.

In Chapter IV: *Murder Ink,* you will find an annotated bibliography of hundreds of well-written, thoroughly researched, nonfiction, "true murder" books, including the classic murder studies: Truman Capote's *In Cold Blood,* Vincent Bugliosi's *Helter Skelter,* and Norman Mailer's *The Executioner's Song.*

Murder is not entertainment, not *The Texas Chainsaw Massacre, Jason, Freddie* or *Chuckie*. The murders described in this book are actual nightmares, not on the mythical "Elm Street," but on all of America's Main Streets. *The Murder Reference* is not about fictional blood and gore, but about actual facts and law.

In the *The Murder Reference* you will find an *A-Z*, coast-to-coast, collection of all the facts and figures of murder in our own time, from Atlanta's "Child Murders" to San Francisco's "Zodiac Killings."

Every American hometown, urban, suburban, rural, has a heinous murderer it cannot forget:

New York City's David Berkowitz. Pensacola, Florida's Ted Bundy. Houston, Texas' Dean Corell. Milwaukee, Wisconsin's Jeffrey Dahmer. Lincoln, Nebraska's Charlie Starkweather. San Antonio, Texas' Genene Jones. Boston's Albert DeSalvo. Plainfield, Wisconsin's Ed Gein. Fort Bragg, North Carolina's Jeffrey MacDonald. Orem, Utah's Gary Gilmore. Yuba City, California's Juan Corona. San Diego's Oliver Huberty. Austin, Texas' Charles Whitman. Chicago's Richard Speck and John Wayne Gacy. Seattle's "Green River Killer." Los Angeles' "Manson Family," "Nightstalker," and "Hillside Stranglers."

Every American hometown, urban, suburban, rural, has an innocent murder victim it will not forget:

Cortland, New York's Grace "Billie" Brown. Atlanta's Mary Phagan. New Brunswick, New Jersey's Edward Hall and Eleanor Mills. Chicago's Bobby Franks. Hopewell, New Jersey's "Lindbergh Baby." New York City's Janice Wylie and Emily Hoffert, Jennifer Levin, John Lennon, Yusef Hawkins, and Kitty Genovese. Holcomb, Kansas' Clutter Family. Amityville, Long Island's DeFeo Family. Clarksville, Pennsylvania's Yablonski Family. San Francisco's Harvey Milk. Boston's Carol Stuart. Los Angeles' Sharon Tate, Dorothy Stratten, Nicole Brown Simpson, and Ronald Goldman. Petaluma, California's Polly Klass. Union, South Carolina's Michael and Alex Smith.

The murderers and victims peopling the pages of *The Murder Reference* are unforgettable, haunting our collective memories and scarring our communal consciences. What murderer, what murder victim, can your hometown not forget?

The more times change:

In the pages of an eighteenth century *Murder Reference* could have been found Pilgrim John Billington who in 1620 murdered a fellow Mayflower passenger in the Plymouth Colony; or Dorothy Talbye who in 1638 murdered her baby daughter in the Massachusetts Bay Colony; or Jeremiah Meacham who in 1715 murdered his wife and sister in Newport, Rhode Island; or Bathsheba Spooner who in 1778 killed her husband in Brookfield, Massachusetts; or William Beadle who in 1783 murdered his whole family in Weathersfield, Connecticut.

And change again:

In the pages of a nineteenth century *Murder Reference* could have been found the 1850 "Harvard Yard" Murder by Professor John Webster in Cambridge, Massachusetts; or Samuel Green, New England's first serial murderer; or New York City's product tampering murderer, "The Bromo Seltzer" Killer; or Hester Vaughn, who in 1868 murdered her newborn baby in Philadelphia; or young Lizzie Borden, acquitted in 1892 for the double murders of her parents in Fall River, Massachusetts; or the execution, in 1896, after a sensational trial, of serial sex murderer H.H. Holmes.

The more murder remains the same:

In the pages of the just-published *Murder Reference* you will find the actual murder laws, up-to-date murder facts and figures, true murder studies, and complete murder stories for the almost completed twentieth century.

If there were to be a twenty-first century *Murder Reference*, we fear that only the names of the murderers and the numbers of their victims would change.

Murder, no matter when committed, is in the exact meaning of Shakespeare's words: *foul* (filthy and obscene), *strange* (bizarre and aberrant) and *unnatural* (monstrous and grotesque). Murder is a brutal fact of life. *The Murder Reference* is about the facts of murder.

- M.H. & S.G.

We wrote this book because in an incomprehensibly obscene act of violence someone we loved was murdered.

We dedicate this book to our cousin Betty with the timeless words of mourning from Shakespeare's *Romeo and Juliet.*

> *Her blood is settled, and her joints are stiff;*
> *Life and these lips have long been separated:*
> *Death lies on her like an untimely frost*
> *Upon the sweetest flower of all the fields.*

> *Thou shall not kill.*
>   **- The Old Testament**

> *Slay no one.*
>   **- The Koran**

Table Of Contents

America's Murder Laws

Every unpunished murder takes away something from the security of every man's life.

- Daniel Webster

Murder is defined as the willful killing of one person by another, committed with either malice aforethought, when done purposely, when done recklessly, or when committed with depraved indifference to the value of a human life.

In *America's Murder Laws* you will find selected excerpts from current murder laws of all fifty states and the District of Columbia, carefully edited into plain non-legal English. These selected edited excerpts are drawn from the official "black letter" law as found in each state's criminal code. These "black letter" laws have gone through a two-step selection/editing process before their inclusion in *The Murder Reference.*

First, we have made "look" and "feel" selections from each jurisdiction's basic murder law. Every state has written into its murder law certain general murder definitions and provisions and we look at many of these basic definitions and provisions to give the reader a feel for how each state protects the innocent, prosecutes the accused, and punishes the guilty.

Second, for all these "look" and "feel" provisions we have made every effort to edit esoteric legalese to easy-to-read plain English without altering either the original content or context of the law. If we have erred in our editing, it was consciously on the side of caution. Where indicated by [brackets] we have added our own plain English definitions of esoteric legal terms and where indicated by ellipses (. . . .) we have deleted redundant "wherefore/therefore" sections.

These selected excerpts do not contain the complete murder laws for any one state. For each state we have provided at the end of the edited selection a citation to the original state criminal code sources of the "black letter" murder law provisions. These provisions can be found in your state's criminal code at either your local public library, law school library, or county law library. It is these official "black letter" murder law provisions, not our selected edited excepts, that are the law in each jurisdiction.

United States Supreme Court Justice Oliver Wendell Holmes, Jr. summed up his feeling on American murder law in this way:

> *Although it is not likely that a criminal will carefully consider the text of the law before he murders, it is reasonable that a fair warning should be given to the world in language that the common world will understand, of what the law intends to do if a certain line is passed. To make the warning fair, so far as possible, the line should be clear.*

The murder laws that follow are the line that has been drawn.

ALABAMA'S MURDER LAWS

Definitions

Homicide. A person commits criminal homicide if he intentionally, knowingly, recklessly, or with criminal negligence causes the death of another person.

Person. Such term, when referring to the victim of a criminal homicide, means a human being who had been born and was alive at the time of the homicidal act.

Criminal Homicide. Murder, manslaughter, or criminally negligent homicide.

(Alabama Criminal Code 13A-6-1)

Murder

A person commits the crime of murder if:

    (1) with intent to cause the death of another person, he causes the death of that person or of another person;

    (2) under circumstances manifesting extreme indifference to human life, he recklessly engages in conduct which creates a grave risk of death to a person other than himself, and thereby causes the death of another person; or

    (3) he commits or attempts to commit arson in the first degree, burglary in the first or second degree, escape in the first degree, kidnapping in the first degree, rape in the first degree, robbery in any degree, sodomy in the first degree or any other felony clearly dangerous to human life and, in the course of and in furtherance of the crime that he is committing or attempting to commit, or in immediate flight therefrom, he, or another participant if there be any, causes the death of any person.

A person does not commit murder under (paragraphs 1 or 2 above) if he was moved to act by a sudden heat of passion caused by provocation recognized by law, and before there had been a reasonable time for the passion to cool and for reason to reassert itself.

Murder is a Class A felony; the punishment for murder or any offense committed under aggravated circumstances . . . is death or life imprisonment without parole.
(Alabama Criminal Code 13A-6-2)

Manslaughter

A person commits the crime of manslaughter if:
> (1) he recklessly causes the death of another person; or
> (2) he causes the death of another person under circumstances that would constitute murder under [the above murder provision]; except, that he causes the death due to a sudden heat of passion caused by provocation recognized by law, and before a reasonable time for the passion to cool and for reason to reassert itself.

Manslaughter is a Class B felony.
(Alabama Criminal Code 13A-6-3)

Criminally Negligent Homicide

A person commits the crime of criminally negligent homicide if he causes the death of another person by criminal negligence. The jury may consider statutes and ordinances regulating the actor's conduct in determining whether he is culpably negligent.

Criminally negligent homicide is a Class A misdemeanor, except in cases in which said criminally negligent homicide is caused by the driver of a motor vehicle who is driving in violation of [the section of the law concerning driving under the influence of alcohol or drugs]; in such cases criminally negligent homicide is a Class C felony.
(Alabama Criminal Code 13A-6-4)

The complete and unedited text of Alabama's murder laws excerpted above can be found in the Criminal Code of the Acts of Alabama.

ALASKA'S MURDER LAWS

Definitions

Person, when referring to the victim of a crime, means a human being who has been born and was alive at the time of the criminal act.

Alive means that there is spontaneous respiratory or cardiac function or, when respiratory and cardiac functions are maintained by artificial means, there is spontaneous brain function. (Alaska Criminal Law 11.41.140)

First Degree Murder

A person commits the crime of murder in the first degree if:

    (1) with intent to cause the death of another person, the person:

      (a) causes the death of any person; or

      (b) compels or induces any person to commit suicide through duress or deception; or

    (2) the person knowingly engages, under circumstances manifesting extreme indifference to the value of human life, in a pattern or practice of assault or torture of a child under the age of sixteen, and one of the acts of assault or torture results in the death of the child; for purposes of this paragraph, a person "engages in a pattern or practice of assault or torture" if the person inflicts serious physical injury to the child by at least two separate acts, and one of the acts results in the death of the child.

Murder in the first degree is an unclassified felony. (Alaska Criminal Law 11.41.100)

Second Degree Murder

A person commits the crime of murder in the second degree if:

    (1) with intent to cause serious physical injury to another person or knowing that the conduct is substantially certain to cause death or serious physical injury to another person, the person causes the death of any person;

    (2) the person knowingly engages in conduct that results in the death of another person under circum-

stances manifesting an extreme indifference to the value of human life; or

(3) acting either alone or with one or more persons, the person commits or attempts to commit arson in the first degree, kidnapping, sexual assault in the first or second degree, burglary in the first degree, escape in the first or second degree, or robbery in any degree and, in the course of or in furtherance of that crime, or in immediate flight from that crime, any person causes the death of a person other than one of the participants.

Murder in the second degree is an unclassified felony.

(Alaska Criminal Law 11.41.110)

Manslaughter

A person commits the crime of manslaughter if the person:

(1) intentionally, knowingly, or recklessly causes the death of another person under circumstances not amounting to murder in the first or second degree; or

(2) intentionally aids another person to commit suicide.

Manslaughter is a Class A felony.

(Alaska Criminal Law 11.41.120)

Criminally Negligent Homicide

A person commits the crime of criminally negligent homicide if, with criminal negligence, the person causes the death of another person.

Criminally negligent homicide is a Class C felony.

(Alaska Criminal Law 11.41.130)

The complete and unedited text of Alaska's murder laws excerpted above can be found in the Criminal Law of the Alaska Session Laws *or Alaska Statutes.*

ARIZONA'S MURDER LAWS

Definitions

Premeditation means that the defendant acts with either the intention or the knowledge that he will kill another human being, when such intention or knowledge precedes the killing by a length of time to permit reflection. An act is not done with premeditation if it is the instant effect of a sudden quarrel or heat of passion

Homicide means first degree murder, second degree murder, manslaughter, or negligent homicide.

Person means a human being.

Adequate provocation means conduct or circumstances sufficient to deprive a reasonable person of self-control.

(Arizona Criminal Code 13-1101)

First Degree Murder

A person commits first degree murder if:

   (1) intending or knowing that his conduct will cause death, such person causes the death of another with premeditation; or

   (2) acting either alone or with one or more other persons such person commits or attempts to commit sexual conduct with a minor, sexual assault, molestation of a child, marijuana offenses, dangerous drug offenses, narcotics offenses that equal or exceed the statutory threshold amount for each offense or combination of offenses, involving or using minors in drug offenses, kidnapping, burglary, arson, robbery, escape, child abuse, or unlawful flight from a pursuing law enforcement vehicle, and in the course of and in furtherance of such offense or immediate flight from such offense, such person or another person causes the death of any person.

Homicide, as defined in [the previous paragraph], requires no specific mental state other than what is required for the commission of any of the enumerated felonies.

First degree murder is a Class 1 felony and is punishable by death or life imprisonment.

(Arizona Criminal Code 13-1105)

Second Degree Murder

A person commits second degree murder if without premeditation:

(1) such person intentionally causes the death of another person;

(2) knowing that his conduct will cause death or serious physical injury, such person causes the death of another person; or

(3) under circumstances manifesting extreme indifference to human life, such person recklessly engages in conduct which creates a grave risk of death and thereby causes the death of another person.

Second degree murder is a Class 1 felony.

(Arizona Criminal Code 13-1104)

Manslaughter

A person commits manslaughter by:

(1) recklessly causing the death of another person;

(2) committing second degree murder [as defined above] upon a sudden quarrel or heat of passion resulting from adequate provocation by the victim;

(3) intentionally aiding another to commit suicide;

(4) committing second degree murder [as defined above] while being coerced to do so by the use or threatened immediate use of unlawful deadly physical force upon such person or a third person which a reasonable person in his situation would have been unable to resist; or

(5) knowingly or recklessly causing the death of an unborn child at any stage of its development by any physical injury to the mother of such child which would be murder if the death of the mother had occurred.

Manslaughter is a Class 2 felony.

(Arizona Criminal Code 13-1103)

Negligent Homicide

A person commits negligent homicide if with criminal negligence such person causes the death of another person.
Negligent homicide is a Class 4 felony.
(Arizona Criminal Code 13-1102)

The complete and unedited text of Arizona's murder laws excerpted above can be found in the Criminal Code of the Arizona Session Laws *or the* Arizona Revised Statutes Annotated.

ARKANSAS' MURDER LAWS

First Degree Murder

A person commits murder in the first degree if:

(1) acting alone or with one or more other persons, he commits or attempts to commit a felony, and in the course of and in the furtherance of the felony or in immediate flight therefrom, he or an accomplice causes the death of any person under circumstances manifesting extreme indifference to the value of human life;

(2) with a purpose of causing the death of another person, he causes the death of another person; or

(3) he knowingly causes the death of a person fourteen years of age or younger at the time the murder was committed.

It is an affirmative defense to any prosecution under [paragraph (1) above] for an offense in which the defendant was not the only participant that the defendant:

(1) did not commit the homicidal act or in any way solicit, command, induce, procure, counsel, or aid its commission;

(2) was not armed with a deadly weapon;

(3) reasonably believed that no other participant was armed with a deadly weapon; and

(4) reasonably believed that no other participant intended to engage in conduct which could result in death or serious physical injury.

Murder in the first degree is a Class Y felony.

(Arkansas Criminal Code 5-10-102)

Second Degree Murder

A person commits murder in the second degree if:

(1) he knowingly causes the death of another person under circumstances manifesting extreme indifference to the value of human life; or

(2) with the purpose of causing serious physical injury to another person, he causes the death of any person.

Murder in the second degree is a Class B felony.
(Arkansas Criminal Code 5-10-103)

Manslaughter

A person commits manslaughter if:

(1) he causes the death of another person under circumstances that would be murder, except that he causes the death under the influence of extreme emotional disturbance for which there is reasonable excuse. The reasonableness of the excuse shall be determined from the viewpoint of a person in the defendant's situation under the circumstances as he believes them to be;

(2) he purposely causes or aids another person to commit suicide;

(3) he recklessly causes the death of another person;

(4) acting alone or with one or more persons, he commits or attempts to commit a felony, and in the course of and in furtherance of the felony or in immediate flight therefrom:

(a) he or an accomplice negligently causes the death of any person; or

(b) another person who is resisting such offense or flight causes the death of any person.

It is an affirmative defense to any prosecution under [paragraph (4) above] for an offense in which the defendant was not the only participant that the defendant:

(1) did not commit the homicidal act or in any way solicit, command, induce, procure, counsel, or aid its commission;

(2) was not armed with a deadly weapon;

(3) reasonably believed that no other participant was armed with a deadly weapon; and

(4) reasonably believed that no other participant intended to engage in conduct which could result in death or serious physical injury.

Manslaughter is a Class C felony.

(Arkansas Criminal Code 5-10-104)

Negligent Homicide

A person commits negligent homicide if he negligently causes the death of another person, not constituting murder or manslaughter, as a result of operating a vehicle, an aircraft, or a watercraft:

(1) while intoxicated; or

(2) if at that time there is one-tenth of one percent or more by weight of alcohol in the person's blood as determined by a chemical test of the person's blood, urine, breath, or other bodily substance.

A person who violates [the above paragraph, being intoxicated] is guilty of a Class D felony.

A person commits negligent homicide if he negligently causes the death of another person [and] is guilty of a Class A misdemeanor.

For the purpose of this section, "intoxicated" means influenced or affected by the ingestion of alcohol, a controlled substance, any intoxicant, or any combination thereof to such a degree that the driver's reactions, motor skills, and judgment are substantially altered and the driver, therefore, constitutes a clear and substantial danger of physical injury or death to himself and other motorists or pedestrians.

(Arkansas Criminal Code 5-10-105)

The complete and unedited text of Arkansas' murder laws excerpted above can be found in The General Acts of Arkansas *or* Arkansas Statutes Annotated.

CALIFORNIA'S MURDER LAWS

Definitions

Murder is the unlawful killing of a human being, or a fetus, with malice aforethought.

Malice may be express or implied. It is express when there is manifested a deliberate intention unlawfully to take away the life of a fellow creature. It is implied, when no considerable provocation appears, or when the circumstances attending the killing show an abandoned and malignant heart.
(California Penal Code 187/188)

Murder

All murder which is perpetrated by means of a destructive device or explosive, knowing use of ammunition designed primarily to penetrate metal or armor, poison, lying in wait, torture, or by any other kind of willful, deliberate, and premeditated killing, or which is committed in the perpetration of, or attempt to perpetrate, arson, rape, carjacking, robbery, burglary, mayhem, kidnapping, train wrecking, or any act punishable under [the sections of the law concerning sodomy, lewd or lascivious acts involving children, or penetration by a foreign object], or any murder which is perpetrated by means of discharging a firearm from a motor vehicle, intentionally at another person outside of the vehicle with the intent to inflict death, is murder of the first degree. All other kinds of murder are of the second degree.

To prove the killing was "deliberate and premeditated," it shall not be necessary to prove the defendant maturely and meaningfully reflected upon the gravity of his or her act.
(California Penal Code 189)

Manslaughter

Manslaughter is the unlawful killing of a human being without malice. It is of three kinds:

(1) voluntary - upon a sudden quarrel or heat of passion;

(2) involuntary - in the commission of an unlawful act, not amounting to felony; or in the commission of a lawful act which might produce death, in an unlaw-

ful manner, or without due caution and circumspection. This subdivision shall not apply to acts committed in the driving of a vehicle;

(3) vehicular.

This section shall not be construed as making any homicide in
the driving of a vehicle punishable which is not a proximate result of the commission of an unlawful act, not amounting to
felony, or of the commission of a lawful act which might produce death, in an unlawful manner.

Gross negligence shall not be construed [interpreted] as pro-
hibiting or precluding a charge of murder upon facts exhibiting
wantonness and a conscious disregard for life to support a find-
ing of implied malice, or upon facts showing malice.

Voluntary manslaughter is punishable by imprisonment in the
state prison for three, six, or eleven years.

Involuntary manslaughter is punishable by imprisonment in the
state prison for two, three, or four years.

(California Penal Code 192/193)

Vehicular Manslaughter

Gross vehicular manslaughter while intoxicated is the unlawful
killing of a human being without malice aforethought, in the
driving of a vehicle, where the driving was in violation of the
Vehicle Code, and the killing was either the proximate result of
the commission of an unlawful act, not amounting to a felony,
and with gross negligence, or the proximate result of the commission of a lawful act which might produce death, in an unlawful manner, and with gross negligence.

Gross vehicular manslaughter while intoxicated is punishable
by imprisonment in the state prison for four, six, or ten years.

(California Penal Code 191.5)

Excusable Homicide

Homicide is excusable in the following cases:

(1) when committed by accident and misfortune, or in
doing any other lawful act by lawful means, with usual and ordinary caution, and without any unlawful intent;

(2) when committed by accident and misfortune, in the heat of passion, upon any sudden and sufficient provocation, or upon a sudden combat, when no undue advantage is taken, nor any dangerous weapon used, and when the killing is not done in a cruel or unusual manner.

The homicide appearing to be excusable, the person indicted must, upon his trial, be fully acquitted and discharged. (California Penal Code 195/199)

Justifiable Homicide

Homicide is justifiable when committed by public officers and those acting by their command in their aid and assistance, either:

(1) in obedience to any judgment of a competent court;

(2) when necessarily committed in overcoming actual resistance to the execution of some legal process, or in the discharge of any other legal duty; or

(3) when necessarily committed in retaking felons who have been rescued or have escaped, or when necessarily committed in arresting persons charged with felony, and who are fleeing from justice or resisting such arrest.

Homicide is also justifiable when committed by any person in any of the following cases:

(1) when resisting any attempt to murder any person, or to commit a felony, or to do some great bodily injury upon any person;

(2) when committed in defense of habitation, property, or person, against one who manifestly intends or endeavors, by violence or surprise, to commit a felony, or against one who manifestly intends and endeavors, in a violent, riotous or tumultuous manner, to enter the habitation of another for the purpose of offering violence to any person therein;

(3) when committed in the lawful defense of such person, or of a wife or husband, parent, child, master, mistress, or servant of such person, when there is rea-

sonable ground to apprehend a design to commit a felony or to do some great bodily injury, and imminent danger of such design being accomplished; but such person, or the person in whose behalf the defense was made, if he was the assailant or engaged in mutual combat, must really and in good faith have endeavored to decline any further struggle before the homicide was committed; or

(4) when necessarily committed in attempting, by lawful ways and means, to apprehend any person for any felony committed, or in lawfully suppressing any riot, or in lawfully keeping and preserving the peace.

The homicide appearing to be justifiable, the person indicted must, upon his trial, be fully acquitted and discharged.

(California Penal Code 196/197/199)

Three Years and A Day

To make the killing either murder or manslaughter, it is requisite that the party die within three years and a day after the stroke received or the cause of death administered. In the computation of such time, the whole of the day on which the act was done shall be reckoned the first.

(California Penal Code 194)

The complete and unedited text of California's murder laws excerpted above can be found in the Penal Code of either West's Annotated California Code *or* Deering's Annotated California Code.

COLORADO'S MURDER LAWS

Definitions

Homicide means the killing of a person by another.

Person, when referring to the victim of a homicide, means a human being who had been born and was alive at the time of the homicidal act.

After deliberation means not only intentionally but also that the decision to commit the act has been made after the exercise of reflection and judgment concerning the act. An act committed after deliberation is never one which has been committed in a hasty or impulsive manner.

(Colorado Criminal Code 18-3-101)

First Degree Murder

A person commits the crime of murder in the first degree if:

(1) after deliberation and with the intent to cause the death of a person other than himself, he causes the death of that person or of another person;

(2) acting either alone or with one or more persons, he commits or attempts to commit arson, robbery, burglary, kidnapping, sexual assault in the first or second degree, or a Class 3 felony for sexual assault on a child, or the crime of escape, and, in the course of or in furtherance of the crime that he is committing or attempting to commit, or of immediate flight therefrom, the death of a person, other than one of the participants, is caused by anyone;

(3) by perjury . . . he procures the conviction and execution of any innocent person; or

(4) under circumstances evidencing an attitude of universal malice manifesting extreme indifference to the value of human life generally, he knowingly engages in conduct which creates a grave risk of death to a person, or persons, other than himself, and thereby causes the death of another.

It is an affirmative defense to a charge of violating (paragraph 2 above) that the defendant:

(1) was not the only participant in the underlying crime;

(2) did not commit the homicidal act or in any way solicit, request, command, importune, cause, or aid the commission thereof;

(3) was not armed with a deadly weapon;

(4) had no reasonable ground to believe that any other participant was armed with such a weapon, instrument, article, or substance;

(5) did not engage himself in or intend to engage in and had no reasonable ground to believe that any other participant intended to engage in conduct likely to result in death or serious bodily injury; and

(6) endeavored to disengage himself from the commission of the underlying crime or flight therefrom immediately upon having reasonable grounds to believe that another participant is armed with a deadly weapon, instrument, article, or substance, or intended to engage in conduct likely to result in death or serious bodily injury.

Murder in the first degree is a Class 1 felony.

(Colorado Criminal Code 8-3-102)

Second Degree Murder

A person commits the crime of murder in the second degree if he causes the death of a person knowingly, but not after deliberation.

Diminished responsibility due to lack of mental capacity or self-induced intoxication is not a defense to murder in the second degree.

Murder in the second degree is a Class 2 felony.

(Colorado Criminal Code 8-3-103)

Manslaughter

A person commits the crime of manslaughter if:

(1) he recklessly causes the death of another person;

(2) he intentionally causes or aids another person to commit suicide; or

(3) he knowingly causes the death of another person under circumstances where the act causing the death

was performed upon a sudden heat of passion, caused by a serious and highly provoking act of the intended victim, affecting the person killing sufficiently to excite an irresistible passion in a reasonable person; but, if between the provocation and the killing there is an interval sufficient for the voice of reason and humanity to be heard, the killing is murder.

Manslaughter is a Class 4 felony.

(Colorado Criminal Code 18-3-104)

Criminally Negligent Homicide

Any person who causes the death of another person by conduct amounting to criminal negligence commits criminally negligent homicide which is a Class 5 felony.

(Colorado Criminal Code 18-3-105)

Vehicular Homicide

If a person operates or drives a motor vehicle in a reckless manner, and such conduct is the proximate cause of the death of another, he commits vehicular homicide.

If a person operates or drives a motor vehicle while under the influence of alcohol or one or more drugs, or a combination of both alcohol and one or more drugs, and such conduct is the proximate cause of the death of another, he commits vehicular homicide.

Driving under the influence means driving a vehicle when a person has consumed alcohol or one or more drugs, or a combination of alcohol and one or more drugs, which alcohol alone, or one or more drugs alone, or alcohol combined with one or more drugs affect him to a degree that he is substantially incapable, either mentally or physically, or both mentally and physically, of exercising clear judgment, sufficient physical control, or due care in the safe operation of a vehicle.

Vehicular homicide is a Class 4 felony.

(Colorado Criminal Code 18-3-106)

The complete and unedited text of Colorado's murder laws ex-cerpted above can be found in Session Laws of Colorado *or* Colorado Revised Statutes.

CONNECTICUT'S MURDER LAWS

Murder

A person is guilty of murder when, with intent to cause the death of another person, he causes the death of such person or of a third person or causes a suicide by force, duress or deception; except that in any prosecution under this subsection, it shall be an affirmative defense that the defendant committed the proscribed act or acts under the influence of extreme emotional disturbance for which there was a reasonable explanation or excuse, the reasonableness of which is to be determined from the viewpoint of a person in the defendant's situation under the circumstances as the defendant believed them to be, provided nothing contained in this subsection shall constitute a defense to a prosecution for, or preclude a conviction of, manslaughter in the first degree or any other crime.

Evidence that the defendant suffered from a mental disease, mental defect or other mental abnormality is admissible, in a prosecution under (the above paragraph), on the question of whether the defendant acted with intent to cause the death of another person.

Murder is punishable as a Class A felony unless it is a capital felony or murder.

(Connecticut Penal Code 53a-54a)

Felony Murder

A person is guilty of murder when, acting either alone or with one or more persons, he commits or attempts to commit robbery, burglary, kidnapping, sexual assault in the first degree, aggravated sexual assault in the first degree, sexual assault in the third degree, sexual assault in the third degree with a firearm, escape in the first degree, or escape in the second degree and, in the course of and in furtherance of such crime or of flight therefrom, he, or another participant, if any, causes the death of a person other than one of the participants, except that in any prosecution under this section, in which the defendant was not the only participant in the underlying crime, it shall be an affirmative defense that the defendant:

(1) did not commit the homicidal act or in any way solicit, request, command, importune, cause or aid the commission thereof;

(2) was not armed with a deadly weapon, or any dangerous instrument;

(3) had no reasonable ground to believe that any other participant was armed with such a weapon or instrument; and

(4) had no reasonable ground to believe that any other participant intended to engage in conduct likely to result in death or serious physical injury.

(Connecticut Penal Code 53a-54c)

First Degree Manslaughter

A person is guilty of manslaughter in the first degree when:

(1) with intent to cause serious physical injury to another person, he causes the death of such person or of a third person;

(2) with intent to cause the death of another person, he causes the death of such person or of a third person under circumstances which do not constitute murder because he committed the proscribed act or acts under the influence of extreme emotional disturbance, as provided in (the section on murder above), except that the fact that homicide was committed under the influence of extreme emotional disturbance constitutes a mitigating circumstance reducing murder to manslaughter in the first degree and need not be proved in any prosecution initiated under this section; or

(3) under circumstances evincing an extreme indifference to human life, he recklessly engages in conduct which creates a grave risk of death to another person, and thereby causes the death of another person.

Manslaughter in the first degree is a Class B felony.

(Connecticut Penal Code 53a-5)

Second Degree Manslaughter

A person is guilty of manslaughter in the second degree when:

    (1) he recklessly causes the death of another person; or

    (2) he intentionally causes or aids another person, other than by force, duress, or deception, to commit suicide.

Manslaughter in the second degree is a Class C felony. (Connecticut Penal Code 53a-56)

Vehicular Manslaughter

A person is guilty of manslaughter in the second degree with a motor vehicle when, while operating a motor vehicle under the influence of intoxicating liquor or any drug or both, he causes the death of another person as a consequence of the effect of such liquor or drug.

Manslaughter in the second degree with a motor vehicle is a Class C felony and the court shall suspend the motor vehicle operator's license or nonresident operating privilege of any person found guilty under this section for one year. (Connecticut Penal Code 53a-56b)

Criminally Negligent Homicide

A person is guilty of criminally negligent homicide when, with criminal negligence, he causes the death of another person, except where the defendant caused such death by a motor vehicle. Criminally negligent homicide is a Class A misdemeanor. (Connecticut Penal Code 53a-58)

The complete and unedited text of Connecticut's murder laws excerpted above can be found in The General Statutes of Connecticut *or* Connecticut Public Acts.

DELAWARE'S MURDER LAWS

First Degree Murder

A person is guilty of murder in the first degree when he, with criminal negligence, causes the death of another person in the course of and in furtherance of the commission or attempted commission of rape, unlawful sexual intercourse in the first or second degree, kidnapping, arson in the first degree, robbery in the first degree, burglary in the first degree, or immediate flight therefrom.

Murder in the first degree is a Class A felony.

(Delaware Criminal Code 636)

Second Degree Murder

A person is guilty of murder in the second degree when:

(1) he recklessly causes the death of another person under circumstances which manifest a cruel, wicked and depraved indifference to human life; or

(2) in the course of and in furtherance of the commission or attempted commission of any felony not specifically enumerated [under first degree murder, above] or immediate flight therefrom, he, with criminal negligence, causes the death of another person.

Murder in the second degree is a Class B felony.

(Delaware Criminal Code 635)

Manslaughter

A person is guilty of manslaughter when:

(1) he recklessly causes the death of another person;

(2) with intent to cause serious physical injury to another person he causes the death of such person, employing means which would to a reasonable man in the defendant's situation, knowing the facts known to him, seem likely to cause death;

(3) he intentionally causes the death of another person under circumstances which do not constitute murder because he acts under the influence of extreme emotional disturbance;

(4) he commits upon a female an abortion which causes her death, unless such abortion is a therapeutic

abortion and the death is not the result of reckless conduct; or

(5) he intentionally causes another person to commit suicide.

Manslaughter is a Class C felony.

(Delaware Criminal Code 632)

Vehicular Homicide

A person is guilty of vehicular homicide in the first degree when while in the course of driving or operating a motor vehicle under the influence of alcohol or drugs, his criminally negligent driving or operation of said vehicle causes the death of another person.

Vehicular homicide in the first degree is a Class E felony.

A person is guilty of vehicular homicide in the second degree when:

(1) while in the course of driving or operating a motor vehicle, his criminally negligent driving or operation of said vehicle causes the death of another person; or

(2) while in the course of driving or operating a motor vehicle, under the influence of alcohol or drugs, his negligent driving or operation of said vehicle causes the death of another person.

Vehicular homicide in the second degree is a Class F felony.

(Delaware Criminal Code 630/630A)

Negligent Homicide

A person is guilty of criminally negligent homicide when, with criminal negligence, he causes the death of another person.

Criminally negligent homicide is a Class E felony.

(Delaware Criminal Code 631)

Assisted Suicide

A person is guilty of promoting suicide when he intentionally causes or aids another person to attempt suicide, or when he intentionally aids another person to commit suicide.

Promoting suicide is a Class F felony.

(Delaware Criminal Code 645)

The complete and unedited text of Delaware's murder laws excerpted above can be found in The Delaware Code Annotated *or* The Laws of Delaware.

DISTRICT OF COLUMBIA'S MURDER LAWS

First Degree Murder

Whoever, being of sound memory and discretion, kills another purposely, either of deliberate and premeditated malice or by means of poison, or in perpetrating or attempting to perpetrate any offense punishable by imprisonment in the penitentiary, or without purpose so to do kills another in perpetrating or in attempting to perpetrate any arson, rape, mayhem, robbery, or kidnapping, or in perpetrating or attempting to perpetrate any housebreaking while armed with or using a dangerous weapon, or in perpetrating or attempting to perpetrate a felony involving a controlled substance, is guilty of murder in the first degree.

The punishment for murder in the first degree shall be life imprisonment, except that the court may impose a punishment of life imprisonment without parole.

In determining the sentence, the court shall consider whether, beyond a reasonable doubt, any of the following aggravating circumstances exist:

(1) the murder was committed in the course of kidnapping or abduction, or an attempt to kidnap or abduct;

(2) the murder was committed for hire;

(3) the murder was committed for the purpose of avoiding or preventing a lawful arrest or effecting an escape from custody;

(4) the murder was especially heinous, atrocious, or cruel;

(5) the murder was a drive-by or random shooting;

(6) there was more than one offense of murder in the first degree arising out of one incident;

(7) the murder was committed because of the victim's race, color, religion, national origin, or sexual orientation;

(8) the murder was committed while committing or attempting to commit a robbery, arson, rape, or sexual offense;

(9) the murder was committed because the victim was or had been a witness in any criminal investigation or judicial proceeding, or the victim was capable of providing or had provided assistance in any criminal investigation or judicial proceeding; or

(10) the murder victim was especially vulnerable due to age or a mental or physical infirmity.

If the court finds that one or more aggravating circumstances exist, a sentence of life imprisonment without parole may be imposed.

[A] person convicted of first-degree murder and upon whom a sentence of life imprisonment is imposed shall be eligible for parole only after the expiration of thirty years from the date of the commencement of the sentence.

(District of Columbia Criminal Code 22-2401/2404/2404.1)

Second Degree Murder

Whoever with malice aforethought . . . kills another, is guilty of murder in the second degree.

(District of Columbia Criminal Code 22-2403)

The complete and unedited text of the District of Columbia's murder laws excerpted above can be found in The District of Columbia Annotated *and* The District of Columbia Statutes at Large.

FLORIDA'S MURDER LAWS

Murder

The unlawful killing of a human being:

(1) when perpetrated from a premeditated design to effect the death of the person killed or any human being;

(2) when committed by a person engaged in the perpetration of, or in the attempt to perpetrate, any:

  (a) trafficking offense prohibited by [law];

  (b) arson;

  (c) sexual battery;

  (d) robbery;

  (e) burglary;

  (f) kidnapping;

  (g) escape;

  (h) aggravated child abuse;

  (i) aircraft piracy;

  (j) unlawful throwing, placing, or discharging of a destructive device or bomb;

  (k) carjacking; or

  (l) home-invasion robbery; or

(3) which resulted from the unlawful distribution of any controlled substance, cocaine, or opium or any synthetic or natural salt, compound, derivative, or preparation of opium by a person eighteen years of age or older, when such drug is proven to be the proximate cause of the death of the user;

is murder in the first degree and constitutes a capital felony.

The unlawful killing of a human being, when perpetrated by any act imminently dangerous to another and evincing a depraved mind regardless of human life, although without any premeditated design to effect the death of any particular individual, is murder in the second degree and constitutes a felony of the first degree, punishable by imprisonment for a term of years not exceeding life.

(Florida Criminal Code 782.04)

Manslaughter

The killing of a human being by the act, procurement, or culpable negligence of another, without lawful justification and in cases in which such killing shall not be excusable homicide or murder, according to the provisions of this chapter, shall be deemed manslaughter and shall constitute a felony of the second degree.

(Florida Criminal Code 782.07)

Excusable Homicide

Homicide is excusable when committed by accident and misfortune in doing any lawful act by lawful means with usual ordinary caution, and without any unlawful intent, or by accident and misfortune in the heat of passion, upon any sudden and sufficient provocation, or upon a sudden combat, without any dangerous weapon being used and not done in a cruel or unusual manner.

(Florida Criminal Code 782.03)

Vehicular Homicide

Vehicular homicide is the killing of a human being by the operation of a motor vehicle by another in a reckless manner likely to cause the death of, or great bodily harm to, another. Vehicular homicide is a felony of the third degree.

Any person who commits vehicular homicide . . . is guilty of a felony of the second degree.

(Florida Criminal Code 782.071)

Assisted Suicide

Every person deliberately assisting another in the commission of self-murder shall be guilty of manslaughter, a felony of the second degree.

(Florida Criminal Code 782.08)

The complete and unedited text of Florida's murder laws excerpted above can be found in Florida Statutes, Florida Statutes Annotated, *or* The Laws of Florida.

GEORGIA'S MURDER LAWS
Murder

A person commits the offense of murder when he unlawfully and with malice aforethought, either express or implied, causes the death of another human being.

Express malice is that deliberate intention unlawfully to take the life of another human being which is manifested by external circumstances capable of proof. [**Implied malice** exists] where no considerable provocation appears and where all the circumstances of the killing show an abandoned and malignant heart.

A person also commits the offense of murder when, in the commission of a felony, he causes the death of another human being irrespective of malice.

A person convicted of the offense of murder shall be punished by death or by imprisonment for life.

(Georgia Criminal Code 26-1101)

Voluntary Manslaughter

A person commits the offense of voluntary manslaughter when he causes the death of another human being under circumstances which would otherwise be murder and if he acts solely as the result of a sudden, violent, and irresistible passion resulting from serious provocation sufficient to excite such passion in a reasonable person; however, if there should have been an interval between the provocation and the killing sufficient for the voice of reason and humanity to be heard, of which the jury in all cases shall be the judge, the killing shall be attributed to deliberate revenge and be punished as murder.

A person who commits the offense of voluntary manslaughter, upon conviction thereof, shall be punished by imprisonment for not less than one nor more than twenty years.

(Georgia Criminal Code 26-1102)

Involuntary Manslaughter

A person commits the offense of involuntary manslaughter in the commission of an unlawful act when he causes the death of another human being without any intention to do so by the commission of an unlawful act other than a felony. A person who commits the offense of involuntary manslaughter in the commission of an unlawful act, upon conviction thereof, shall be punished by imprisonment for not less than one year nor more than ten years.

A person commits the offense of involuntary manslaughter in the commission of a lawful act in an unlawful manner when he causes the death of another human being without any intention to do so, by the commission of a lawful act in an unlawful manner likely to cause death or great bodily harm. A person who commits the offense of involuntary manslaughter in the commission of a lawful act in an unlawful manner, upon conviction thereof, shall be punished as for a misdemeanor.

(Georgia Criminal Code 26-1103)

The complete and unedited text of Georgia's murder laws excerpted above can be found in The Official Code of Georgia Annotated, The Code of Georgia Annotated, *or* Georgia Laws.

HAWAII'S MURDER LAWS

Murder

Except as provided in [the following section on manslaughter], a person commits the offense of murder if he intentionally or knowingly causes the death of another person.
Murder is a Class A felony.
(Hawaii Penal Code 707-701)

Manslaughter

A person commits the offense of manslaughter if:

(1) he recklessly causes the death of another person; or

(2) he intentionally causes another person to commit suicide.

In a prosecution for murder it is a defense, which reduces the offense to manslaughter, that the defendant was, at the time he caused the death of the other person, under the influence of extreme mental or emotional disturbance for which there is a reasonable explanation. The reasonableness of the explanation shall be determined from the viewpoint of a person in the defendant's situation under the circumstances as he believed them to be.
Manslaughter is a Class B felony.
(Hawaii Penal Code 707-702)

Negligent Homicide

A person is guilty of the offense of negligent homicide in the first degree if he causes the death of another person by the operation of a vehicle in a negligent manner.
Negligent homicide in the first degree is a Class C felony.
A person is guilty of the offense of negligent homicide in the second degree if he causes the death of another person by the operation of a vehicle in a manner which is simple negligence.
[A]s used in this section:

(1) a person acts with simple negligence with respect to his conduct when he should be aware of a risk that he engages in such conduct;

(2) a person acts with simple negligence with respect to attendant circumstances when he should be aware of a risk that such circumstances exist;

(3) a person acts with simple negligence with respect to a result of his conduct when he should be aware of a risk that his conduct will cause such a result;

(4) a risk is within the meaning of this subsection if the person's failure to perceive it, considering the nature and purpose of his conduct and the circumstances known to him, involves a deviation from the standard of care that a law-abiding person would observe in the same situation.

Negligent homicide in the second degree is a misdemeanor. (Hawaii Penal Code 707-703/704)

The complete and unedited text of Hawaii's murder laws excerpted above can be found in Hawaii Revised Statutes *or in the* Session Laws of Hawaii.

IDAHO'S MURDER LAWS

Definitions

Murder is the unlawful killing of a human being with malice aforethought or the intentional application of torture to a human being, which results in the death of a human being. **Torture** is the intentional infliction of extreme and prolonged pain with the intent to cause suffering. It shall also be torture to inflict on a human being extreme and prolonged acts of brutality irrespective of proof of intent to cause suffering. The death of a human being caused by such torture is murder irrespective of proof of specific intent to kill; torture causing death shall be deemed the equivalent of intent to kill.

Malice may be express or implied. It is express when there is manifested a deliberate intention unlawfully to take away the life of a fellow creature. It is implied when no considerable provocation appears, or when the circumstances attending the killing show an abandoned and malignant heart.

(Idaho Code 18-4001/4002)

First Degree Murder

All murder which is perpetrated by means of poison, or lying in wait, or torture, when torture is inflicted with the intent to cause suffering, to execute vengeance, to extort something from the victim, or to satisfy some sadistic inclination, or which is perpetrated by any kind of wilful, deliberate and premeditated killing is murder of the first degree.

Any murder of any peace officer, executive officer, officer of the court, fireman, judicial officer or prosecuting attorney who was acting in the lawful discharge of an official duty, and was known or should have been known by the perpetrator of the murder to be an officer so acting, shall be murder of the first degree.

Any murder committed by a person under a sentence for murder of the first or second degree, including such persons on parole or probation from such sentence, shall be murder of the first degree.

Any murder committed in the perpetration of, or attempt to perpetrate, aggravated battery on a child under twelve years of age, arson, rape, robbery, burglary, kidnapping or mayhem is murder of the first degree.

Any murder committed by a person incarcerated in a penal institution upon a person employed by the penal institution, another inmate of the penal institution or a visitor to the penal institution shall be murder of the first degree.

Any murder committed by a person while escaping or attempting to escape from a penal institution is murder of the first degree.

[E]very person guilty of murder of the first degree shall be punished by death or by imprisonment for life, provided that whenever the court shall impose a sentence of life imprisonment, the court shall set . . . a minimum period of confinement of not less than ten years during which period of confinement the offender shall not be eligible for parole or discharge or credit or reduction of sentence for good conduct, except for meritorious service.

(Idaho Code 18-4003/4004)

Manslaughter

Manslaughter is the unlawful killing of a human being, without malice. It is of three kinds:

> (1) voluntary - upon a sudden quarrel or heat of passion;
>
> (2) involuntary - in the perpetration of or attempt to perpetrate any unlawful act, other than arson, rape, robbery, kidnapping, burglary, or mayhem; or in the commission of a lawful act which might produce death, in an unlawful manner, or without due caution and circumspection; or in the operation of any firearm or deadly weapon in a reckless, careless, or negligent manner which produces death;
>
> (3) vehicular.

(Idaho Code 18-4006)

Justifiable Homicide

Homicide is . . . justifiable when committed by any person in either of the following cases:

(1) when resisting any attempt to murder any person, or to commit a felony, or to do some great bodily injury upon any person;

(2) when committed in defense of habitation, property or person, against one who manifestly intends or endeavors, by violence or surprise, to commit a felony, or against one who manifestly intends and endeavors, in a violent, riotous or tumultuous manner, to enter the habitation of another for the purpose of offering violence to any person therein;

(3) when committed in the lawful defense of such person, or of a wife or husband, parent, child, master, mistress or servant of such person, when there is reasonable ground to apprehend a design to commit a felony or to do some great bodily injury, and imminent danger of such design being accomplished; but such person, or the person in whose behalf the defense was made, if he was the assailant or engaged in mortal combat, must really and in good faith have endeavored to decline any further struggle before the homicide was committed; or

(4) when necessarily committed in attempting, by lawful ways and means, to apprehend any person for any felony committed, or in lawfully suppressing any riot, or in lawfully keeping and preserving the peace.

The homicide appearing to be justifiable, the person indicted must, upon his trial, be fully acquitted and discharged. (Idaho Code 18-4009/4013)

Excusable Homicide

Homicide is excusable in the following cases:

(1) when committed by accident and misfortune in doing any lawful act by lawful means, with usual and ordinary caution, and without any unlawful intent;

(2) when committed by accident and misfortune, in the heat of passion, upon any sudden and sufficient provocation, or upon a sudden combaat when no un-

due advantage is taken nor any dangerous weapon used, and when the killing is not done in a cruel or unusual manner.

The homicide appearing to be excusable, the person indicted must, upon his trial, be fully acquitted and discharged.
(Idaho Code 18-4012/4013)

Year-and-a-Day

To make the killing either murder or manslaughter it is requisite that the party die within a year and a day after the stroke received or the cause of death administered; in the computation of which the whole of the day on which the act was done, shall be reckoned first.
(Idaho Code 18-4008)

The complete and unedited text of Idaho's murder laws excerpted above can be found in The Idaho Code *or* The Session Laws of Idaho.

ILLINOIS' MURDER LAWS
First Degree Murder

A person who kills an individual without lawful justification commits first degree murder if, in performing the acts which cause the death:

(1) he either intends to kill or do great bodily harm to that individual or another, or knows that such acts will cause death to that individual or another;

(2) he knows that such acts create a strong probability of death or great bodily harm to that individual or another; or

(3) he is attempting or committing a forcible felony other than second degree murder.

(Illinois Code 5/9.1)

Second Degree Murder

A person commits the offense of second degree murder when he commits the offense of first degree murder as defined [above] and either of the following mitigating factors are present:

(1) at the time of the killing he is acting under a sudden and intense passion resulting from serious provocation by the individual killed or another whom the offender endeavors to kill, but he negligently or accidentally causes the death of the individual killed; or

(2) at the time of the killing he believes the circumstances to be such that, if they existed, would justify or exonerate the killing . . . , but his belief is unreasonable.

Serious provocation is conduct sufficient to excite an intense passion in a reasonable person.

Second degree murder is a Class 1 felony.

(Illinois Code 5/9-2)

Manslaughter and Reckless Homicide

A person who unintentionally kills an individual without lawful justification commits involuntary manslaughter if his acts whether lawful or unlawful which cause the death are such as are likely to cause death or great bodily harm to some individudual, and he performs them recklessly, except in cases in which the cause of the death consists of the driving of a motor vehicle, in which case the person commits reckless homicide.

In cases involving reckless homicide, being under the influence of alcohol or any other drug or drugs at the time of the alleged violation shall be presumed to be evidence of a reckless act unless disproved by evidence to the contrary.

Involuntary manslaughter is a Class 3 felony.

Reckless homicide is a Class 3 felony.

(Illinois Code 5/9-3)

The complete and unedited text of Illinois' murder laws excerpted above can be found in Illinois Revised Statutes, Illinois Annotated Statutes, *or* Laws of Illinois.

INDIANA'S MURDER LAWS
Murder

A person who:

(1) knowingly or intentionally kills another human being;

(2) kills another human being while committing or attempting to commit arson, burglary, child molesting, consumer product tampering, criminal deviate conduct, kidnapping, rape, robbery, or carjacking; or

(3) kills another human being while committing or attempting to commit:

(a) dealing in cocaine or a narcotic drug; or

(b) dealing in a controlled substance;

commits murder, a felony.
(Indiana Criminal Code 35-42-1.1)

Voluntary Manslaughter

A person who knowingly or intentionally kills another human being while acting under sudden heat commits voluntary manslaughter, a Class B felony. However, the offense is a Class A felony if it is committed by means of a deadly weapon.

The existence of sudden heat is a mitigating factor that reduces what otherwise would be murder . . . to voluntary manslaughter.
(Indiana Criminal Code 35-42-1-3)

Involuntary Manslaughter

A person who kills another human being while committing or attempting to commit:

(1) a Class C or Class D felony that inherently poses a risk of serious bodily injury;

(2) a Class A misdemeanor that inherently poses a risk of serious bodily injury; or

(3) battery;

commits involuntary manslaughter, a Class C felony. However, if the killing results from the operation of a vehicle, the offense is a Class D felony.
(Indiana Criminal Code 35-42-1-4)

Reckless Homicide

A person who recklessly kills another human being commits reckless homicide, a Class C felony.
(Indiana Criminal Code 35-42-1-5)

Assisted Suicide

This section does not apply to the following:

(1) a licensed health care provider who administers, prescribes, or dispenses medications or procedures to relieve a person's pain or discomfort, even if the medication or procedure may hasten or increase the risk of death, unless such medications or procedures are intended to cause death;

(2) the withholding or withdrawing of medical treatment or life-prolonging procedures by a licensed health care provider, including [living wills and life-prolonging procedures, health care consent, or power of attorney].

A person who has knowledge that another person intends to commit or attempt to commit suicide and who intentionally does either of the following commits assisting suicide, a Class C felony:

(1) provides the physical means by which the other person attempts or commits suicide;

(2) participates in a physical act by which the other person attempts or commits suicide.

(Indiana Criminal Code 34-42-1-2.5)

The complete and unedited text of Indiana's murder laws excerpted above can be found in The Indiana Code, Indiana Statutes Annotated, Annotated Indiana Code, *and* The Acts of Indiana.

IOWA'S MURDER LAWS

First Degree Murder

A person commits murder in the first degree when the person commits murder under any of the following circumstances:

(1) the person willfully, deliberately, and with premeditation kills another person;

(2) the person kills another person while participating in a forcible felony;

(3) the person kills another person while escaping or attempting to escape from lawful custody;

(4) the person intentionally kills a peace officer, correctional officer, public employee, or hostage while the person is imprisoned in a correctional institution under the jurisdiction of the Iowa department of corrections, or in a city or county jail;

(5) the person kills a child while committing child endangerment, or while committing assault upon the child, and the death occurs under circumstances manifesting an extreme indifference to human life.

Murder in the first degree is a Class A felony.

(Iowa Criminal Code 707.2)

Second Degree Murder

A person commits murder in the second degree when the person commits murder which is not murder in the first degree. Murder in the second degree is a Class B felony. [T]he maximum sentence for a person convicted under this section shall be a period of confinement of not more than fifty years.

(Iowa Criminal Code 707.3)

Voluntary Manslaughter

A person commits voluntary manslaughter when that person causes the death of another person, under circumstances which would otherwise be murder, if the person causing the death acts solely as the result of sudden, violent, and irresistible passion resulting from serious provocation sufficient to excite such passion in a person and there is not an interval between the provocation and the killing in which a person of ordinary reason and temperament would regain control and suppress the impulse to kill.

Voluntary manslaughter is a Class C felony.

(Iowa Criminal Code 707.4)

Involuntary Manslaughter

A person commits a Class D felony when the person unintentionally causes the death of another person by the commission of a public offense other than a forcible felony or escape.

A person commits an aggravated misdemeanor when the person unintentionally causes the death of another person by the commission of an act in a manner likely to cause death or serious injury.

(Iowa Criminal Code 707.5)

Vehicular Homicide

A person commits a Class C felony when the person unintentionally causes the death of another by any of the following means:

(1) operating a motor vehicle while under the influence of alcohol or other drug or a combination of such substances or while having an alcohol concentration of .10 or more. Upon a plea or verdict of guilty of a violation of this paragraph, the court shall order the state department of transportation to revoke the defendant's motor vehicle license or nonresident operating privileges for a period of six years. The defendant shall surrender to the court any Iowa license or permit and the court shall forward it to the department with a copy of the revocation order;

(2) driving a motor vehicle in a reckless manner with willful or wanton disregard for the safety of persons or property;

(3) eluding or attempting to elude a pursuing law enforcement vehicle if the death of the other person directly or indirectly results from the violation.

A person commits a Class D felony when the person unintentionally causes the death of another while drag racing. (Iowa Criminal Code 707.6A)

The complete and unedited text of Iowa's murder laws excerpted above can be found in The Code of Iowa, The Iowa Code Annotated, *and* The Acts of Iowa.

KANSAS' MURDER LAWS

First Degree Murder

Murder in the first degree is the killing of a human being committed maliciously, willfully, deliberately and with premeditation or committed in the perpetration or attempt to perpetrate any felony.

Murder in the first degree is a Class A felony.

(Kansas Criminal Code 21-3401)

Second Degree Murder

Murder in the second degree is the malicious killing of a human being, committed without deliberation or premeditation and not in the perpetration or attempt to perpetrate a felony.

Murder in the second degree is a Class B felony.

(Kansas Criminal Code 21-3402)

Voluntary Manslaughter

Voluntary manslaughter is the unlawful killing of a human being, without malice, which is done intentionally upon a sudden quarrel or in the heat of passion.

Voluntary manslaughter is a Class C felony.

(Kansas Criminal Code 21-3403)

Involuntary Manslaughter

Involuntary manslaughter is the unlawful killing of a human being, without malice, which is done unintentionally in the wanton commission of an unlawful act not amounting to felony, or in the commission of a lawful act in an unlawful or wanton manner.

An **unlawful act** is any act which is prohibited by a statute of the United States or the state of Kansas or an ordinance of any city within the state, which statute or ordinance is enacted for the protection of human life or safety.

Involuntary manslaughter is a Class D felony.

(Kansas Criminal Code 21-3404)

Vehicular Homicide

Aggravated vehicular homicide is the unintentional killing of a human being, without malice, which is done while committing a violation of [the Kansas laws concerning reckless driving, driving under the influence of alcohol or drugs, or fleeing a police officer], and amendments thereto, or the ordinance of a city which prohibits any of the acts prohibited by those statutes.

This section shall be applicable only when the death of the injured person ensues within one year as a proximate result of the operation of a vehicle in the manner described [above].

Aggravated vehicular homicide is a Class E felony.

(Kansas Criminal Code 21-3405a)

Assisted Suicide

Assisting suicide is intentionally advising, encouraging or assisting another in the taking of his own life.

Assisting suicide is a Class E felony.

(Kansas Criminal Code 21-3406)

The complete and unedited text of Kansas' murder laws excerpted above can be found in The Kansas Statutes Annotated *and* The Laws of Kansas.

KENTUCKY'S MURDER LAWS

Murder

A person is guilty of murder when:

> (1) with intent to cause the death of another person, he causes the death of such person or of a third person; except that in any prosecution a person shall not be guilty if he acted under the influence of extreme emotional disturbance for which there was a reasonable explanation or excuse, the reasonableness of which is to be determined from the viewpoint of a person in the defendant's situation under the circumstances as the defendant believed them to be. . . ; or

> (2) including, but not limited to, the operation of a motor vehicle under circumstances manifesting extreme indifference to human life, he wantonly engages in conduct which creates a grave risk of death to another person and thereby causes the death of another person.

Murder is a capital offense.

(Kentucky Criminal Code 507.020)

First Degree Manslaughter

A person is guilty of manslaughter in the first degree when:

> (1) with intent to cause serious physical injury to another person, he causes the death of such person or of a third person; or

> (2) with intent to cause the death of another person, he causes the death of such person or of a third person under circumstances which do not constitute murder because he acts under the influence of extreme emotional disturbance.

Manslaughter in the first degree is a Class B felony.

(Kentucky Criminal Code 507.030)

Second Degree Manslaughter

A person is guilty of manslaughter in the second degree when, including, but not limited to, the operation of a motor vehicle,

he wantonly causes the death of another person.
Manslaughter in the second degree is a Class C felony.
(Kentucky Criminal Code 507.040)

Reckless Homicide

A person is guilty of reckless homicide when, with recklessness
he causes the death of another person.
Reckless homicide is a Class D felony.
(Kentucky Criminal Code 507.050)

*The complete and unedited text of Kentucky's murder laws ex-
cerpted above can be found in* Kentucky Revised Statutes Annotated *and* Kentucky Acts.

LOUISIANA'S MURDER LAWS

First Degree Murder

First degree murder is the killing of a human being:

(1) when the offender has specific intent to kill or to inflict great bodily harm and is engaged in the perpetration or attempted perpetration of aggravated kidnapping, second degree kidnapping, aggravated escape, aggravated arson, aggravated rape, forcible rape, aggravated burglary, armed robbery, drive-by shooting, first degree robbery, or simple robbery;

(2) when the offender has a specific intent to kill or to inflict great bodily harm upon a fireman or peace officer engaged in the performance of his lawful duties;

(3) when the offender has a specific intent to kill or to inflict great bodily harm upon more than one person;

(4) when the offender has specific intent to kill or inflict great bodily harm and has offered, has been offered, has given, or has received anything of value for the killing;

(5) when the offender has the specific intent to kill or to inflict great bodily harm upon a victim under the age of twelve or sixty-five years of age or older;

(6) when the offender has the specific intent to kill or to inflict great bodily harm while engaged in the distribution, exchange, sale, or purchase, or any attempt thereof, of a controlled dangerous substance;

(7) when the offender has specific intent to kill and is engaged in the activities prohibited by [the law concerning ritualisitic acts].

Whoever commits the crime of first degree murder shall be punished by death or life imprisonment at hard labor without benefit of parole, probation, or suspension of sentence in accordance with the determination of the jury.

(Louisiana Criminal Code 14:30)

Second Degree Murder

Second degree murder is the killing of a human being:

(1) when the offender has a specific intent to kill or to inflict great bodily harm; or

(2) when the offender is engaged in the perpetration or attempted perpetration of aggravated rape, forcible rape, aggravated arson, aggravated burglary, aggravated kidnapping, aggravated escape, drive-by shooting, armed robbery, first degree robbery, or simple robbery, even though he has no intent to kill or to inflict great bodily harm;

(3) when the offender unlawfully distributes or dispenses a controlled dangerous substance which is the direct cause of the death of the recipient who ingested or consumed the controlled dangerous substance;

(4) when the offender unlawfully distributes or dispenses a controlled dangerous substance to another who subsequently distributes or dispenses such controlled dangerous substance which is the direct cause of the death of the person who ingested or consumed the controlled dangerous substance.

Whoever commits the crime of second degree murder shall be punished by life imprisonment at hard labor without benefit of parole, probation, or suspension of sentence. (Louisiana Criminal Code 14:30.1)

Manslaughter

Manslaughter is:

(1) a homicide which would be murder under (the sections on first degree murder or second degree murder, above), but the offense is committed in sudden passion or heat of blood immediately caused by provocation sufficient to deprive an average person of his self-control and cool reflection. Provocation shall not reduce a homicide to manslaughter if the jury finds that the offender's blood had actually cooled, or that an average person's blood would have cooled, at the time the offense was committed; or

(2) a homicide committed, without any intent to cause death or great bodily harm:

(a) when the offender is engaged in the perpetration or attempted perpetration of any felony not enumerated in [the sections on first degree murder or second degree murder], or of any intentional misdemeanor directly affecting the person; or

(b) when the offender is resisting lawful arrest by means, or in a manner, not inherently dangerous, and the circumstances are such that the killing would not be murder under [the sections on first degree murder or second degree murder].

Whoever commits manslaughter shall be imprisoned at hard labor for not more than forty years. However, if the victim was killed as a result of receiving a battery and was under the age of ten years, the offender shall be imprisoned at hard labor, without benefit of probation or suspension of sentence, for not less than ten years nor more than forty years. (Louisiana Criminal Code 14:31)

Negligent Homicide

Negligent homicide is the killing of a human being by criminal negligence.

Whoever commits the crime of negligent homicide shall be imprisoned with or without hard labor for not more than five years, fined not more than five thousand dollars, or both. However, if the victim was killed as a result of receiving a battery and was under the age of ten years, the offender shall be imprisoned at hard labor, without benefit of probation or suspension of sentence, for not less than two nor more than five years. (Louisiana's Criminal Code 14:32)

Vehicular Homicide

Vehicular homicide is the killing of a human being caused proximately or caused directly by an offender engaged in the operation of, or in actual physical control of, any motor vehicle, aircraft, vessel, or other means of conveyance whether or not the offender had the intent to cause death or great bodily harm whenever any one of the following conditions exists:

   (1) the operator is under the influence of alcoholic beverages as determined by chemical tests;

   (2) the operator's blood alcohol concentration is 0.10 percent or more by weight based upon grams of alcohol per one hundred cubic centimeters of blood;

   (3) the operator is under the influence of any controlled dangerous substance.

Whoever commits the crime of vehicular homicide shall be fined not less than two thousand dollars nor more than fifteen thousand dollars and shall be imprisoned with or without hard labor for not less than two years nor more than fifteen years. At least one year of the sentence of imprisonment shall be imposed without benefit of probation, parole, or suspension of sentence.

(Louisiana's Criminal Code 14:32.1)

The complete and unedited text of Louisiana's murder laws excerpted above can be found in Louisiana Revised Statutes Annotated *and* Acts of the State of Louisiana.

MAINE'S MURDER LAWS

Murder

A person is guilty of murder if:

(1) he intentionally or knowingly causes the death of another human being;

(2) he engages in conduct which manifests a depraved indifference to the value of human life and which in fact causes the death of another human being; or

(3) he intentionally or knowingly causes another human being to commit suicide by the use of force, duress or deception.

(Maine Criminal Code 201)

Manslaughter

A person is guilty of manslaughter if that person:

(1) recklessly, or with criminal negligence, causes the death of another human being;

(2) intentionally or knowingly causes the death of another human being under circumstances which do not constitute murder because the person causes the death while under the influence of extreme anger or extreme fear brought about by adequate provocation; or

(3) has direct and personal management or control of any employment, place of employment or other employee, and intentionally or knowingly violates any occupational safety or health standard of this State or the Federal Government, and that violation in fact causes the death of an employee and that death is a reasonably foreseeable consequence of the violation.

Manslaughter is a Class A crime except that:

(1) it is a defense to a prosecution of a manslaughter based upon the reckless or criminally negligent operation of a motor vehicle, which reduces the crime to a Class B crime, that the death of the victim resulted from conduct that would otherwise be defined only as a civil violation or civil infraction; and

(2) [manslaughter by an employer, as outlined above]
is a Class C crime.
(Maine Criminal Code 203)

Assisted Suicide

A person is guilty of aiding or soliciting suicide if he intentionally aids or solicits another to commit suicide, and the other
commits or attempts suicide.
Aiding or soliciting suicide is a Class D crime.
(Maine Criminal Code 204)

*The complete and unedited text of Maine's murder laws ex-
cerpted above can be found in* Maine Revised Statutes *and* The
Laws of Maine.

MARYLAND'S MURDER LAWS

First Degree Murder

All murder which shall be perpetrated by means of poison, or lying in wait, or by any kind of wilful, deliberate and premeditated killing shall be murder in the first degree.

All murder which shall be committed in the perpetration of, or attempt to perpetrate, arson in the first degree shall be murder in the first degree.

All murder which shall be committed in the burning or attempting to burn any barn, tobacco house, stable, warehouse or other outhouse, not parcel of any dwelling house, having therein any tobacco, hay, grain, horses, cattle, goods, wares or merchandise, shall be murder in the first degree.

All murder which shall be committed in the perpetration of, or attempt to perpetrate, any rape in any degree, sexual offense in the first or second degree, sodomy, mayhem, robbery, carjacking or armed carjacking, burglary in the first, second, or third degree, kidnapping, or in the escape or attempt to escape from the Maryland Penitentiary, the house of correction, the Baltimore City Detention Center, or from any jail or penal institution in any of the counties of this State, shall be murder in the first degree.

If a person is found guilty of murder, the court or jury that determined the person's guilt shall state in the verdict whether the person is guilty of murder in the first degree or murder in the second degree.

Except [for penalties for defendants less than eighteen years of age or mentally retarded], a person found guilty of murder in the first degree shall be sentenced to death, imprisonment for life, or imprisonment for life without the possibility of parole. If a person found guilty of murder in the first degree was, at the time the murder was committed, less than eighteen years old or if the person establishes by a preponderance of the evidence that the person was, at the time the murder was committed, mentally retarded, the person shall be sentenced to imprisonment for life or imprisonment for life without the possibility of parole and may not be sentenced to death.

(Maryland Criminal Code 27-407/408/409/410/412)

Second Degree Murder

All other kinds of murder shall be deemed murder in the second degree.

A person found guilty of murder in the second degree shall be sentenced to imprisonment for not more than thirty years. (Maryland Criminal Code 27-411/412)

The complete and unedited text of Maryland's murder laws excerpted above can be found in The Maryland Code Annotated *and* The Laws of Maryland.

MASSACHUSETTS' MURDER LAWS

Murder

Murder committed with deliberately premeditated malice aforethought, or with extreme atrocity or cruelty, or in the commission or attempted commission of a crime punishable with death or imprisonment for life, is murder in the first degree. Murder which does not appear to be in the first degree is murder in the second degree.

Whoever is guilty of murder committed with deliberately premeditated malice aforethought or with extreme atrocity or cruelty, and who had attained the age of eighteen years at the time of the murder, may suffer the punishment of death. . . . Any other person who is guilty of murder in the first degree shall be punished by imprisonment in the state prison for life. Whoever is guilty of murder in the second degree shall be punished by imprisonment in state prison for life. No person shall be eligible for parole . . . while he is serving a life sentence for murder in the first degree, but if his sentence is commuted therefrom by the governor and council . . . he shall thereafter be subject to the provisions of law governing parole for persons sentenced for lesser offenses.

(Massachusetts Criminal Code 265-1/-2)

Manslaughter

Whoever commits manslaughter shall, except as hereinafter provided, be punished by imprisonment in the state prison for not more than twenty years or by a fine of not more than one thousand dollars and imprisonment in jail or a house of correction for not more than two and one half years.

(Massachusetts Criminal Code 265-13)

Attempted Murder

Whoever assaults another with intent to commit murder . . . shall be punished by imprisonment in the state prison for not more than ten years or by a fine of not more than one thousand dollars and imprisonment in jail for not more than two and one half years.

Whoever attempts to commit murder by poisoning, drowning or strangling another person, or by any means not constituting an assault with intent to commit murder, shall be punished by imprisonment in the state prison for not more than twenty years or by a fine of not more than one thousand dollars and imprisonment in jail for not more than two and one half years. (Massachusetts Criminal Code 265-15/16)

The complete and unedited text of Massachusetts' murder laws excerpted above can be found in General Laws of the Commonwealth of Massachusetts, Massachusetts General Laws Annotated, Annotated Laws of Massachusetts, *and* Acts and Resolves of Massachusetts.

MICHIGAN'S MURDER LAWS

First Degree Murder

A person who commits any of the following is guilty of first degree murder and shall be punished by imprisonment for life:

(1) murder perpetrated by means of poison, lying in wait, or any other willful, deliberate, and premeditated killing;

(2) murder committed in the perpetration of, or attempt to perpetrate, arson, criminal sexual conduct in the first or third degree, child abuse in the first degree, a major controlled substance offense, robbery, breaking and entering of a dwelling, larceny of any kind, extortion, or kidnapping;

(3) a murder of a peace officer or a corrections officer committed while the peace officer or corrections officer is lawfully engaged in the performance of any of his or her duties as a peace officer or corrections officer, with knowledge that the peace officer or corrections officer is . . . engaged in the performance of his or her duty as [an officer].

(Michigan Criminal Code 750.316)

Second Degree Murder

All other kinds of murder shall be murder of the second degree, and shall be punished by imprisonment in the state prison for life, or any term of years, in the discretion of the court trying the same.

(Michigan Criminal Code 750.317)

Manslaughter

Any person who shall wound, maim or injure any other person by the discharge of any firearm, pointed or aimed, intentionally but without malice, at any such person, shall, if death ensue from such wounding, maiming or injury, be deemed guilty of the crime of manslaughter.

Any person who shall commit the crime of manslaughter shall be guilty of a felony punishable by imprisonment in the state

prison, not more than fifteen years or by fine of not more than $7,500, or both, at the discretion of the court.
(Michigan Criminal Code 750.321/.329)

Negligent Homicide

Any person who, by the operation of any vehicle upon any highway or upon any other property, public or private, at an immoderate rate of speed or in a careless, reckless or negligent manner, but not wilfully or wantonly, shall cause the death of another, shall be guilty of a misdemeanor, punishable by imprisonment in the state prison not more than two years or by a fine of not more than $2,000, or by both such fine and imprisonment.

The crime of negligent homicide shall be deemed to be included within every crime of manslaughter charged to have been committed in the operation of any vehicle, and in any case where a defendant is charged with manslaughter committed in the operation of any vehicle, if the jury shall find the defendant not guilty of the crime of manslaughter, it may render a verdict of guilty of negligent homicide.
(Michigan Criminal Code 750.324/325)

Assisted Suicide

A person who has knowledge that another person intends to commit or attempt to commit suicide and who intentionally does either of the following is guilty of criminal assistance to suicide, a felony punishable by imprisonment for not more than four years or by a fine of not more than $2,000, or both:

(1) provides the physical means by which the other person attempts or commits suicide; or

(2) participates in a physical act by which the other person attempts or commits suicide.

[The above] shall not apply to withholding or withdrawing medical treatment.

[The above] does not apply to prescribing, dispensing, or administering medication or procedures if the intent is to relieve pain or discomfort and not to cause death, even if the medication or procedure may hasten or increase the risk of death. (Michigan Criminal Code 752.1027)

The complete and unedited text of Michigan's murder laws excerpted above can be found in Michigan Compiled Laws, Michigan Compiled Laws Annotated, Michigan Statutes Annotated, *and* Public Acts of the State of Michigan.

MINNESOTA'S MURDER LAWS

First Degree Murder

Whoever does any of the following is guilty of murder in the first degree and shall be sentenced to imprisonment for life:

(1) causes the death of a human being with premeditation and with intent to effect the death of the person or of another;

(2) causes the death of a human being while committing or attempting to commit criminal sexual conduct in the first or second degree with force or violence, either upon or affecting the person or another;

(3) causes the death of a human being with intent to effect the death of the person or another, while committing or attempting to commit burglary, aggravated robbery, kidnapping, arson in the first or second degree, tampering with a witness in the first degree, escape from custody, or any felony violation involving the unlawful sale of a controlled substance;

(4) causes the death of a peace officer or a guard employed at a Minnesota state or local correctional facility, with intent to effect the death of that person or another, while the peace officer or guard is engaged in the performance of official duties;

(5) causes the death of a minor under circumstances other than those described in clause (1) or (2) while committing child abuse, when the perpetrator has engaged in a past pattern of child abuse upon the child and the death occurs under circumstances manifesting an extreme indifference to human life; or

(6) causes the death of a human being under circumstances other than those described in clause (1), (2), or (5) while committing domestic abuse, when the perpetrator has engaged in a past pattern of domestic abuse upon the victim and the death occurs under circumstances manifesting an extreme indifference to human life.

(Minnesota Criminal Code 609.185)

Second Degree Murder

Whoever does any of the following is guilty of murder in the second degree and may be sentenced to imprisonment for not more than forty years:

(1) causes the death of a human being with intent to effect the death of that person or another, but without premeditation;

(2) causes the death of a human being, without intent to effect the death of any person, while committing or attempting to commit a felony offense other than criminal sexual conduct in the first or second degree with force or violence; or

(3) causes the death of a human being without intent to effect the death of any person, while intentionally inflicting or attempting to inflict bodily harm upon the victim, when the perpetrator is restrained under an order for protection . . . and the victim is a person designated to receive protection under the order.

(Minnesota Criminal Code 609.19)

Third Degree Murder

Whoever, without intent to effect the death of any person, causes the death of another by perpetrating an act eminently dangerous to others and evincing a depraved mind, without regard for human life, is guilty of murder in the third degree and may be sentenced to imprisonment for not more than twenty-five years.

Whoever, without intent to cause death, proximately causes the death of a human being by, directly or indirectly, unlawfully selling, giving away, bartering, delivering, exchanging, distributing, or administering a controlled substance, is guilty of murder in the third degree and may be sentenced to imprisonment for not more than twenty-five years or to payment of a fine of not more than $40,000, or both.

(Minnesota Criminal Code 609.195)

First Degree Manslaughter

Whoever does any of the following is guilty of manslaughter in the first degree and may be sentenced to imprisonment for not more than fifteen years or to payment of a fine of not more than $30,000, or both:

(1) intentionally causes the death of another person in the heat of passion provoked by such words or acts of another as would provoke a person of ordinary self-control under like circumstances, provided that the crying of a child does not constitute provocation;

(2) causes the death of another in committing or attempting to commit a misdemeanor or gross misdemeanor offense with such force and violence that death of or great bodily harm to any person was reasonably foreseeable, and murder in the first or second degree was not committed thereby;

(3) intentionally causes the death of another person because the actor is coerced by threats made by someone other than the actor's coconspirator and which cause the actor reasonably to believe that the act performed by the actor is the only means of preventing imminent death to the actor or another; or

(4) proximately causes the death of another, without intent to cause death by, directly or indirectly, unlawfully selling, giving away, bartering, delivering, exchanging, distributing, or administering a controlled substance.

(Minnesota Criminal Code 609.20)

Second Degree Manslaughter

A person who causes the death of another by any of the following means is guilty of manslaughter in the second degree and may be sentenced to imprisonment for not more than ten years or to payment of a fine of not more than $20,000, or both:

(1) by the person's culpable negligence whereby the person creates an unreasonable risk, and consciously takes chances of causing death or great bodily harm to another;

(2) by shooting another with a firearm or other dangerous weapon as a result of negligently believing the other to be a deer or other animal;

(3) by setting a spring gun, pit fall, deadfall, snare, or other like dangerous weapon or device; or

(4) by negligently or intentionally permitting any animal, known by the person to have vicious propensities or have caused great or substantial bodily harm in the past, to run uncontrolled off the owner's premises, or negligently failing to keep it properly confined.

If proven by a preponderance of the evidence, it shall be an affirmative defense to criminal liability under clause (4) that the victim provoked the animal to cause the victim's death.
(Minnesota Criminal Code 609.205)

Vehicular Homicide

Whoever causes the death of a human being [or of an unborn child] not constituting murder or manslaughter as a result of operating a motor vehicle:

(1) in a grossly negligent manner;

(2) in a negligent manner while under the influence of alcohol, a controlled substance, or any combination of those elements;

(3) while having an alcohol concentration of 0.10 or more; or

(4) while having an alcohol concentration of 0.10 or more, as measured within two hours of the time of driving;

is guilty of criminal vehicular homicide resulting in death and may be sentenced to imprisonment for not more than ten years or to payment of a fine of not more than $20,000, or both.
(Minnesota Criminal Code 609.21)

Assisted Suicide

Whoever intentionally advises, encourages, or assists another in taking the other's own life may be sentenced to imprisonment for not more than fifteen years or to payment of a fine of not more than $30,000, or both.

Whoever intentionally advises, encourages, or assists another who attempts but fails to take the other's own life may be sentenced to imprisonment for not more than seven years or to payment of a fine of not more than $14,000, or both.

A health care provider who administers, prescribes, or dispenses medications or procedures to relieve another person's pain or discomfort, even if the medication or procedure may hasten or increase the risk of death, does not violate this section unless the medications or procedures are knowingly administered, prescribed, or dispensed to cause death.

A health care provider who withholds or withdraws a life-sustaining procedure . . . in accordance with reasonable medical practice does not violate this section.

(Minnesota Criminal Code 609.215)

The complete and unedited text of Minnesota's murder laws excerpted above can be found in Minnesota Statutes, Minnesota Statutes Annotated, *and* The Laws of Minnesota.

MISSISSIPPI'S MURDER LAWS
Murder
The killing of a human being without the authority of law by any means or in any manner shall be murder in the following cases:

(1) when done with deliberate design to effect the death of the person killed, or of any human being;

(2) when done in the commission of an act eminently dangerous to others and evincing a depraved heart, regardless of human life, although without any premeditated design to effect the death of any particular individual; [or]

(3) when done without any design to effect death by any person engaged in the commission of any felony other than rape, kidnapping, burglary, arson, robbery, sexual battery, unnatural intercourse with any child under the age of twelve, or nonconsensual unnatural intercourse with mankind, or felonious abuse and/or battery of a child, or in any attempt to commit such felonies.

Every person who shall be convicted of murder shall be sentenced by the court to imprisonment for life in the State Penitentiary.

(Mississippi Criminal Code 97-3-19/21)

Manslaughter
The killing of a human being without malice, by the act, procurement, or culpable negligence of another, while such other is engaged in the perpetration of any felony, except [rape, burglary, kidnapping, arson, robbery, sexual battery, unnatural intercourse with any child under the age of twelve, nonconsensual unnatural intercourse with mankind, felonious abuse, and/or battery of a child with intent to cause bodily harm], or while such other is attempting to commit any felony besides such as are above enumerated and excepted, shall be manslaughter.

The killing of a human being without malice, by the act, procurement, or culpable negligence of another, while such other is engaged in the perpetration of any crime or misdemeanor not amounting to felony, or in the attempt to commit any crime or misdemeanor, where such killing would be murder at common law, shall be manslaughter.

Every person who shall unnecessarily kill another, either while resisting an attempt by such other person to commit any felony, or to do any unlawful act, or after such attempt shall have failed, shall be guilty of manslaughter.

The involuntary killing of a human being by the act, procurement, or culpable negligence of another, while such human being is engaged in the commission of a trespass or other injury to private rights or property, or is engaged in an attempt to commit such injury, shall be manslaughter.

The killing of a human being, without malice, in the heat of passion, but in a cruel or unusual manner, or by the use of a dangerous weapon, without authority of law, and not in necessary self-defense, shall be manslaughter.

The wilful killing of an unborn quick child, by an injury to the mother of such child, which would be murder if it resulted in the death of the mother, shall be manslaughter.

If any physician or other person, while in a state of intoxication, shall, without a design to effect death, administer or cause to be administered, any poison, drug, or other medicine, or shall perform any surgical operation on another, which shall cause the death of such other person, he shall be guilty of manslaughter.

Any person convicted of manslaughter shall be fined in a sum not less than five hundred dollars, or imprisoned in the county jail not more than one year, or both, or in the penitentiary not less than two years, nor more than twenty years.
(Mississippi Criminal Code 97-3-25/27/29/31/33/35/37/39)

Justifiable Homicide

The killing of a human being by the act, procurement, or omission of another shall be justifiable in the following cases:

(1) when committed by public officers, or those acting by their aid and assistance, in obedience to any judgment of a competent court;

(2) when necessarily committed by public officers, or those acting by their command in their aid and assistance, in overcoming actual resistance to the execution

of some legal process, or to the discharge of any other legal duty;

(3) when necessarily committed by public officers, or those acting by their command in their aid and assistance, in retaking any felon who has been rescued or has escaped;

(4) when necessarily committed by public officers, or those acting by their command in their aid and assistance, in arresting any felon fleeing from justice;

(5) when committed by any person in resisting any attempt unlawfully to kill such person or to commit any felony upon him, or upon or in any dwelling house in which such person shall be;

(6) when committed in the lawful defense of one's own person or any other human being, where there shall be reasonable ground to apprehend a design to commit a felony or to do some great personal injury, and there shall be imminent danger of such design being accomplished;

(7) when necessarily committed in attempting by lawful ways and means to apprehend any person for any felony committed;

(8) when necessarily committed in lawfully suppressing any riot or in lawfully keeping and preserving the peace.

When necessarily committed [as used in paragraphs 3 and 4 above] means that a public officer or a person acting by or at the officer's command, aid or assistance is authorized to use such force as necessary in securing and detaining the felon offender, overcoming the offender's resistance, preventing the offender's escape, recapturing the offender if the offender escapes or in protecting himself or others from bodily harm; but such officer or person shall not be authorized to resort to deadly or dangerous means when to do so would be unreasonable under the circumstances. The public officer or person acting by or at the officer's command may act upon a reasonable apprehension of the surrounding circumstances; however, such officer or person shall not use excessive force or force that is greater than reasonably necessary in securing and detaining the offender, overcoming the offender's resistance, preventing the offender's escape, recapturing the offender if the offender escapes or in protecting himself or others from bodily harm.

Felon [as used in paragraphs 3 and 4 above] shall include an offender who has been convicted of a felony and shall also include an offender who is in custody, or whose custody is being sought, on a charge or for an offense which is punishable, upon conviction, by death or confinement in the penitentiary.

(Mississippi Criminal Code 97-3-15)

Excusable Homicide

The killing of any human being by the act, procurement, or omission of another shall be excusable:

(1) when committed by accident and misfortune in doing any lawful act by lawful means, with usual and ordinary caution, and without any unlawful intent;

(2) when committed by accident and misfortune, in the heat of passion, upon any sudden and sufficient provocation; [or]

(3) when committed upon any sudden combat, without undue advantage being taken, and without any dangerous weapon being used, and not done in a cruel or unusual manner.

(Mississippi Criminal Code 97-3-17)

Assisted Suicide

A person who wilfully, or in any manner, advises, encourages, abets, or assists another person to take, or in taking, the latter's life, or in attempting to take the latter's life, is guilty of felony and, on conviction, shall be punished by imprisonment in the penitentiary not exceeding ten years, or by fine not exceeding one thousand dollars, and imprisonment in the county jail not exceeding one year.

(Mississippi Criminal Code 97-3-49)

The complete and unedited text of Mississippi's murder laws excerpted above can be found in The Mississippi Code Annotated *and* The General Laws of Mississippi.

MISSOURI'S MURDER LAWS
Definitions

Adequate cause means cause that would reasonably produce a degree of passion in a person of ordinary temperament sufficient to substantially impair an ordinary person's capacity for self control.

Deliberation means cool reflection for any length of time no matter how brief.

Intoxicated condition means under the influence of alcohol, a controlled substance, or drug, or any combination thereof.

Operates means physically driving or operating or being in actual physical control of a motor vehicle.

Serious physical injury means physical injury that creates a substantial risk of death or that causes serious disfigurement or protracted loss or impairment of the function of any part of the body.

Sudden passion means passion directly caused by and arising out of provocation by the victim or another acting with the victim which passion arises at the time of the offense and is not solely the result of former provocation.

(Missouri Criminal Code 565.002)

First Degree Murder

A person commits the crime of murder in the first degree if he knowingly causes the death of another person after deliberation upon the matter.

Murder in the first degree is a Class A felony, and the punishment shall be either death or imprisonment for life without eligibility for probation or parole, or release except by act of the governor; except that, if a person has not reached his sixteenth birthday at the time of the commission of the crime, the punishment shall be imprisonment for life without eligibility for probation or parole, or release except by act of the governor.

(Missouri Criminal Code 565.020)

Second Degree Murder

A person commits the crime of murder in the second degree if he:

    (1) knowingly causes the death of another person or, with the purpose of causing serious physical injury to another person, causes the death of another person; or
    (2) commits or attempts to commit any felony, and, in the perpetration or the attempted perpetration of such felony or in the flight from the perpetration or attempted perpetration of such felony, another person is killed as a result of the perpetration or attempted perpetration of such felony or immediate flight from the perpetration of such felony or attempted perpetration of such felony.

Murder in the second degree is a Class A felony, and the punishment for second degree murder shall be in addition to the punishment for commission of a related felony or attempted felony, other than murder or manslaughter.
(Missouri Criminal Code 565.021)

Voluntary Manslaughter

A person commits the crime of voluntary manslaughter if he:
    (1) causes the death of another person under circumstances that would constitute murder in the second degree under [second degree murder, paragraph (1), above], except that he caused the death under the influence of sudden passion arising from adequate cause; or
    (2) knowingly assists another in the commission of self-murder.

Voluntary manslaughter is a Class B felony.
(Missouri Criminal Code 565.023)

Involuntary Manslaughter

A person commits the crime of involuntary manslaughter if he:
    (1) recklessly causes the death of another person; or
    (2) while in an intoxicated condition operates a motor vehicle in this state and, when so operating, acts with criminal negligence to cause the death of any person.

Involuntary manslaughter is a Class C felony.
(Missouri Criminal Code 565.024)

The complete and unedited text of Missouri's murder laws excerpted above can be found in Missouri Revised Statutes, The Annotated Missouri Statutes *and* The Laws of Missouri.

MONTANA'S MURDER LAWS

Deliberate Homicide

A person commits the offense of deliberate homicide if:

(1) he purposely or knowingly causes the death of another human being; or

(2) he attempts to commit, commits, or is legally accountable for the attempt or commission of robbery, sexual intercourse without consent, arson, burglary, kidnapping, aggravated kidnapping, felonious escape, felony assault, aggravated assault, or any other forcible felony and in the course of the forcible felony or flight thereafter, he or any person legally accountable for the crime causes the death of another human being.

A person convicted of the offense of deliberate homicide shall be punished by death, by life imprisonment, or by imprisonment in the state prison for a term of not less than ten years or more than one hundred years, except as provided in [the section of the law on sentence enhancement, which allows an additional sentence for an offense committed because of the victim's race, creed, religion, color, national origin, or involvement in civil or human rights activities].

(Montana Criminal Code 45-5-102)

Negligent Homicide

A person commits the offense of negligent homicide if he negligently causes the death of another human being.

A person convicted of negligent homicide shall be imprisoned in the state prison for any term not to exceed ten years or be fined an amount not to exceed $50,000, or both.

(Montana Criminal Code 45-5-104)

Assisted Suicide

A person who purposely aids or solicits another to commit suicide, but such suicide does not occur, commits the offense of aiding or soliciting suicide.

A person convicted of the offense of aiding or soliciting a suicide shall be imprisoned in the state prison for any term not to exceed ten years or be fined an amount not to exceed $50,000, or both.
(Montana Criminal Code 45-5-105)

The complete and unedited text of Montana's murder laws excerpted above can be found in The Montana Code Annotated *and* The Laws of Montana.

NEBRASKA'S MURDER LAWS
First Degree Murder
A person commits murder in the first degree if he kills another person:
> (1) purposely and with deliberate and premeditated malice; or
>
> (2) in the perpetration of or attempt to perpetrate any sexual assault in the first degree, arson, robbery, kidnapping, hijacking of any public or private means of transportation, or burglary; or
>
> (3) by administering poison or causing the same to be done;

or if by willful and corrupt perjury . . . he purposely procures the conviction and execution of any innocent person.

Murder in the first degree is a Class I or Class IA felony.
(Nebraska Criminal Code 28-303)

Second Degree Murder
A person commits murder in the second degree if he causes the death of a person intentionally, but without premeditation.
Murder in the second degree is a Class IB felony.
(Nebraska Criminal Code 28-304)

Manslaughter
A person commits manslaughter if he kills another without malice, either upon a sudden quarrel, or causes the death of another unintentionally while in the commission of an unlawful act.
Manslaughter is a Class III felony.
(Nebraska Criminal Code 28-305)

Vehicular Homicide
A person who causes the death of another unintentionally while engaged in the operation of a motor vehicle in violation of the law of the State of Nebraska or in violation of any city or village ordinance commits motor vehicle homicide.
Except as provided [below], motor vehicle homicide is a Class I misdemeanor.

If the proximate cause of the death of another is the operation of a motor vehicle in violation of [the sections of the law concerning reckless driving], motor vehicle homicide is a Class IV felony.

If the proximate cause of the death of another is the operation of a motor vehicle in violation of [the section of the law concerning driving under the influence of alcohol or drugs], motor vehicle homicide is a Class IV felony and the court shall, as part of the judgment of conviction, order the person not to drive any motor vehicle for any purpose for a period of at least sixty days and not more than fifteen years from the date ordered by the court and shall order that the operator's license of such person be revoked for the same period. The revocation shall not run concurrently with any jail term imposed.

If the proximate cause of the death of another is the operation of a motor vehicle in violation of [the section of the law concerning driving under the influence of alcohol or drugs], motor vehicle homicide is a Class III felony if the defendant has a prior conviction under [that section] or a city or village ordinance enacted pursuant to such section and the court shall, as part of the judgment of conviction, order the person not to drive any motor vehicle for any purpose for a period of at least sixty days and not more than fifteen years from the date ordered by the court and shall order that the operator's license of such person be revoked for the same period. The revocation shall not run concurrently with any jail term imposed.
(Nebraska Criminal Code 28-306)

Assisted Suicide

A person commits assisting suicide when, with intent to assist another person in committing suicide, he aids and abets him in committing or attempting to commit suicide.

Assisting suicide is a Class IV felony.
(Nebraska Criminal Code 28-307)

The complete and unedited text of Nebraska's murder laws excerpted above can be found in Revised Statutes of Nebraska *and* The Laws of Nebraska.

NEVADA'S MURDER LAWS

Definitions

Murder is the unlawful killing of a human being, with malice aforethought, either express or implied, or caused by a controlled substance which was sold, given, traded or otherwise made available to a person in violation of [the law]. The unlawful killing may be effected by any of the various means by which death may be occasioned.

Express malice is that deliberate intention unlawfully to take away the life of a fellow creature, which is manifested by external circumstances capable of proof.

[Implied malice exists] when no considerable provocation appears, or when all the circumstances of the killing show an abandoned and malignant heart.

Child abuse means physical injury of a nonaccidental nature to a child under the age of eighteen years.

Sexual abuse of a child means [incest, lewdness with a child, annoyance or molestation of a child, sado-masochistic abuse, sexual assault, statutory sexual seduction, or open or gross lewdness].

Sexual molestation means any willful and lewd or lascivious act, other than acts constituting the crime of sexual assault, upon or with the body, or any part or member thereof, of a child under the age of fourteen years, with the intent of arousing, appealing to, or gratifying the lust, passions or sexual desires of the perpetrator or of the child.

(Nevada Criminal Code 200.010/.020/.030)

First Degree Murder

Murder of the first degree is murder which is:

(1) perpetrated by means of poison, lying in wait, torture or child abuse, or by any other kind of willful, deliberate and premeditated killing;

(2) committed in the perpetration or attempted perpetration of sexual assault, kidnapping, arson, robbery, burglary, invasion of the home, sexual abuse of a chid or sexual molestation of a child under the age of fourteen years; or

(3) committed to avoid or prevent the lawful arrest of
any person by a peace officer or to effect the escape
of any person from legal custody.

Every person convicted of murder of the first degree shall be
punished:

(1) by death, only if one or more aggravating circumstances are found and any mitigating circumstance or
circumstances which are found do not outweigh the
aggravating circumstance or circumstances.

(2) otherwise, by imprisonment in the state prison for
life with or without possibility of parole. If the penalty is fixed at life imprisonment with possibility of
parole, eligibility for parole begins when a minimum
of ten years has been served.

(Nevada Criminal Code 200.030)

Second Degree Murder

Murder of the second degree is all other kinds of murder.

Every person convicted of murder of the second degree shall be
punished by imprisonment in the state prison for life or for a
definite term of not less than five years. Under either sentence, eligibility for parole begins when a minimum of five
years has been served.

(Nevada Criminal Code 200.030)

Manslaughter

Manslaughter:

(1) is the unlawful killing of a human being, without
malice express or implied, and without any mixture of
deliberation; or

(2) results from the accidental death of another human being as a result of a violation of [the section of
the law concerning fleeing a police officer].

Manslaughter must be voluntary, upon a sudden heat of passion, caused by a provocation apparently sufficient to make the
passion irresistible; or, involuntary, in the commission of an unlawful act, or a lawful act without due caution or circumspection.

In cases of voluntary manslaughter, there must be a serious and highly provoking injury inflicted upon the person killing, sufficient to excite an irresistible passion in a reasonable person, or an attempt by the person killed to commit a serious personal injury on the person killing.

Every person convicted of the crime of voluntary manslaughter shall be punished by imprisonment in the state prison for a term of not less than one year nor more than ten years, and may be further punished by a fine of not more than $10,000.

Every person convicted of involuntary manslaughter shall be punished by imprisonment in the state prison for not less than one year nor more than six years, or by imprisonment in the county jail for not more than one year, or by a fine of not more than $5,000, or by both fine and imprisonment.

If imprisonment in the county jail, or fine, or both, shall be prescribed for the punishment of involuntary manslaughter, the crime shall for all purposes be deemed a gross misdemeanor. (Nevada Criminal Code 200.040/.050/.080/.090)

Justifiable Homicide

Homicide is justifiable when committed by a public officer, or person acting under his command and in his aid, in the following cases:

(1) in obedience to the judgment of a competent court;

(2) when necessary to overcome actual resistance to the execution of the legal process, mandate or order of a court or officer, or in the discharge of a legal duty;

(3) when necessary:

(a) in retaking an escaped or rescued prisoner who has been committed, arrested for, or convicted of a felony;

(b) in attempting, by lawful ways or means, to apprehend or arrest a person; or

(c) in lawfully suppressing a riot or preserving the peace.

Justifiable homicide is the killing of a human being in necessary self-defense, or in defense of habitation, property or person, against one who manifestly intends, or endeavors, by violence or surprise, to commit a felony, or against any person or persons who manifestly intend and endeavor, in a violent, riotous, tumultuous or surreptitious manner, to enter the habitation of another for the purpose of assaulting or offering personal violence to any person dwelling or being therein.

Homicide is also justifiable when committed either:

(1) in the lawful defense of the slayer, or his or her husband, wife, parent, child, brother or sister, or of any other person in his presence or company, when there is reasonable ground to apprehend a design on the part of the person slain to commit a felony or to do some great personal injury to the slayer or to any such person, and there is imminent danger of such design being accomplished;

(2) in the actual resistance of an attempt to commit a felony upon the slayer, in his presence, or upon or in a dwelling, or other place of abode in which he is; or

(3) by any person, when committed upon the person of another who is engaged in the commission of a felony or an attempted felony, or who after the commission or attempted commission of any such felony is fleeing from the premises or resisting lawful pursuit and arrest within twenty miles of the premises where such felony was committed or attempted to be committed.

(Nevada Criminal Code 200.120/.140/.160/.200)

Year-and-a-Day

In order to make the killing either murder or manslaughter, it is requisite that the party die within a year and a day after the stroke received, or the cause of death administered, in the computation of which the whole of the day on which the act was done shall be reckoned the first.

(Nevada Criminal Code 200.100)

The complete and unedited text of Nevada's murder laws excerpted above can be found in Nevada Revised Statutes Annotated *and* Statutes of Nevada.

NEW HAMPSHIRE'S MURDER LAWS
First Degree Murder

A person is guilty of murder in the first degree if he:

    (1) purposely causes the death of another; or

    (2) knowingly causes the death of:

        (a) another before, after, while engaged in the commission of, or while attempting to commit felonious sexual assault;

        (b) another before, after, while engaged in the commission of, or while attempting to commit robbery or burglary while armed with a deadly weapon, the death being caused by the use of such weapon;

        (c) another in perpetrating or attempting to perpetrate arson;

        (d) the president or president-elect or vice-president or vice-president-elect of the United States, the governor or governor-elect of New Hampshire or any state or any member or member-elect of the congress of the United States, or any candidate for such office after such candidate has been nominated at his party's primary, when such killing is motivated by knowledge of the foregoing capacity of the victim.

Purposely shall mean that the actor's conscious object is the death of another, and that his act or acts in furtherance of that object were deliberate and premeditated.

A person convicted of a murder in the first degree shall be sentenced to life imprisonment and shall not be eligible for parole at any time.

(New Hampshire Criminal Code 630:1-a)

Second Degree Murder

A person is guilty of murder in the second degree if:

    (1) he knowingly causes the death of another; or

    (2) he causes such death recklessly under circumstances manifesting an extreme indifference to the value of human life. Such recklessness and indifference are presumed if the actor causes the death by the

use of a deadly weapon in the commission of, or in an attempt to commit, or in immediate flight after committing or attempting to commit any Class A felony.

Murder in the second degree shall be punishable by imprisonment for life or such term as the court may order.

(New Hampshire Criminal Code 630:1-b)

Manslaughter

A person is guilty of manslaughter when he causes the death of another:

(1) under the influence of extreme mental or emotional disturbance caused by extreme provocation but which would otherwise constitute murder; or

(2) recklessly.

Manslaughter shall be punishable by imprisonment for a term of not more than thirty years.

(New Hampshire Criminal Code 630:2)

Negligent Homicide

A person is guilty of a Class B felony when he causes the death of another negligently.

A person is guilty of a Class A felony when in consequence of being under the influence of intoxicating liquor or a controlled drug or any combination of intoxicating liquor and controlled drug while operating a propelled vehicle, or a boat, he causes the death of another.

In addition to any other penalty imposed, if the death of another person resulted from the negligent driving of a motor vehicle, the court may revoke the license or driving privilege of the convicted person for up to seven years.

(New Hampshire Criminal Code 630:3)

Assisted Suicide

A person is guilty of causing or aiding suicide if he purposely aids or solicits another to commit suicide.

Causing or aiding suicide is a Class B felony if the actor's conduct causes such suicide or an attempted suicide. Otherwise it is a misdemeanor.
(New Hampshire Criminal Code 630:4)

The complete and unedited text of New Hampshire's murder laws excerpted above can be found in The New Hampshire Revised Statutes Annotated *and* The Laws of the State of New Hampshire.

NEW JERSEY'S MURDER LAWS
Definitions
Bodily injury means physical pain, illness or any impairment of physical conditions.

Serious bodily injury means bodily injury which creates a substantial risk of death or which causes serious, permanent disfigurement, or protracted loss or impairment of the function of any bodily member or organ.

Deadly weapon means any firearm or other weapon, device, instrument, material or substance, whether animate or inanimate, which in the manner it is used or is intended to be used, is known to be capable of producing death or serious bodily injury or which in the manner it is fashioned would lead the victim reasonably to believe it to be capable of producing death or serious bodily injury.
(New Jersey Criminal Code 2C:11-1)

Murder
Except as provided in [the section on manslaughter, below], criminal homicide constitutes murder when:

(1) the actor purposely causes death or serious bodily injury resulting in death;

(2) the actor knowingly causes death or serious bodily injury resulting in death;

(3) it is committed when the actor, acting either alone or with one or more other persons, is engaged in the commission of, or an attempt to commit, or flight after committing or attempting to commit robbery, sexual assault, arson, burglary, kidnapping, or criminal escape, and in the course of such crime or of immediate flight therefrom, any person causes the death of a person other than one of the participants; except that any prosecution under this subsection, in which the defendant was not the only participant in the underlying crime, it is an affirmative defense that the defendant:

(a) did not commit the homicidal act or in any way solicit, request, command, importune, cause or aid the commission thereof; and

(b) was not armed with a deadly weapon, or any instrument, article or substance readily capable of causing death or serious physical injury and of a sort not ordinarily carried in public places by law-abiding persons; and

(c) had no reasonable ground to believe that any other participant was armed with such a weapon, instrument, article or substance; and

(d) had no reasonable ground to believe that any other participant intended to engage in conduct likely to result in death or serious physical injury.

Murder is a crime of the first degree. [A] person convicted of murder [as outlined in section 3, above] shall be sentenced . . . to a term of thirty years, during which the person shall not be eligible for parole or to a specific term of years which shall be between thirty years and life imprisonment of which the person shall serve thirty years before being eligible for parole. [A person convicted of murder as outlined in sections 1 and 2, above, may be sentenced to death.]

(New Jersey Criminal Code 2C:11-3)

Manslaughter

Criminal homicide constitutes aggravated manslaughter when the actor recklessly causes death under circumstances manifesting extreme indifference to human life.

Criminal homicide constitutes manslaughter when:

(1) it is committed recklessly;

(2) a homicide which would otherwise be murder is committed in the heat of passion resulting from a reasonable provocation; or

(3) the actor causes the death of another person while fleeing or attempting to elude a law enforcement officer. . . .

Aggravated manslaughter is a crime of the first degree and upon conviction thereof a person may . . . be sentenced to an ordinary term of imprisonment between ten and thirty years. Manslaughter is a crime of the second degree.

(New Jersey Criminal Code 2C:11-4)

Vehicular Homicide

Criminal homicide constitutes death by auto or vessel when it is caused by driving a vehicle or vessel recklessly.

Death by auto or vessel is a crime of the third degree. [T]he court may not suspend the imposition of sentence on any defendant convicted under this section, who was operating the auto or vessel under the influence of an intoxicating liquor, narcotic, hallucinogenic or habit-producing drug, or with a blood alcohol concentration of 0.10% or more by weight of alcohol in his blood and any sentence imposed under this section shall include either a fixed minimum term of 270 days imprisonment, during which the defendant shall be ineligible for parole, or a requirement that the defendant perform a community related service for a minimum of 270 days.

Auto or vessel means all means of conveyance propelled otherwise than by muscular power.

(New Jersey Criminal Code 2C:11-5)

Assisted Suicide

A person who purposely aids another to commit suicide is guilty of a crime of the second degree if his conduct causes such suicide or an attempted suicide, and otherwise of a crime of the fourth degree.

(New Jersey Criminal Code 2C:11-6)

The complete and unedited text of New Jersey's murder laws excerpted above can be found in New Jersey Revised Statutes, New Jersey Statutes Annotated, *and* The Laws of New Jersey.

NEW MEXICO'S MURDER LAWS

First Degree Murder

Murder in the first degree is the killing of one human being by another without lawful justification or excuse, by any of the means with which death may be caused:

(1) by any kind of willful, deliberate and premeditated killing;

(2) in the commission of or attempt to commit any felony; or

(3) by any act greatly dangerous to the lives of others, indicting a depraved mind regardless of human life.

Whoever commits murder in the first degree is guilty of a capital felony.

(New Mexico Criminal Code 30-2-1)

Second Degree Murder

Unless he is acting upon sufficient provocation, upon a sudden quarrel or in the heat of passion, a person who kills another human being without lawful justification or excuse commits murder in the second degree if in performing the acts which cause the death he knows that such acts create a strong probability of death or great bodily harm to that individual or another.

Whoever commits murder in the second degree is guilty of a second degree felony resulting in the death of a human being.

(New Mexico Criminal Code 30-2-1)

Manslaughter

Manslaughter is the unlawful killing of a human being without malice.

Voluntary manslaughter consists of manslaughter committed upon a sudden quarrel or in the heat of passion.

Whoever commits voluntary manslaughter is guilty of a third degree felony resulting in the death of a human being.

Involuntary manslaughter consists of manslaughter committed in the commission of an unlawful act not amounting to felony, or in the commission of a lawful act which might produce death in an unlawful manner or without due caution and circumspection.

Whoever commits involuntary manslaughter is guilty of a fourth degree felony.
(New Mexico Criminal Code 30-2-3)

Excusable Homicide

Homicide is excusable in the following cases:

(1) when committed by accident or misfortune in doing any lawful act, by lawful means, with usual and ordinary caution and without any unlawful intent; or

(2) when committed by accident or misfortune in the heat of passion, upon any sudden and sufficient provocation, or upon a sudden combat, if no undue advantage is taken, nor any dangerous weapon used and the killing is not done in a cruel or unusual manner.

Whenever any person is prosecuted for a homicide, and upon his trial the killing shall be found to have been excusable, the jury shall find such person not guilty and he shall be discharged.
(New Mexico Criminal Code 30-2-5/8)

Justifiable Homicide

Homicide is justifiable when committed by a public officer or public employee or those acting by their command and in their aid and assistance:

(1) in obedience to any judgment of a competent court;

(2) when necessarily committed in overcoming actual resistance to the execution of some legal process or to the discharge of any other legal duty;

(3) when necessarily committed in retaking felons who have been rescued or who have escaped or when necessarily committed in arresting felons fleeing from justice; or

(4) when necessarily committed in order to prevent the escape of a felon from any place of lawful custody or confinement.

[H]omicide is necessarily committed when a public officer or public employee has probable cause to believe he or another is threatened with serious harm or deadly force while performing those lawful duties described in this section. Whenever feasible, a public officer or employee should give warning prior to using deadly force.

Homicide is justifiable when committed by any person in any of the following cases:

(1) when committed in the necessary defense of his life, his family or his property, or in necessarily defending against any unlawful action directed against himself, his wife or family;

(2) when committed in the lawful defense of himself or of another and when there is a reasonable ground to believe a design exists to commit a felony or to do some great personal injury against such person or another, and there is imminent danger that the design will be accomplished; or

(3) when necessarily committed in attempting, by lawful ways and means, to apprehend any person for any felony committed in his presence, or in lawfully suppressing any riot, or in necessarily and lawfully keeping and preserving the peace.

Whenever any person is prosecuted for a homicide, and upon his trial the killing shall be found to have been justifiable, the jury shall find such person not guilty and he shall be discharged.

(New Mexico Criminal Code 30-2-6/7/8)

Assisted Suicide

Assisting suicide consists of deliberately aiding another in the taking of his own life. Whoever commits assisting suicide is guilty of a fourth degree felony.

(New Mexico Criminal Code 30-2-4)

The complete and unedited text of New Mexico's murder laws excerpted above can be found in New Mexico Statutes Annotated *and* The Laws of New Mexico.

NEW YORK'S MURDER LAWS

Definitions

Homicide means conduct which causes the death of a person or an unborn child with which a female has been pregnant for more than twenty-four weeks under circumstances constituting murder, manslaughter in the first degree, manslaughter in the second degree, criminally negligent homicide, abortion in the first degree or self-abortion in the first degree.

Person, when referring to the victim of a homicide, means a human being who has been born and is alive.

Abortional act means an act committed upon or with respect to a female, whether by another person or by the female herself, whether she is pregnant or not, whether directly upon her body or by the administering, taking or prescription of drugs or in any other manner, with intent to cause a miscarriage of such female.

Justifiable abortional act. An abortional act is justifiable when committed upon a female with her consent by a duly licensed physician acting:

> (1) under a reasonable belief that such is necessary to preserve her life; or
>
> (2) within twenty-four weeks from the commencement of her pregnancy.

The submission by a female to an abortional act is justifiable when she believes that it is being committed by a duly licensed physician, acting under a reasonable belief that such act is necessary to preserve her life, or, within twenty-four weeks from the commencement of her pregnancy.
(New York Criminal Code 125.00/.05)

Negligent Homicide

A person is guilty of criminally negligent homicide when, with criminal negligence, he causes the death of another person.
Criminally negligent homicide is a Class E felony.
(New York Criminal Code 125.10)

Second Degree Murder

A person is guilty of murder in the second degree when:

(1) with intent to cause the death of another person, he causes the death of such person or of a third person; except that in any prosecution under this subdivision, it is an affirmative defense that:

(a) the defendant acted under the influence of extreme emotional disturbance for which there was a reasonable explanation or excuse, the reasonableness of which is to be determined from the viewpoint of a person in the defendant's situation under the circumstances as the defendant believed them to be. Nothing contained in this paragraph shall constitute a defense to a prosecution for, or preclude a conviction of, manslaughter in the first degree or any other crime;

(b) the defendant's conduct consisted of causing or aiding, without the use of duress or deception, another person to commit suicide. Nothing contained in this paragraph shall constitute a defense to a prosecution for, or preclude a conviction of, manslaughter in the second degree or any other crime;

(2) under circumstances evincing a depraved indifference to human life, he recklessly engages in conduct which creates a grave risk of death to another person, and thereby causes the death of another person;

(3) acting either alone or with one or more other persons, he commits or attempts to commit robbery, burglary, kidnapping, arson, rape in the first degree, sodomy in the first degree, sexual abuse in the first degree, aggravated sexual abuse, escape in the first degree, or escape in the second degree, and, in the course of and in furtherance of such crime or of immediate flight therefrom, he, or another participant, if there be any, causes the death of a person other than one of the participants; except that in any prosecution under this subdivision, in which the defendant was not the only

participant in the underlying crime, it is an affirmative defense that the defendant:

(a) did not commit the homicidal act or in any way solicit, request, command, importune, cause or aid the commission thereof; and

(b) was not armed with a deadly weapon, or any instrument, article or substance readily capable of causing death or serious physical injury and of a sort not ordinarily carried in public places by law-abiding persons; and

(c) had no reasonable ground to believe that any other participant was armed with such a weapon, instrument, article or substance; and

(d) had no reasonable ground to believe that any other participant intended to engage in conduct likely to result in death or serious physical injury; or

(4) under circumstances evincing a depraved indifference to human life, and being eighteen years old or more the defendant recklessly engages in conduct which creates a grave risk of serious physical injury or death to another person less than eleven years old and thereby causes the death of such person.

Murder in the second degree is a Class A-I felony.
(New York Criminal Code 125.25)

First Degree Manslaughter

A person is guilty of manslaughter in the first degree when:

(1) with intent to cause serious physical injury to another person, he causes the death of such person or of a third person; or

(2) with intent to cause the death of another person, he causes the death of such person or of a third person under circumstances which do not constitute murder because he acts under the influence of extreme emotional disturbance, as defined in [the section on second degree manslaughter, below] The fact that homicide was committed under the influence of extreme emotional disturbance constitutes a mitigating circum-

stance reducing murder to manslaughter in the first degree and need not be proved in any prosecution initiated under this subdivision;

(3) he commits upon a female pregnant for more than twenty-four weeks an abortional act which causes her death, unless such abortional act is justifiable [as outlined above, under definitions]; or

(4) being eighteen years old or more and with intent to cause physical injury to a person less than eleven years old, the defendant recklessly engages in conduct which creates a grave risk of serious physical injury to such person and thereby causes the death of such person.

Manslaughter in the first degree is a Class B felony.
(New York Criminal Code 125.20)

Second Degree Manslaughter

A person is guilty of manslaughter in the second degree when:

(1) he recklessly causes the death of another person;

(2) he commits upon a female an abortional act which causes her death, unless such abortional act is justifiable; or

(3) he intentionally causes or aids another person to commit suicide.

Manslaughter in the second degree is a Class C felony.
(New York Criminal Code 125.15)

Vehicular Manslaughter

A person is guilty of vehicular manslaughter in the first degree when he:

(1) commits the crime of vehicular manslaughter in the second degree; and

(2) commits such crime while knowing or having reason to know that his license or his privilege of operating a motor vehicle in the state or his privilege of obtaining a license issued by the commissioner of motor vehicles is suspended or revoked and such suspension or revocation is based upon either a refusal to submit

to a chemical test pursuant to the vehicle and traffic law or following a conviction for a violation of the vehicle and traffic law.

Vehicular manslaughter in the first degree is a Class C felony. (New York Criminal Code 125.13)

The complete and unedited text of New York's murder laws excerpted above can be found in McKinney's Consolidated Laws of New York *and* The Laws of New York.

NORTH CAROLINA'S MURDER LAWS

First Degree Murder

A murder which shall be perpetrated by means of poison, lying in wait, imprisonment, starving, torture, or by any other kind of willful, deliberate, and premeditated killing, or which shall be committed in the perpetration or attempted perpetration of any arson, rape or a sex offense, robbery, kidnapping, burglary, or other felony committed or attempted with the use of a deadly weapon shall be deemed to be murder in the first degree, a Class A felony, and any person who commits such murder shall be punished with death or imprisonment in the State's prison for life as the court shall determine, except that any such person who was under seventeen years of age at the time of the murder shall be punished with imprisonment in the State's prison for life. Provided, however, any person under the age of seventeen who cmmmits murder in the first degree while serving a prison sentence imposed for a prior murder or while on escape from a prison sentence imposed for a prior murder shall be punished with death or imprisonment in the State's prison for life as the court shall determine. (North Carolina Criminal Code 14-17)

Second Degree Murder

All other kinds of murder [not mentioned above], including that which shall be proximately caused by the unlawful distribution of opium or any synthetic or natural salt, compound, derivative, or preparation of opium, or cocaine . . . ., when the ingestion of such substance causes the death of the user, shall be deemed murder in the second degree, and any person who commits such murder shall be punished as a Class B felon. (North Carolina Criminal Code 14-17)

Manslaughter

Voluntary manslaughter shall be punishable as a Class E felony, and involuntary manslaughter shall be punishable as a Class F felony. (North Carolina Criminal Code 14-18)

The complete and unedited text of North Carolina's murder laws excerpted above can be found in The General Statutes of North Carolina *and* The Laws of North Carolina.

NORTH DAKOTA'S MURDER LAWS

Murder

A person is guilty of murder, a Class AA felony, if the person:

 (1) intentionally or knowingly causes the death of another human being;

 (2) causes the death of another human being under circumstances manifesting extreme indifference to the value of human life; or

 (3) acting either alone or with one or more other persons, commits or attempts to commit treason, robbery, burglary, kidnapping, felonious restraint, arson, gross sexual imposition, a felony offense against a child, or escape and, in the course of and in furtherance of such crime or of immediate flight therefrom, the person or any other participant in the crime causes the death of any person. In any prosecution under this subsection in which the defendant was not the only participant in the underlying crime, it is an affirmative defense that the defendant:

  (a) did not commit the homicidal act or in any way solicit, command, induce, procure, counsel, or aid the commission thereof;

  (b) was not armed with a firearm, destructive device, dangerous weapon, or other weapon which under the circumstances indicated a readiness to inflict serious bodily injury;

  (c) reasonably believed that no other participant was armed with such a weapon; and

  (d) reasonably believed that no other participant intended to engage in conduct likely to result in death or serious bodily injury.

A person is guilty of murder, a Class A felony, if the person causes the death of another human being under circumstances which would be Class AA felony murder, except that the person causes the death under the influence of extreme emotional disturbance for which there is reasonable excuse. The reasonableness of the excuse must be determined from the viewpoint of a person in that person's situation under the circumstances as that person believes them to be. An extreme emotional disturbance is excusable, within the meaning of this subsection

only, if it is occasioned by substantial provocation, or a serious event, or situation for which the offender was not culpably responsible.
(North Dakota Criminal Code 12.1-16-01)

Manslaughter

A person is guilty of manslaughter, a Class B felony, if he recklessly causes the death of another human being. (North Dakota Criminal Code 12.1-16-02)

Negligent Homicide

A person is guilty of a Class C felony if he negligently causes the death of another human being. (North Dakota Criminal Code 12.1-16-03)

Assisted Suicide

Any person who intentionally or knowingly aids, abets, facilitates, solicits, or incites another person to commit suicide, or who provides to, delivers to, procures for, or prescribes for another person any drug or instrument with knowledge that the other person intends to attempt to commit suicide with the drug or instrument is guilty of a Class C felony.

Any person who, through deception, coercion, or duress, willfully causes the death of another person by suicide is guilty of a Class AA felony.
(North Dakota Criminal Code 12.1-16-04)

The complete and unedited text of North Dakota's murder laws excerpted above can be found in The North Dakota Century Code *and* The Laws of North Dakota.

OHIO'S MURDER LAWS

Murder

No person shall purposely cause the death of another.
Whoever violates this section is guilty of murder.
(Ohio Criminal Code 2903.02)

Voluntary Manslaughter

No person, while under the influence of sudden passion or in a
sudden fit of rage, either of which is brought on by serious
provocation occasioned by the victim that is reasonably sufficient to incite the person into using deadly force, shall knowingly cause the death of another.

Whoever violates this section is guilty of voluntary manslaughter, an aggravated felony of the first degree.
(Ohio Criminal Code 2903.03)

Involuntary Manslaughter

No person shall cause the death of another as a proximate result of the offender's committing or attempting to commit a
felony.

No person shall cause the death of another as a proximate result of the offender's committing or attempting to commit a
misdemeanor of the first, second, third, or fourth degree or a
minor misdemeanor.

Whoever violates this section is guilty of involuntary manslaughter. Violation of [the above felony section] is an aggravated felony of the first degree. Violation of [the above misdemeanor section] is an aggravated felony of the third degree.
(Ohio Criminal Code 2903.04)

Negligent Homicide

No person shall negligently cause the death of another by
means of a deadly weapon or dangerous ordnance.

Whoever violates this section is guilty of negligent homicide, a
misdemeanor of the first degree.
(Ohio Criminal Code 2903.05)

Vehicular Homicide

No person, while operating or participating in the operation of a motor vehicle, motorcycle, snowmobile, locomotive, watercraft, or aircraft, shall negligently cause the death of another.
Whoever violates this section is guilty of vehicular homicide, a misdemeanor of the first degree.
(Ohio Criminal Code 2903.07)

The complete and unedited text of Ohio's murder laws excerpted above can be found in The Ohio Revised Code Annotated *and* Ohio Laws.

OKLAHOMA'S MURDER LAWS

Definitions

Homicide is the killing of one human being by another.
Premeditation is a design to effect death sufficient to constitute murder performed instantly before committing the act by which it is carried into execution.
(Oklahoma Criminal Code 21-691/703)

First Degree Murder

A person commits murder in the first degree when he unlawfully and with malice aforethought causes the death of another human being. Malice is that deliberate intention unlawfully to take away the life of a human being, which is manifested by external circumstances capable of proof.

A person also commits the crime of murder in the first degree when he takes the life of a human being, regardless of malice, in the commission of forcible rape, robbery with a dangerous weapon, kidnapping, escape from lawful custody, first degree burglary, first degree arson, unlawful distributing or dispensing of controlled dangerous substances, or trafficking in illegal drugs.

A person commits murder in the first degree when the death of a child results from the willful or malicious injuring, torturing, maiming or using of unreasonable force by said person or who shall willfully cause, procure or permit any of said acts to be done upon the child.

A person commits murder in the first degree when he unlawfully and with malice aforethought solicits another person or persons to cause the death of a human being in furtherance of unlawfully manufacturing, distributing or dispensing controlled dangerous substances . . . , unlawfully possessing with intent to distribute or dispense controlled dangerous substances, or trafficking in illegal drugs.

No person can be convicted of murder . . . , unless the death of the person alleged to have been killed and the fact of the killing by the accused are each established as independent facts beyond a reasonable doubt.

A person who is convicted of or pleads guilty or *nolo contendere* [no contest] to murder in the first degree shall be pun-

ished by death, by imprisonment for life without parole or by
imprisonment for life.
(Oklahoma Criminal Code 21-693/701.7)

Second Degree Murder

Homicide is murder in the second degree in the following cases:

    (1) when perpetrated by an act imminently dangerous
to another person and evincing a depraved mind, regardless of human life, although without any premeditated design to effect the death of any particular individual; or

    (2) when perpetrated by a person engaged in the com-
mission of any felony other than the unlawful acts set
out in [the section on first degree murder, above].

A person who is convicted of or pleads guilty or *nolo contendere* [no contest] to murder in the second degree shall be punished by imprisonment in a state penal institution for not less
than ten years nor more than life.
(Oklahoma Criminal Code 21-701.8/701.9)

First Degree Manslaughter

Homicide is manslaughter in the first degree in the following
cases:

    (1) when perpetrated without a design to effect death
by a person while engaged in the commission of a
misdemeanor;

    (2) when perpetrated without a design to effect death,
and in a heat of passion, but in a cruel and unusual
manner, or by means of a dangerous weapon; unless it
is committed under such circumstances as constitute
excusable or justifiable homicide.

    (3) when perpetrated unnecessarily either while resist-
ing an attempt by the person killed to commit a crime,
or after such attempt shall have failed.

Every physician who being in a state of intoxication without a
design to effect death, administers any poison, drug or medi-

cine, or does any other act as such physician to another person, which produces the death of such other person, is guilty of manslaughter in the first degree.

The willful killing of an unborn quick child by any injury committed upon the person of the mother of such child . . . is manslaughter in the first degree.

Every person guilty of manslaughter in the first degree is punishable by imprisonment in the penitentiary for not less than four years.

No person can be convicted of . . . manslaughter . . . unless the death of the person alleged to have been killed and the fact of the killing by the accused are each established as independent facts beyond a reasonable doubt.

(Oklahoma Criminal Code 21-693/711/712/713/715)

Second Degree Manslaughter

Every killing of one human being by the act, procurement or culpable negligence of another, which, under the provisions of this chapter, is not murder, nor manslaughter in the first degree, nor excusable nor justifiable homicide, is manslaughter in the second degree.

Every person guilty of manslaughter in the second degree is punishable by imprisonment in the penitentiary not more than four years and not less than two years, or by imprisonment in a county jail not exceeding one year, or by a fine not exceeding one thousand dollars, or both fine and imprisonment.

No person can be convicted of . . . manslaughter, . . . unless the death of the person alleged to have been killed and the fact of the killing by the accused are each established as independent facts beyond a reasonable doubt.

(Oklahoma Criminal Code 21-693/716/722)

Justifiable Homicide

A peace officer, correctional officer, or any person acting by his command in his aid and assistance, is justified in using deadly force when:

(1) the officer is acting in obedience to and in accordance with any judgment of a competent court in executing a penalty of death;

(2) in effecting an arrest or preventing an escape from custody following arrest and the officer reasonably believes both that:

(a) such force is necessary to prevent the arrest from being defeated by resistance or escape; and

(b) there is probable cause to believe that the person to be arrested has committed a crime involving the infliction or threatened infliction of serious bodily harm, or the person to be arrested is attempting to escape by use of a deadly weapon, or otherwise indicates that he will endanger human life or inflict great bodily harm unless arrested without delay;

(3) the officer is in the performance of his legal duty or the execution of legal process and reasonably believes the use of the force is necessary to protect himself or others from the infliction of serious bodily harm; or

(4) the force is necessary to prevent an escape from a penal institution or other place of confinement used primarily for the custody of persons convicted of felonies or from custody while in transit thereto or therefrom unless the officer has reason to know:

(a) the person escaping is not a person who has committed a felony involving violence; and

(b) the person escaping is not likely to endanger human life or to inflict serious bodily harm if not apprehended.

Homicide is also justifiable when committed by any person in either of the following cases:

(1) when resisting any attempt to murder such person, or to commit any felony upon him, or upon or in any dwelling house in which such person is;

(2) when committed in the lawful defense of such person, or of his or her husband, wife, parent, child, master, mistress, or servant, when there is a reasonable

ground to apprehend a design to commit a felony, or to do some great personal injury, and imminent danger of such design being accomplished; or
(3) when necessarily committed in attempting, by lawful ways and means, to apprehend any person for any felony committed; or in lawfully suppressing any riot; or in lawfully keeping and preserving the peace.
(Oklahoma Criminal Code 21-732/733)

Assisted Suicide

No person can be convicted of . . . aiding suicide, unless the death of the person alleged to have been killed and the fact of the killing by the accused are each established as independent facts beyond a reasonable doubt.
(Oklahoma Criminal Code 21-693)

The complete and unedited text of Oklahoma's murder laws excerpted above can be found in Oklahoma Statutes *and* Oklahoma Statutes Annotated.

OREGON'S MURDER LAWS

Definitions

Criminal homicide is murder, manslaughter, or criminally negligent homicide.

Human being means a person who has been born and was alive at the time of the criminal act.

(Oregon Criminal Code 163.005)

Murder

Except as provided in [the section on manslaughter, below], criminal homicide constitutes murder:

(1) when it is committed intentionally, except that it is an affirmative defense that, at the time of the homicide, the defendant was under the influence of an extreme emotional disturbance;

(2) when it is committed by a person, acting either alone or with one or more persons, who commits or attempts to commit any of the following crimes and in the course of and in furtherance of the crime the person is committing or attempting to commit, or during the immediate flight therefrom, the person, or another participant if there be any, causes the death of a person other than one of the participants:

(a) arson in the first degree;

(b) criminal mischief in the first degree by means of an explosive;

(c) burglary in the first degree;

(d) escape in the first degree;

(e) kidnapping in the second degree;

(f) kidnapping in the first degree;

(g) robbery in the first degree;

(h) any felony sexual offense in the first degree; or

(i) compelling prostitution; or

(3) by abuse when a person, recklessly under circumstances manifesting extreme indifference to the value of human life, causes the death of a child under fourteen years of age or a dependent person, and the person has previously engaged in a pattern or practice of

assault or torture of the victim or another child under fourteen years of age or a dependent person.
(Oregon Criminal Code 163.115)

Manslaughter

Criminal homicide constitutes manslaughter in the first degree when:

(1) it is committed recklessly under circumstances manifesting extreme indifference to the value of human life; or

(2) it is committed intentionally by a defendant under the influence of extreme emotional disturbance. The fact that the homicide was committed under the influence of extreme emotional disturbance constitutes a mitigating circumstance reducing the homicide which would otherwise be murder to manslaughter in the first degree and need not be proved in any prosecution.

Manslaughter in the first degree is a Class A felony.

Criminal homicide constitutes manslaughter in the second degree when:

(1) it is committed recklessly; or

(2) a person intentionally causes or aids another person to commit suicide.

Manslaughter in the second degree is a Class B felony.
(Oregon Criminal Code 163.118/.125)

Negligent Homicide

A person commits the crime of criminally negligent homicide when, with criminal negligence, the person causes the death of another person.

Criminally negligent homicide is a Class C felony.
(Oregon Criminal Code 163.145)

Assisted Suicide

It is a defense to a charge of murder that the defendant's conduct consisted of causing or aiding, without the use of duress or deception, another person to commit suicide. Nothing con-

tained in this section shall constitute a defense to a prosecution for, or preclude a conviction of, manslaughter or any other crime.
(Oregon Criminal Code 163.117)

The complete and unedited text of Oregon's murder laws ex-cerpted above can be found in Oregon Revised Statutes *and* Oregon Laws.

PENNSYLVANIA'S MURDER LAWS

Definitions

Intentional killing means killing by means of poison, or by any other kind of willful, deliberate, and premeditated killing.

Perpetration of a felony means the act of the defendant in engaging in or being an accomplice in the commission of, or an attempt to commit, or flight after committing, or attempting to commit, robbery, rape, or deviate sexual intercourse by force or threat of force, arson, burglary, or kidnapping.

(Pennsylvania Criminal Code 2502d)

First Degree Murder

A criminal homicide constitutes murder of the first degree when it is committed by an intentional killing.

(Pennsylvania Criminal Code 2502a)

Second Degree Murder

A criminal homicide constitutes murder of the second degree when it is committed while defendant was engaged as a principal or an accomplice in the perpetration of a felony.

(Pennsylvania Criminal Code 2502b)

Third Degree Murder

All other kinds of murder [not mentioned in the sections on first or second degree murder, above] shall be murder of the third degree. Murder of the third degree is a felony of the first degree.

(Pennsylvania Criminal Code 2502c)

Voluntary Manslaughter

A person who kills an individual without lawful justification commits voluntary manslaughter if at the time of the killing he is acting under a sudden and intense passion resulting from serious provocation by:

(1) the individual killed; or

(2) another whom the actor endeavors to kill, but he negligently or accidentally causes the death of the individual killed.

A person who intentionally or knowingly kills an individual commits voluntary manslaughter if at the time of the killing he believes the circumstances to be such that, if they existed, would justify the killing . . . , but his belief is unreasonable.
Voluntary manslaughter is a felony of the second degree.
(Pennsylvania Criminal Code 2503)

Involuntary Manslaughter

A person is guilty of involuntary manslaughter when as a direct result of the doing of an unlawful act in a reckless or grossly negligent manner, or the doing of a lawful act in a reckless or grossly negligent manner, he causes the death of another person.
Involuntary manslaughter is a misdemeanor of the first degree.
(Pennsylvania Criminal Code 2504)

Assisted Suicide

A person may be convicted of criminal homicide for causing another to commit suicide only if he intentionally causes such suicide by force, duress, or deception.
A person who intentionally aids or solicits another to commit suicide is guilty of a felony of the second degree if his conduct causes such suicide or an attempted suicide, and otherwise of a misdemeanor of the second degree.
(Pennsylvania Criminal Code 2505)

The complete and unedited text of Pennsylvania's murder laws excerpted above can be found in Pennsylvania Consolidated Statutes *and* The Laws of Pennsylvania.

RHODE ISLAND'S MURDER LAWS

First Degree Murder

The unlawful killing of a human being with malice aforethought is murder. Every murder perpetrated by poison, lying in wait, or any other kind of wilful, deliberate, malicious, and premeditated killing, or committed in the perpetration of, or attempt to perpetrate, any arson, . . . or rape, any degree of sexual assault or child molestation, burglary or breaking and entering, robbery, kidnapping, or committed during the course of the perpetration, or attempted perpetration, of felony manufacture, sale, delivery, or other distribution of a controlled substance otherwise prohibited by [law], or while resisting arrest by, or under arrest of, any state trooper or police officer in the performance of his or her duty; or perpetrated from a premeditated design unlawfully and maliciously to effect the death of any human being other than him or her who is killed is murder in the first degree.

Every person guilty of murder in the first degree shall be imprisoned for life. Every person guilty of murder in the first degree:

(1) committed intentionally while engaged in the commission of another capital offense or other felony for which life imprisonment may be imposed;

(2) committed in a manner creating a great risk of death to more than one person by means of a weapon or device or substance which would normally be hazardous to the life of more than one person;

(3) committed at the direction of another person in return for money or any other thing of monetary value from that person;

(4) committed in a manner involving torture or an aggravated battery to the victim;

(5) committed against any member of the judiciary, law enforcement officer, corrections employee, or firefighter arising from the lawful performance of his or her official duties;

(6) committed by a person who at the time of the murder was committed to confinement in the adult

correctional institutions or the state reformatory for
women upon conviction of a felony; or

(7) committed during the course of the perpetration
or attempted perpetration of felony manufacture, sale,
delivery or other distribution of a controlled substance otherwise prohibited by [law];

shall be imprisoned for life and if ordered by the court . . .
such person shall not be eligible for parole from imprisonment.

If any person under the age of eighteen who is kidnapped by a
person other than his or her natural or adopted parent dies as a
direct result of such kidnapping, then the person convicted of
the offense shall be guilty of murder in the first degree and
shall be punished by imprisonment for life, and the court may
. . . order that that person not be eligible for parole.

Every person guilty of murder in the first degree shall serve
not less than fifteen years of his or her sentence before being
eligible for parole.

(Rhode Island Criminal Code 11-23-1/-2/-2.1/-2.2)

Second Degree Murder

[Any murder other than those described under first degree
murder, above] is murder in the second degree.

Every person guilty of murder in the second degree shall be
imprisoned for not less than ten years and may be imprisoned
for life.

(Rhode Island Criminal Code 11-23-1/-2)

Manslaughter

Every person who shall commit manslaughter shall be imprisoned not exceeding thirty years.

(Rhode Island Criminal Code 11-23-3)

*The complete and unedited text of Rhode Island's murder laws
excerpted above can be found in* The General Laws of Rhode
Island *and* The Public Laws of Rhode Island.

SOUTH CAROLINA'S MURDER LAWS

Murder

Murder is the killing of any person with malice aforethought, either express or implied.

A person who is convicted of or pleads guilty to murder must be punished by death or by imprisonment for life and is not eligible for parole until the service of twenty years; provided, however, that when the State seeks the death penalty and an aggravating circumstance is specifically found beyond a reasonable doubt . . . , and a recommendation of death is not made, the court must impose a sentence of life imprisonment without eligibility for parole until the service of thirty years.
(South Carolina Criminal Code 16-3-10/-20)

Manslaughter

Manslaughter, or the unlawful killing of another without malice, express or implied, must be imprisoned not more than thirty years nor less than two years.
(South Carolina Criminal Code 16-3-50)

Involuntary Manslaughter

With regard to the crime of involuntary manslaughter, criminal negligence is defined as the reckless disregard of the safety of others. A person charged with the crime of involuntary manslaughter may be convicted only upon a showing of criminal negligence. . . . A person convicted of involuntary manslaughter must be imprisoned not more than five years.
(South Carolina Criminal Code 16-3-60)

Homicide by Child Abuse

A person is guilty of homicide by child abuse who:

(1) causes the death of a child under the age of eleven while committing child abuse or neglect . . . and the death occurs under circumstances manifesting an extreme indifference to human life; or

(2) knowingly aids and abets another person to commit child abuse or neglect . . . and the child abuse or

neglect results in the death of a child under the age of eleven.

Homicide by child abuse is a felony and a person who is convicted of or pleads guilty to homicide by child abuse:

(1) under [paragraph 1, above] may be imprisoned for life but not less than a term of twenty years; or

(2) under [paragraph 2, above] must be imprisoned for a term not exceeding twenty years nor less than ten years.

(South Carolina Criminal Code 16-3-85)

The complete and unedited text of South Carolina's murder laws excerpted above can be found in The Code of Laws of South Carolina *and* The Acts of South Carolina.

SOUTH DAKOTA'S MURDER LAWS

First Degree Murder

Homicide is murder in the first degree when perpetrated without authority of law and with a premeditated design to effect the death of the person killed or of any other human being, or when committed by a person engaged in the perpetration of, or attempt to perpetrate, any arson, rape, robbery, burglary, kidnapping, or unlawful throwing, placing, or discharging of a destructive device or explosive. Homicide is also murder in the first degree if committed by a person who perpetrated, or who attempted to perpetrate, any arson, rape, robbery, burglary, kidnapping or unlawful throwing, placing, or discharging of a destructive device or explosive and who subsequently effects the death of any victim of such crime to prevent detection or prosecution of the crime.

Murder in the first degree is a Class A felony.

(South Dakota Criminal Code 22-16-4/-12)

Second Degree Murder

Homicide is murder in the second degree when perpetrated by any act imminently dangerous to others and evincing a depraved mind, regardless of human life, although without any premeditated design to effect the death of any particular individual.

Homicide is murder in the second degree when perpetrated without any design to effect death by a person engaged in the commission of any felony other than as provided in [the section on first degree murder, above].

Murder in the second degree is a Class B felony.

(South Dakota Criminal Code 22-16-7/-9/-12)

Manslaughter

Homicide is manslaughter in the first degree when perpetrated:

(1) without a design to effect death by a person while engaged in the commission of a misdemeanor involving moral turpitude;

(2) without a design to effect death, and in a heat of passion, but in a cruel and unusual manner;

(3) without a design to effect death, but by means of a dangerous weapon;

(4) unnecessarily, either while resisting an attempt by the person killed to commit a crime or after such attempt shall have failed.

Manslaughter in the first degree is a Class 1 felony.

Any reckless killing of one human being, including an unborn child, by the act or procurement of another which . . . is neither murder nor manslaughter in the first degree, nor excusable nor justifiable homicide, is manslaughter in the second degree. Manslaughter in the second degree is a Class 4 felony.

(South Dakota Criminal Code 22-16-15/-20)

Excusable Homicide

Homicide is excusable when committed by accident and misfortune in doing any lawful act, with usual and ordinary caution.

Homicide is excusable when committed by accident and misfortune in the heat of passion, upon sudden and sufficient provocation, or upon a sudden combat; provided that no undue advantage is taken nor any dangerous weapon used and that killing is not done in a cruel or unusual manner.

(South Dakota Criminal Code 22-16-30/-31)

Justifiable Homicide

Homicide is justifiable when committed by law enforcement officers and those acting by their command in their aid and assistance:

(1) when necessarily committed in overcoming actual resistance to the execution of some legal process, or to the discharge of any other legal duty; or

(2) when necessarily committed in retaking felons who have been rescued, or who have escaped, or when necessarily committed in arresting felons fleeing from justice.

Homicide is justifiable when necessarily committed in attempting by lawful ways and means to apprehend any person for any felony committed, or in lawfully suppressing any riot, or in lawfully keeping and preserving the peace.

Homicide is justifiable when committed by any person when resisting any attempt to murder such person, or to commit any felony upon him or her, or upon or in any dwelling house in which such person is.

Homicide is justifiable when committed by any person in the lawful defense of such person, or of his or her husband, wife, parent, child, master, mistress, or servant when there is reasonable ground to apprehend a design to commit a felony, or to do some great personal injury, and imminent danger of such design being accomplished.

(South Dakota Criminal Code 22-16-32/-33/-34/-35)

Vehicular Homicide

Any person who, while under the influence of an alcoholic beverage, any controlled drug or substance, or a combination thereof, without design to effect death, operates or drives a motor vehicle of any kind in a negligent manner and thereby causes the death of another person is guilty of vehicular homicide. Vehicular homicide is a Class 4 felony. In addition to any other penalty prescribed by law, the court may also order that the driver's license of any person convicted of vehicular homicide be revoked for a period of two years subsequent to release from incarceration.

(South Dakota Criminal Code 22-16-41)

Assisted Suicide

Suicide is the intentional taking of one's own life.

Any person who intentionally in any manner advises, encourages, abets, or assists another in taking his own life is guilty of a Class 6 felony.

It is no defense to a prosecution for aiding suicide that the person who committed or attempted to commit suicide was not a person deemed capable of committing crime.

It shall be the duty of any law enforcement officer who has knowledge that any party has attempted to take his own life to immediately notify the state's attorney.

(South Dakota Criminal Code 22-16-36/-37/-39/-40)

The complete and unedited text of South Dakota's murder laws excerpted above can be found in South Dakota Codified Laws Annotated *and* The Laws of South Dakota.

TENNESSEE'S MURDER LAWS

First Degree Murder

First degree murder is:

(1) a premeditated and intentional killing of another;

(2) a killing of another committed in the perpetration of or attempt to perpetrate any first degree murder, arson, rape, robbery, burglary, theft, kidnapping, aggravated child abuse or aircraft piracy; or

(3) a killing of another committed as the result of the unlawful throwing, placing, or discharging of a destructive device or bomb.

No culpable mental state is required for conviction under [paragraphs 2 or 3, above] except the intent to commit the enumerated offenses or acts in such [paragraphs].

A person convicted of first degree murder shall be punished by:

(1) death;

(2) imprisonment for life without possibility of parole; or

(3) imprisonment for life.

Premeditation is an act done after the exercise of reflection and judgment. [It] means that the intent to kill must have been formed prior to the act itself. It is not necessary that the purpose to kill pre-exist in the mind of the accused for any definite period of time. The mental state of the accused at the time the accused allegedly decided to kill must be carefully considered in order to determine whether the accused was sufficiently free from excitement and passion as to be capable of premeditation.

(Tennessee Criminal Code 39-13-202)

Second Degree Murder

Second degree murder is:

(1) a knowing killing of another; or

(2) a killing of another which results from the unlawful distribution of any [illegal] drug when such drug is the proximate cause of the death of the user.

Second degree murder is a Class A felony.

(Tennessee Criminal Code 39-13-210)

Voluntary Manslaughter

Voluntary manslaughter is the intentional or knowing killing of another in a state of passion produced by adequate provocation sufficient to lead a reasonable person to act in an irrational manner.

Voluntary manslaughter is a Class C felony.

(Tennessee Criminal Code 39-13-211)

Criminally Negligent Homicide

Criminally negligent conduct which results in death constitutes criminally negligent homicide.

Criminally negligent homicide is a Class E felony.

(Tennessee Criminal Code 39-13-212)

Vehicular Homicide

Vehicular homicide is the reckless killing of another by the operation of an automobile, airplane, motorboat or other motor vehicle:

> (1) as the proximate result of conduct creating a substantial risk of death or serious bodily injury to a person; or
>
> (2) as the proximate result of the driver's intoxication. . . . For the purposes of this section, **intoxication** includes alcohol intoxication . . . , drug intoxication, or both.

Vehicular homicide is a Class C felony, unless it is the proximate result of driver intoxication as set forth in [paragraph 2, above], in which case it is a Class B felony.

The court shall prohibit a defendant convicted of vehicular homicide from driving a vehicle in this state for a period of time not less than three years nor more than ten years.

(Tennessee Criminal Code 39-13-213)

Assisted Suicide

A person commits the offense of assisted suicide who:

> (1) intentionally provides another person with the means by which such person directly and intentionally brings about such person's own death; or

(2) intentionally participates in a physical act by which another person directly and intentionally brings about such person's own death; and

(3) provides the means or participates in the physical act with:

(a) actual knowledge that the other person intends to bring about such person's own death; and

(b) the clear intent that the other person bring about such person's own death.

It is not an offense under this section to:

(1) withhold or withdraw medical care. . . ;

(2) prescribe, dispense, or administer medications or perform medical procedures calculated or intended to relieve another person's pain or discomfort (but not calculated or intended to cause death), even if the medications or medical procedures may hasten or increase the risk of death; or

(3) fail to prevent another from bringing about that person's own death.

This section shall not in any way affect, impair, impede, or otherwise omit or render invalid the rights, privileges, and policies set forth in the Tennessee Right to Natural Death Act . . . , the provisions for the durable power of attorney for health care . . . , or the Do-Not-Resuscitate (DNR) regulations of the Tennessee Board for licensing health care facilities . . . .

Assisted suicide is a Class D felony.

(Tennessee Criminal Code 39-13-216)

The complete and unedited text of Tennessee's murder laws excerpted above can be found in The Tennessee Code Annotated *and* The Public Acts of Tennessee.

TEXAS' MURDER LAWS

Murder

In this section:

(1) **Adequate cause** means cause that would commonly produce a degree of anger, rage, resentment, or terror in a person of ordinary temper, sufficient to render the mind incapable of cool reflection.

(2) **Sudden passion** means passion directly caused by and arising out of provocation by the individual killed or another acting with the person killed which passion arises at the time of the offense and is not solely the result of former provocation.

A person commits an offense if he:

(1) intentionally or knowingly causes the death of an individual;

(2) intends to cause serious bodily injury and commits an act clearly dangerous to human life that causes the death of an individual; or

(3) commits or attempts to commit a felony, other than manslaughter, and in the course of and in furtherance of the commission or attempt, or in immediate flight from the commission or attempt, he commits or attempts to commit an act clearly dangerous to human life that causes the death of an individual.

Except as provided by [the paragraph below], an offense under this section is a felony of the first degree.

At the punishment stage of a trial, the defendant may raise the issue as to whether he caused the death under the immediate influence of sudden passion arising from an adequate cause. If the defendant proves the issue in the affirmative by a preponderance of the evidence, the offense is a felony of the second degree.

(Texas Criminal Code 19.02)

Manslaughter

A person commits an offense if he recklessly causes the death of an individual.

An offense under this section is a felony of the second degree.

(Texas Criminal Code 19.04)

Negligent Homicide

A person commits an offense if he causes the death of an individual by criminal negligence.

An offense under this section is a state jail felony.

(Texas Criminal Code 19.05)

The complete and unedited text of Texas' murder laws excerpted above can be found in Texas Revised Statutes Annotated, Texas Statutes Annotated, *and* The Laws of the State of Texas.

UTAH'S MURDER LAWS

Murder

Criminal homicide constitutes murder if the actor:

(1) intentionally or knowingly causes the death of another;

(2) intending to cause serious bodily injury to another commits an act clearly dangerous to human life that causes the death of another;

(3) acting under circumstances evidencing a depraved indifference to human life engages in conduct which creates a grave risk of death to another and thereby causes the death of another;

(4) while in the commission, attempted commission, or immediate flight from the commission or attempted commission of aggravated robbery, robbery, rape, object rape, forcible sodomy, or aggravated sexual assault, aggravated arson, arson, aggravated burglary, burglary, aggravated kidnapping, kidnapping, child kidnapping, rape of a child, object rape of a child, sodomy upon a child, forcible sexual abuse, sexual abuse of a child, aggravated sexual abuse of a child, or child abuse . . . ; or

(5) causes the death of a peace officer while in the commission or attempted commission of:

(a) an assault against a peace officer . . . ; or

(b) interference with a peace officer while making a lawful arrest . . . if the actor uses force against a peace officer.

Murder is a first degree felony.
(Utah Criminal Code 76-5-203)

Manslaughter

Criminal homicide constitutes manslaughter if the actor:

(1) recklessly causes the death of another;

(2) causes the death of another under the influence of extreme emotional disturbance for which there is a reasonable explanation or excuse; or

(3) causes the death of another under circumstances where the actor reasonably believes the circumstances

provide a legal justification or excuse for his conduct although the conduct is not legally justifiable or excusable under the existing circumstances.

Under [paragraph 2, above], emotional disturbance does not include a condition resulting from mental illness as defined [by law].

The reasonableness of an explanation or excuse under [paragraph 2, above], or the reasonable belief of the actor under [paragraph 3, above], shall be determined from the viewpoint of a reasonable person under the then existing circumstances.

Manslaughter is a felony of the second degree.
(Utah Criminal Code 76-5-205)

Negligent Homicide

Criminal homicide constitutes negligent homicide if the actor, acting with criminal negligence, causes the death of another.

Negligent homicide is a Class A misdemeanor.
(Utah Criminal Code 76-5-206)

Vehicular Homicide

Criminal homicide is automobile homicide, a third degree felony, if the actor operates a motor vehicle while having a blood alcohol content of .08% or greater by weight, or while under the influence of alcohol, any drug, or the combined influence of alcohol and any drug, to a degree that renders the actor incapable of safely operating the vehicle, and causes the death of another by operating the vehicle in a negligent manner.

The fact that a person charged with violating this section is on or has been legally entitled to use alcohol or a drug is not a defense to any charge of violating this section.

For purposes of this section, **motor vehicle** means any self-propelled vehicle and includes any automobile, truck, van, motorcycle, train, engine, watercraft, or aircraft.
(Utah Criminal Code 76-5-207)

The complete and unedited text of Utah's murder laws excerpted above can be found in The Utah Code Annotated *and* The Laws of Utah.

VERMONT'S MURDER LAWS
Murder

Murder committed by means of poison, or by lying in wait, or by wilful, deliberate and premeditated killing, or committed in perpetrating or attempting to perpetrate arson, sexual assault, aggravated sexual assault, robbery or burglary, shall be murder in the first degree. All other kinds of murder shall be murder in the second degree.

The punishment for murder in the first degree shall be imprisonment for life and for a minimum term of thirty-five years unless the court finds that there are aggravating or mitigating factors which justify a different minimum term.
(Vermont Criminal Code 2301/2303)

Manslaughter

A person who commits manslaughter shall be fined not more than $3,000, or imprisoned for not less than one year nor more than fifteen years.
(Vermont Criminal Code 2304)

Justifiable Homicide

If a person kills or wounds another . . . in the suppression of a person attempting to commit murder, sexual assault, aggravated sexual assault, burglary or robbery, with force or violence [he shall be guiltless].
(Vermont Criminal Code 2305)

Attempted Murder

Any person who shall attempt to commit the crimes of aggravated murder or murder shall be imprisoned not more than twenty years or fined not more than $3,000, or both.
(Vermont Criminal Code 2307)

False Testimony

A person who wilfully and corruptly bears false testimony with intent to take away the life of a person and thereby causes the

life of such person to be taken, shall be guilty of murder in the first degree.
(Vermont Criminal Code 2308)

The complete and unedited text of Vermont's murder laws excerpted above can be found in Vermont Statutes Annotated *and* The Laws of Vermont.

VIRGINIA'S MURDER LAWS

Murder

Any person who commits capital murder, murder of the first degree, murder of the second degree, voluntary manslaughter, or involuntary manslaughter, shall be guilty of a felony.

The following offenses shall constitute capital murder, punishable as a Class 1 felony:

(1) the willful, deliberate, and premeditated killing of any person in the commission of abduction, when such abduction was committed with the intent to extort money or a pecuniary benefit;

(2) the willful, deliberate, and premeditated killing of any person by another for hire;

(3) the willful, deliberate, and premeditated killing of any person by a prisoner confined in a state or local correctional facility, or while in the custody of an employee thereof;

(4) the willful, deliberate, and premeditated killing of any person in the commission of robbery or attempted robbery while armed with a deadly weapon;

(5) the willful, deliberate, and premeditated killing of any person in the commission of, or subsequent to, rape or attempted rape, forcible sodomy or attempted forcible sodomy or object sexual penetration;

(6) the willful, deliberate, and premeditated killing of a law-enforcement officer when such killing is for the purpose of interfering with the performance of his official duties;

(7) the willful, deliberate, and premeditated killing of more than one person as a part of the same act or transaction;

(8) the willful, deliberate, and premeditated killing of a child under the age of twelve years in the commission of abduction when such abduction was committed with the intent to extort money or a pecuniary benefit, or with the intent to defile the victim of such abduction; and

(8) the willful, deliberate, and premeditated killing of any person in the commission of or attempted commission of a violation of [the law] involving a con-

trolled substance, when such killing is for the purpose of furthering the commission or attempted commission of such violation.

Murder, other than capital murder, by poison, lying in wait, imprisonment, starving, or by any willful, deliberate, and premeditated killing, or in the commission of, or attempt to commit, arson, rape, forcible sodomy, inanimate object sexual penetration, robbery, burglary or abduction, except as provided [above], is murder of the first degree, punishable as a Class 2 felony.

All murder other than capital murder and murder in the first degree is murder of the second degree and is punishable by confinement in a state correctional facility for not less than five nor more than forty years.

The killing of one accidentally, contrary to the intention of the parties, while in the prosecution of some felonious act other than those specified [above] is murder of the second degree and is punishable as a Class 3 felony.

(Virginia Criminal Code 18.2-30/31/32/33)

Manslaughter

Voluntary manslaughter is punishable as a Class 5 felony.

Involuntary manslaughter is punishable as a Class 5 felony.

Any person who, as a result of driving under the influence, unintentionally causes the death of another person, shall be guilty of involuntary manslaughter.

If, in addition, the conduct of the defendant was so gross, wanton and culpable as to show a reckless disregard for human life, he shall be guilty of aggravated involuntary manslaughter, a felony punishable by a term of imprisonment of not less than one nor more than twenty years, one year of which shall be a mandatory, minimum term of imprisonment.

The provisions of this section shall not preclude prosecution under any other homicide statute. The driver's license of any person convicted under this section may be suspended for a period of up to five years. This section shall not preclude any other revocation or suspension required by law.

(Virginia Criminal Code 18.2-35/36/36.1)

The complete and unedited text of Virginia's murder laws excerpted above can be found in The Code of Virginia Annotated *and* Acts of the Commonwealth of Virginia.

WASHINGTON'S MURDER LAWS

First Degree Murder

A person is guilty of murder in the first degree when:

(1) with a premeditated intent to cause the death of another person, he or she causes the death of such person or of a third person;

(2) under circumstances manifesting an extreme indifference to human life, he or she engages in conduct which creates a grave risk of death to any person, and thereby causes the death of a person; or

(3) he or she commits or attempts to commit the crime of either:

(a) robbery in the first or second degree;

(b) rape in the first or second degree;

(c) burglary in the first degree;

(d) arson in the first or second degree; or

(e) kidnapping in the first or second degree;

and in the course of or in furtherance of such crime or in immediate flight therefrom, he or she, or another participant, causes the death of a person other than one of the participants, except that in any prosecution under this subdivision in which the defendant was not the only participant in the underlying crime, if established by the defendant by a preponderance of the evidence, it is a defense that the defendant:

(a) did not commit the homicidal act or in any way solicit, request, command, importune, cause, or aid the commission thereof;

(b) was not armed with a deadly weapon, or any instrument, article, or substance readily capable of causing death or serious physical injury;

(c) had no reasonable grounds to believe that any other participant was armed with such a weapon, instrument, article, or substance; and

(d) had no reasonable grounds to believe that any other participant intended to engage in conduct likely to result in death or serious physical injury.

Murder in the first degree is a Class A felony.

[A]ny person convicted of the crime of murder in the first degree shall be sentenced to life imprisonment.
(Washington Criminal Code 9A.32.030/040)

Second Degree Murder

A person is guilty of murder in the second degree when:

(1) with intent to cause the death of another person but without premeditation, he causes the death of such person or of a third person; or

(2) he commits or attempts to commit any felony other than those enumerated in [paragraph 3 of first degree murder, above], and, in the course of and in furtherance of such crime or in immediate flight therefrom, he, or another participant, causes the death of a person other than one of the participants; except that in any prosecution under this subdivision in which the defendant was not the only participant in the underlying crime, if established by the defendant by a preponderance of the evidence, it is a defense that the defendant:

(a) did not commit the homicidal act or in any way solicit, request, command, importune, cause, or aid the commission thereof;

(b) was not armed with a deadly weapon, or any instrument, article, or substance readily capable of causing death or serious physical injury;

(c) had no reasonable grounds to believe that any other participant was armed with such a weapon, instrument, article, or substance; and

(d) had no reasonable grounds to believe that any other participant intended to engage in conduct likely to result in death or serious physical injury.

Murder in the second degree is a Class A felony.
(Washington Criminal Code 9A.32.050)

Manslaughter

A person is guilty of manslaughter in the first degree when:

(1) he recklessly causes the death of another person;

or

(2) he intentionally and unlawfully kills an unborn quick child by inflicting any injury upon the mother of such child.

Manslaughter in the first degree is a Class B felony.

A person is guilty of manslaughter in the second degree when, with criminal negligence, he causes the death of another person.

Manslaughter in the second degree is a Class C felony.

(Washington Criminal Code 9A.32.060/070)

The complete and unedited text of Washington's murder laws excerpted above can be found in The Revised Code of Washington, The Revised Code of Washington Annotated, *and* The Laws of Washington.

WEST VIRGINIA'S MURDER LAWS
Murder

Murder by poison, lying in wait, imprisonment, starving, or by any willful, deliberate and premeditated killing, or in the commission of, or attempt to commit, arson, kidnapping, sexual assault, robbery, burglary, breaking and entering, escape from lawful custody, or a felony offense of manufacturing or delivering a controlled substance, is murder of the first degree. All other murder is murder of the second degree.

In an indictment for murder and manslaughter, it shall not be necessary to set forth the manner in which, or the means by which, the death of the deceased was caused, but it shall be sufficient in every such indictment to charge that the defendant did feloniously, willfully, maliciously, deliberately and unlawfully slay, kill and murder the deceased.

Murder of the first degree shall be punished by confinement in the penitentiary for life.

Murder of the second degree shall be punished by confinement in the penitentiary not less than five nor more than eighteen years.

(West Virginia Criminal Code 61-2-1/2/3)

Manslaughter

Voluntary manslaughter shall be punished by confinement in the penitentiary not less than one nor more than five years.

Involuntary manslaughter is a misdemeanor, and any person convicted thereof shall be confined in jail not to exceed one year, or fined not to exceed one thousand dollars, or both, in the discretion of the court.

(West Virginia Criminal Code 61-2-4/5)

Poisoning

If any person administer, or attempt to administer, any poison or other destructive thing in food, drink, medicine or otherwise, or poison any spring, well, reservoir, conduit or pipe of water, with intent to kill . . . another person, he shall be guilty of a felony, and upon conviction, shall be confined in the penitentiary not less than three nor more than eighteen years.

(West Virginia Criminal Code 61-2-7)

The complete and unedited text of West Virginia's murder laws excerpted above can be found in The West Virginia Code *and* The Acts of West Virginia.

WISCONSIN'S MURDER LAWS

Murder

Whoever causes the death of another human being while committing or attempting to commit [first degree sexual assault, second degree sexual assault by use of threat of force or violence, arson, armed burglary, or armed robbery] may be imprisoned for not more than twenty years in excess of the maximum period of imprisonment provided by law for that crime or attempt.

(Wisconsin Criminal Code 940.03)

Reckless Homicide

Whoever recklessly causes the death of another human being under circumstances which show utter disregard for human life is guilty of a Class B felony.

Whoever causes the death of another human being under any of the following circumstances is guilty of a Class B felony:

(1) by manufacture or delivery of a controlled substance . . . which another human being uses and dies as a result of that use; [or]

(2) by administering or assisting in administering a controlled substance . . . , without lawful authority to do so, to another human being and that human being dies as a result of the use of the substance.

Whoever recklessly causes the death of another human being is guilty of a Class C felony.

(Wisconsin Criminal Code 940.02/.06)

Negligent Homicide

Whoever knowing the vicious propensities of any animal intentionally allows it to go at large or keeps it without ordinary care, if such animal, while so at large or not confined, kills any human being who has taken all the precautions which the circumstances may permit to avoid such animal, is guilty of a Class C felony.

Whoever causes the death of another human being by the negligent operation or handling of a dangerous weapon, explosives or fire is guilty of a Class D felony.

Whoever causes the death of another human being by the negligent operation or handling of a vehicle is guilty of a Class E felony.
(Wisconsin Criminal Code 940.07/.08/.10)

Assisted Suicide

Whoever with intent that another take his or her own life assists such person to commit suicide is guilty of a Class D felony.
(Wisconsin Criminal Code 940.12)

The complete and unedited text of Wisconsin's murder laws excerpted above can be found in Wisconsin Statutes, Wisconsin Statutes Annotated, *and* The Laws of Wisconsin.

WYOMING'S MURDER LAWS

First Degree Murder

Whoever purposely and with premeditated malice, or in the perpetration of, or attempt to perpetrate, any sexual assault, arson, robbery, burglary, escape, resisting arrest or kidnapping, or by administering poison or causing the same to be done, kills any human being is guilty of murder in the first degree.

A person convicted of murder in the first degree shall be punished by death or life imprisonment according to law.

(Wyoming Criminal Code 6-2-101)

Second Degree Murder

Whoever purposely and maliciously, but without premeditation, kills any human being is guilty of murder in the second degree, and shall be imprisoned in the penitentiary for any term not less than twenty years, or during life.

(Wyoming Criminal Code 6-2-104)

Manslaughter

A person is guilty of manslaughter if he unlawfully kills any human being without malice, expressed or implied, either:

> (1) voluntarily, upon a sudden heat of passion; or
> (2) involuntarily, but recklessly except under circumstances constituting a violation of [the paragraph on aggravated homicide by vehicle, below].

Manslaughter is a felony punishable by imprisonment in the penitentiary for not more than twenty years.

(Wyoming Criminal Code 6-2-105)

Vehicular Homicide

Except as provided in [the paragraph below on aggravated homicide by vehicle], a person is guilty of homicide by vehicle and shall be fined not more than two thousand dollars or imprisoned in the county jail for not more than one year, or both, if he operates or drives a vehicle in a criminally negligent manner, and his conduct is the proximate cause of the death of another person.

A person is guilty of aggravated homicide by vehicle and shall be punished by imprisonment in the penitentiary for not more than twenty years, if:

> (1) while operating or driving a vehicle in violation of [the section of the law concerning driving under the influence of alcohol or drugs], he causes the death of another person and the violation is the proximate cause of death; or
>
> (2) he operates or drives a vehicle in a reckless manner, and his conduct is the proximate cause of the death of another person.

The division of motor vehicles shall revoke the license or permit to drive and the nonresident operating privilege of any person convicted of aggravated homicide by vehicle or of homicide by vehicle.

(Wyoming Criminal Code 6-2-106)

Negligent Homicide

Except under circumstances constituting a violation of [the section on vehicular homicide, above], a person is guilty of criminally negligent homicide if he causes the death of another person by conduct amounting to criminal negligence.

Criminally negligent homicide is a misdemeanor punishable by imprisonment for not more than one year, a fine of not more than two thousand dollars, or both.

(Wyoming Criminal Code 6-2-107)

The complete and unedited text of Wyoming's murder laws excerpted above can be found in Wyoming Statutes and The Session Laws of Wyoming.

Murder Statistics

Whoever destroys a single life is as guilty as if he had destroyed the whole world.

- The Talmud

Murder Statistics is a comprehensive collection of both up-to-date and historic murder facts and figures, presented in two mutually supporting sections. The current decade is covered in *Murder Statistics For The 1990's.* The previous nine decades are covered in *Body Count: Ninety Years Of Murder In America.*

Murder Statistics For The 1990's is broken down into three interrelated, mutually supporting, geographic divisions - Regions, States, and Cities - and is presented in two forms: reported number of murders, and reported murder rates per each 100,000 people.

In *Murder Statistics By Region*, you will find murder statistics for the first five years of the 1990's for each geographic region of the United States, broken down by *Reported Number Of Murders* and *Reported Murder Rates.*

In *Murder Statistics By States*, you will find murder statistics for the first five years of the 1990's for all fifty U.S. States and the District of Columbia, broken down by *Reported Number Of Murders* and *Reported Murder Rates.*

In *Murder Statistics By Cities*, you will find the *Reported Number Of Murders* for the first five and one-half years of the 1990's for all 207 U.S. cities over 100,000 in population.

All of these murder statistics are drawn from the Federal Bureau of Investigation's *Uniform Crime Reports*, the single most authoritative criminal justice statistical source available, which is published annually, with semi-annual supplements. *Uniform Crime Reports* uses this definition of murder:

Murder: *The wilful (non-negligent) killing of one human being by another. Excluded under this definition are deaths caused by negligence, suicide, or accident; justifiable homicides; and attempts to murder.*

Body Count: Ninety Years Of Murder In America is a comprehensive collection of historic murder statistics presented alongside *Murder Statistics For The 1990's* for easy reference and comparison. *Body Count: Ninety Years Of Murder In America* is presented in four mutually supporting sections for the period January 1, 1900 to December 31, 1989. In the first section you will find *Murder Victims By Decade.* In the second section you will find *Reported Number Of Murders By Year.* In the third section you will find *Reported Number Of Murders By Sex/Year.* In the fourth section you will find *Reported Murder Rates By Year.* These murder facts and figures have been drawn from both *The Historical Statistics of the United States* (1900 - 1970) and *The Statistical Abstract of the United States* (1971 - 1989) to give the reader a complete statistical study of murder in the almost completed twentieth century.

MURDER STATISTICS FOR THE 1990'S

Murder Statistics By Region

Reported Number Of Murders By Region
Number of people reported murdered in geographic regions
from January 1990 - December 1994

United States

1990	23,438	1993	24,526
1991	24,703	1994	23,305
1992	23,760		

Northeast

1990	4,359	1993	4,203
1991	4,275	1994	3,644
1992	4,007		

New England (CT, MA, ME, NH, RI, VT)

1990	521	1993	542
1991	540	1994	520
1992	467		

Middle Atlantic (NJ, NY, PA)

1990	3,838	1993	3,661
1991	3,735	1994	3,124
1992	3,540		

Midwest

1990	4,165	1993	4,654
1991	4,709	1994	4,606
1992	4,642		

East North Central (IL, IN, MI, OH, WI)

1990	3,385	1993	3,584
1991	3,754	1994	3,647
1992	3,666		

West North Central (IW, KS, MN, MI, NE, ND, SD)

1990	780	1993	1,070
1991	955	1994	959
1992	976		

South

1990 **10.113**		1993 **10,113**	
1991 **10,517**		1994 **9,708**	
1992 **9,761**			

South Atlantic (DE, DC, FL, GA, MD, NC, SC, VA, WV)

1990 **4,951**		1993	**4,961**
1991 **5,050**		1994	**4,674**
1992 **4,795**			

East South Central (AL, KY, MS, TN)

1990 **1,555**		1993	**1,611**
1991 **1,601**		1994	**1,636**
1992 **1,511**			

West South Central (AK, LA, OK, TX)

1990 **3,607**		1993	**3,541**
1991 **3,866**		1994	**3,398**
1992 **3,455**			

West

1990 **4,801**		1993 **5,556**	
1991 **5,202**		1994 **5,347**	
1992 **5,350**			

Mountain (AZ, CO, ID, MT, NV, NM, UT, WY)

1990 **817**	1993	**950**	
1991 **912**	1994	**1,112**	
1992 **946**			

Pacific (AK, CA, HI, OR, WA)

1990 **3,984**		1993	**4,606**
1991 **4,290**		1994	**4,235**
1992 **4,404**			

Reported Murder Rates By Region
Rates of murders reported per 100,000 people in
geographic regions from January 1990 - December 1994

nited States

990	9.4	1993	9.5
991	9.8	1994	9.0
992	9.3		

Northeast

1990	8.6	1993	8.2
1991	8.4	1994	7.1
1992	7.8		

New England (CT, MA, ME, NH, RI, VT)

1990	3.9	1993	4.1
1991	4.1	1994	3.9
1992	3.5		

Middle Atlantic (NJ, NY, PA)

1990	10.2	1993	9.6
1991	9.9	1994	8.2
1992	9.3		

Midwest

1990	7.0	1993	7.6
1991	7.8	1994	7.5
1992	7.6		

East North Central (IL, IN, MI, OH, WI)

1990	8.1	1993	8.3
1991	8.9	1994	8.4
1992	8.6		

West North Central (IW, KS, MN, MI, NE, ND, SD)

1990	4.4	1993	5.9
1991	5.4	1994	5.3
1992	5.4		

South

1990	**11.8**	1993	**11.3**
1991	**12.1**	1994	**10.7**
1992	**11.1**		

South Atlantic (DE, DC, FL, GA, MD, NC, SC, VA, WV)

1990	**11.4**	1993	**10.8**
1991	**11.4**	1994	**10.1**
1992	**10.6**		

East South Central (AL, KY, MS, TN)

1990	**10.2**	1993	**10.3**
1991	**10.4**	1994	**10.3**
1992	**9.7**		

West South Central (AK, LA, OK, TX)

1990	**13.5**	1993	**12.7**
1991	**14.2**	1994	**12.0**
1992	**12.5**		

West

1990	**9.1**	1993	**9.9**
1991	**9.6**	1994	**9.4**
1992	**9.7**		

Mountain (AZ, CO, ID, MT, NV, NM, UT, WY)

1990	**6.0**	1993	**6.4**
1991	**6.5**	1994	**7.3**
1992	**6.6**		

Pacific (AK, CA, HI, OR, WA)

1990	**10.2**	1993	**11.2**
1991	**10.7**	1994	**10.2**
1992	**10.8**		

Murder Statistics By States

Reported Number Of Murders By State
Number of people reported murdered by states
from January 1990 - December 1994

Alabama

1990	467	1993	484
1991	469	1994	501
1992	455		

Alaska

1990	41	1993	54
1991	42	1994	38
1992	44		

Arizona

1990	284	1993	339
1991	291	1994	426
1992	312		

Arkansas

1990	241	1993	247
1991	264	1994	294
1992	259		

California

1990	3553	1993	4096
1991	3859	1994	3703
1992	3921		

Colorado

1990	138	1993	206
1991	199	1994	199
1992	216		

Connecticut

1990	166	1993	206
1991	187	1994	215
1992	166		

Delaware

1990	33	1993	35
1991	37	1994	33
1992	32		

District Of Columbia

1990	472	1993	454
1991	482	1994	399
1992	443		

Florida

1990	1379	1993	1224
1991	1248	1994	1165
1992	1208		

Georgia

1990	767	1993	789
1991	849	1994	703
1992	741		

Hawaii

1990	44	1993	45
1991	45	1994	50
1992	42		

Idaho

1990	27	1993	32
1991	19	1994	40
1992	37		

Illinois

1990	1182	1993	1332
1991	1300	1994	1378
1992	1322		

Indiana

1990	344	1993	430
1991	423	1994	453
1992	454		

Iowa

1990	54	1993	66
1991	57	1994	47
1992	44		

Kansas

1990	98	1993	161
1991	153	1994	149
1992	151		

Kentucky

1990	264	1993	249
1991	253	1994	244
1992	216		

Louisiana

1990	724	1993	874
1991	720	1994	856
1992	747		

Maine

1990	30	1993	20
1991	15	1994	28
1992	21		

Maryland

1990	552	1993	632
1991	569	1994	579
1992	596		

Massachusetts

1990	243	1993	233
1991	249	1994	214
1992	214		

Michigan

1990	971	1993	933
1991	1009	1994	927
1992	938		

Minnesota

1990	117	1993	155
1991	131	1994	147
1992	150		

Mississippi

1990	313	1993	357
1991	332	1994	409
1992	320		

Missouri

1990	449	1993	590
1991	543	1994	554
1992	547		

Montana

1990	39	1993	25
1991	21	1994	28
1992	24		

Nebraska

1990	43	1993	63
1991	52	1994	51
1992	68		

Nevada

1990	116	1993	144
1991	152	1994	170
1992	145		

New Hampshire

1990	21	1993	23
1991	40	1994	16
1992	18		

New Jersey

1990	432	1993	418
1991	406	1994	396
1992	397		

New Mexico

1990	139	1993	130
1991	163	1994	177
1992	141		

New York

1990	2605	1993	2420
1991	2571	1994	2016
1992	2397		

North Carolina

1990	711	1993	785
1991	769	1994	772
1992	723		

North Dakota

1990	5	1993	11
1991	7	1994	1
1992	12		

Ohio

1990	663	1993	667
1991	783	1994	662
1992	724		

Oklahoma

1990	253	1993	273
1991	230	1994	226
1992	210		

Oregon

1990	108	1993	140
1991	133	1994	150
1992	139		

Pennsylvania

1990	801	1993	823
1991	758	1994	712
1992	746		

Rhode Island

1990	48	1993	39
1991	37	1994	41
1992	36		

South Carolina

1990	390	1993	377
1991	402	1994	353
1992	373		

South Dakota

1990	14	1993	24
1991	12	1994	10
1992	4		

Tennessee

1990	511	1993	521
1991	547	1994	482
1992	520		

Texas

1990	2389	1993	2147
1991	2652	1994	2022
1992	2239		

Utah

1990	52	1993	58
1991	52	1994	56
1992	54		

Vermont

1990	13	1993	21
1991	12	1994	6
1992	12		

Virginia

1990	545	1993	539
1991	583	1994	571
1992	564		

Washington

1990	238	1993	271
1991	211	1994	294
1992	258		

West Virginia

1990	102	1993	126
1991	111	1994	99
1992	115		

Wisconsin

1990	225	1993	222
1991	239	1994	227
1992	218		

Wyoming

1990	22	1993	16
1991	15	1994	16
1992	17		

United States

1990	23,438
1991	24,703
1992	23,760
1993	24,526
1994	23,305

Reported Murder Rates By State
Rates of murders reported per 100,000 people by states
from January 1990 - December 1994

Alabama
1990	11.6	1993	11.6
1991	11.5	1994	11.9
1992	11.0		

Alaska
1990	7.5	1993	9.0
1991	7.4	1994	6.3
1992	7.5		

Arizona
1990	7.7	1993	8.6
1991	7.8	1994	10.5
1992	8.1		

Arkansas
1990	10.3	1993	10.2
1991	11.1	1994	12.0
1992	10.8		

California
1990	11.9	1993	13.1
1991	12.7	1994	11.8
1992	12.7		

Colorado
1990	4.2	1993	5.8
1991	5.9	1994	5.4
1992	6.2		

Connecticut
1990	5.1	1993	6.3
1991	5.7	1994	6.6
1992	5.1		

Delaware
1990	5.0	1993	5.0
1991	5.4	1994	4.7
1992	4.6		

District Of Columbia
1990	77.8	1993	78.5
1991	80.6	1994	70.0
1992	75.2		

Florida
1990	10.7	1993	8.9
1991	9.4	1994	8.3
1992	9.0		

Georgia
1990	11.8	1993	11.4
1991	12.8	1994	10.0
1992	11.0		

Hawaii
1990	4.0	1993	3.8
1991	4.0	1994	4.2
1992	3.6		

Idaho
1990	2.7	1993	2.9
1991	1.8	1994	3.5
1992	3.5		

Illinois
1990	10.3	1993	11.4
1991	11.3	1994	11.7
1992	11.4		

Indiana

1990	6.2	1993	7.5
1991	7.5	1994	7.9
1992	8.2		

Iowa

1990	1.9	1993	2.3
1991	2.0	1994	1.7
1992	1.6		

Kansas

1990	4.0	1993	6.4
1991	6.1	1994	5.8
1992	6.0		

Kentucky

1990	7.2	1993	6.6
1991	6.8	1994	6.4
1992	5.8		

Louisiana

1990	17.2	1993	20.3
1991	16.9	1994	19.8
1992	17.4		

Maine

1990	2.4	1993	1.6
1991	1.2	1994	2.3
1992	1.7		

Maryland

1990	11.5	1993	12.7
1991	11.7	1994	11.6
1992	12.1		

Massachusetts

1990	4.0	1993	3.9
1991	4.2	1994	3.5
1992	3.6		

Michigan

1990	10.4	1993	9.8
1991	10.8	1994	9.8
1992	9.9		

Minnesota

1990	2.7	1993	3.4
1991	3.0	1994	3.2
1992	3.3		

Mississippi

1990	12.2	1993	13.5
1991	12.8	1994	15.3
1992	12.2		

Missouri

1990	8.8	1993	11.3
1991	10.5	1994	10.5
1992	10.5		

Montana

1990	4.9	1993	3.0
1991	2.6	1994	3.3
1992	2.9		

Nebraska

1990	2.7	1993	3.9
1991	3.3	1994	3.1
1992	4.2		

Nevada

1990	9.7	1993	10.4
1991	11.8	1994	11.7
1992	10.9		

New Hampshire

1990	1.9	1993	2.0
1991	3.6	1994	1.4
1992	1.6		

New Jersey

1990	5.6	1993	5.3
1991	5.2	1994	5.0
1992	5.1		

New Mexico

1990	9.2	1993	8.0
1991	10.5	1994	10.7
1992	8.9		

New York

1990	14.5	1993	13.3
1991	14.2	1994	11.1
1992	13.2		

North Carolina

1990	10.7	1993	11.3
1991	11.4	1994	10.9
1992	10.6		

North Dakota

1990	.8	1993	1.7
1991	1.1	1994	.2
1992	1.9		

Ohio

1990	6.1	1993	6.0
1991	7.2	1994	6.0
1992	6.6		

Oklahoma

1990	8.0	1993	8.4
1991	7.2	1994	6.9
1992	6.5		

Oregon

1990	3.8	1993	4.6
1991	4.6	1994	4.9
1992	4.7		

Pennsylvania

1990	6.7	1993	6.8
1991	6.3	1994	5.9
1992	6.2		

Rhode Island

1990	4.8	1993	3.9
1991	3.7	1994	4.1
1992	3.6		

South Carolina

1990	11.2	1993	10.3
1991	11.3	1994	9.6
1992	10.4		

South Dakota

1990	2.0	1993	3.4
1991	1.7	1994	1.4
1992	.6		

Tennessee

1990	10.5	1993	10.2
1991	11.0	1994	9.3
1992	10.4		

Texas

1990	14.1	1993	11.9
1991	15.3	1994	11.0
1992	12.7		

Utah

1990	3.0	1993	3.1
1991	2.9	1994	2.9
1992	3.0		

Vermont

1990	2.3	1993	3.6
1991	2.1	1994	1.0
1992	2.1		

Virginia

1990	8.8	1993	8.3
1991	9.3	1994	8.7
1992	8.8		

Washington

1990	4.9	1993	5.2
1991	4.2	1994	5.5
1992	5.0		

West Virginia

1990	5.7	1993	6.9
1991	6.2	1994	5.4
1992	6.3		

Wisconsin

1990	4.6	1993	4.4
1991	4.8	1994	4.5
1992	4.4		

Wyoming

1990	4.9	1993	3.4
1991	3.3	1994	3.4
1992	3.6		

United States

1990	9.4
1991	9.8
1992	9.3
1993	9.5
1994	9.0

Murder Statistics by Cities

Reported Numbers Of Murders By Cities
Number of people reported murdered in cities over 100,000
in population for four full years, January 1990 - December 1994,
and one half-year, January - June 1995

Abilene, Texas

1990	7	1993	8
1991	15	1994	6
1992	4	1995	2

Amarillo, Texas

1990	22	1993	11
1991	15	1994	25
1992	17	1995	7

Akron, Ohio

1990	18	1993	19
1991	40	1994	23
1992	24	1995	9

Amherst Town, NY

1990	1	1993	1
1991	1	1994	1
1992	6	1995	1

Albany, New York

1990	9	1993	6
1991	12	1994	13
1992	8	1995	2

Anaheim, California

1990	20	1993	33
1991	25	1994	24
1992	35	1995	16

Albuquerque, NM

1990	34	1993	50
1991	51	1994	na
1992	42	1995	na

Anchorage, Alaska

1990	10	1993	23
1991	25	1994	22
1992	17	1995	10

Alexandria, Virginia

1990	8	1993	9
1991	7	1994	9
1992	4	1995	0

Ann Arbor, Michigan

1990	1	1993	2
1991	2	1994	4
1992	1	1995	1

Allentown, PA

1990	2	1993	6
1991	7	1994	11
1992	11	1995	6

Arlington, Texas

1990	8	1993	7
1991	26	1994	18
1992	16	1995	8

Arlington, Virginia

1990	12	1993	4
1991	11	1994	na
1992	11	1995	na

Atlanta, Georgia

1990	231	1993	203
1991	205	1994	191
1992	198	1995	82

Aurora, Colorado

1990	8	1993	19
1991	11	1994	15
1992	16	1995	12

Aurora, Illinois

1990	11	1993	17
1991	13	1994	13
1992	14	1995	na

Austin, Texas

1990	46	1993	37
1991	49	1994	37
1992	37	1995	na

Bakersfield, California

1990	25	1993	27
1991	20	1994	35
1992	16	1995	na

Baltimore, Maryland

1990	305	1993	353
1991	304	1994	321
1992	335	1995	144

Baton Rouge, Louisiana

1990	49	1993	74
1991	58	1994	64
1992	58	1995	27

Beaumont, Texas

1990	19	1993	23
1991	15	1994	25
1992	23	1995	10

Berkeley, California

1990	11	1993	8
1991	14	1994	8
1992	12	1995	5

Birmingham, Alabama

1990	125	1993	121
1991	139	1994	135
1992	133	1995	61

Boise, Idaho

1990	3	1993	3
1991	3	1994	4
1992	5	1995	1

Boston, Massachusetts

1990	143	1993	98
1991	113	1994	85
1992	73	1995	37

Bridgeport, Connecticut

1990	57	1993	60
1991	51	1994	50
1992	57	1995	14

Brownsville, Texas

1990	13	1993	17
1991	18	1994	12
1992	15	1995	3

Buffalo, New York

1990	37	1993	76
1991	50	1994	90
1992	76	1995	28

Cedar Rapids Iowa

1990	1	1993	na
1991	na	1994	na
1992	na	1995	na

Chandler, Arizona

1990	1	1993	0
1991	7	1994	6
1992	2	1995	2

Charlotte, North Carolina

1990	93	1993	122
1991	114	1994	87
1992	99	1995	48

Chattanooga, Tennessee

1990	32	1993	38
1991	49	1994	43
1992	31	1995	9

Chesapeake, Virginia

1990	7	1993	13
1991	11	1994	19
1992	9	1995	4

Chicago, Illinois

1990	851	1993	845
1991	925	1994	928
1992	939	1995	388

Chula Vista, California

1990	7	1993	14
1991	8	1994	7
1992	7	1995	3

Cincinnati, Ohio

1990	49	1993	39
1991	54	1994	38
1992	49	1995	25

Clearwater, Florida

1990	na	1993	3
1991	2	1994	4
1992	2	1995	1

Cleveland, Ohio

1990	168	1993	167
1991	175	1994	132
1992	157	1995	69

Colorado Springs, CO

1990	9	1993	19
1991	25	1994	14
1992	17	1995	8

Columbia, South Carolina

1990	22	1993	22
1991	25	1994	19
1992	15	1995	na

Columbus, Georgia

1990	23	1993	32
1991	23	1994	20
1992	15	1995	11

Columbus, Ohio

1990	89	1993	105
1991	138	1994	100
1992	113	1995	32

Concord, California

1990	3	1993	5
1991	3	1994	4
1992	5	1995	2

Corpus Christi, Texas

1990	29	1993	34
1991	32	1994	13
1992	30	1995	19

Dallas, Texas

1990	447	1993	317
1991	500	1994	295
1992	387	1995	148

Dayton, Ohio

1990	47	1993	49
1991	54	1994	57
1992	57	1995	22

Denver, Colorado

1990	67	1993	74
1991	88	1994	81
1992	95	1995	42

Des Moines, Iowa

1990	16	1993	9
1991	na	1994	12
1992	7	1995	5

Detroit, Michigan

1990	582	1993	579
1991	615	1994	541
1992	595	1995	234

Durham, North Carolina

1990	23	1993	26
1991	30	1994	35
1992	31	1995	13

Elizabeth, New Jersey

1990	11	1993	17
1991	11	1994	11
1992	13	1995	8

El Monte, California

1990	9	1993	19
1991	13	1994	16
1992	17	1995	22

El Paso, Texas

1990	34	1993	47
1991	49	1994	44
1992	44	1995	22

Erie, Pennsylvania

1990	2	1993	7
1991	7	1994	8
1992	3	1995	1

Escondido, California

1990	4	1993	8
1991	11	1994	9
1992	8	1995	4

Eugene, Oregon

1990	1	1993	3
1991	0	1994	2
1992	2	1995	1

Evansville, Indiana

1990	6	1993	7
1991	12	1994	8
1992	8	1995	2

Flint, Michigan

1990	55	1993	48
1991	52	1994	58
1992	52	1995	19

Fontana, California

1990	11	1993	14
1991	13	1994	19
1992	18	1995	9

Fort Lauderdale, Florida

1990	31	1993	31
1991	27	1994	33
1992	12	1995	13

Fort Wayne, Indiana

1990	17	1993	28
1991	23	1994	38
1992	18	1995	11

Fort Worth, Texas

1990	130	1993	133
1991	195	1994	132
1992	153	1995	51

Fremont, California

1990	2	1993	4
1991	2	1994	6
1992	6	1995	1

Fresno, California

1990	66	1993	87
1991	52	1994	84
1992	81	1995	25

Fullerton, California

1990	6	1993	2
1991	3	1994	6
1992	4	1995	3

Garden Grove, CA

1990	16	1993	13
1991	7	1994	7
1992	5	1995	3

Garland, Texas

1990	11	1993	12
1991	13	1994	10
1992	15	1995	2

Gary, Indiana

1990	65	1993	105
1991	59	1994	80
1992	82	1995	54

Glendale, Arizona

1990	15	1993	16
1991	8	1994	3
1992	12	1995	4

Glendale, California

1990	3	1993	9
1991	8	1994	5
1992	7	1995	4

Grand Prairie, Texas

1990	5	1993	9
1991	7	1994	14
1992	9	1995	6

Grand Rapids, Michigan

1990	18	1993	33
1991	22	1994	23
1992	13	1995	10

Green Bay, Wisconsin

1990	3	1993	2
1991	2	1994	4
1992	1	1995	2

Greensboro, NC

1990	20	1993	27
1991	35	1994	21
1992	23	1995	15

Hampton, Virginia

1990	14	1993	14
1991	14	1994	11
1992	10	1995	8

Hartford, Connecticut

1990	19	1993	30
1991	24	1994	55
1992	13	1995	16

Hayward, California

1990	4	1993	8
1991	10	1994	12
1992	5	1995	4

Hialeah, Florida

1990	14	1993	na
1991	28	1994	na
1992	na	1995	7

Hollywood, Florida

1990	11	1993	9
1991	7	1994	8
1992	5	1995	1

Honolulu, Hawaii

1990	34	1993	31
1991	29	1994	35
1992	31	1995	18

Houston, Texas

1990	568	1993	446
1991	608	1994	375
1992	465	1995	138

Huntington Beach, CA

1990	5	1993	3
1991	6	1994	5
1992	8	1995	6

Huntsville, Alabama			
1990	18	1993	18
1991	na	1994	18
1992	20	1995	4

Jacksonville, Florida			
1990	176	1993	125
1991	128	1994	106
1992	123	1995	40

Independence, Missouri			
1990	1	1993	4
1991	5	1994	6
1992	1	1995	2

Jersey City, New Jersey			
1990	28	1993	20
1991	22	1994	37
1992	25	1995	12

Indianapolis, Indiana			
1990	58	1993	68
1991	95	1994	108
1992	88	1995	na

Kansas City, Kansas			
1990	28	1993	na
1991	44	1994	na
1992	60	1995	na

Inglewood, California			
1990	55	1993	45
1991	46	1994	46
1992	37	1995	15

Kansas City, Missouri			
1990	121	1993	153
1991	135	1994	142
1992	150	1995	47

Irvine, California			
1990	0	1993	1
1991	0	1994	1
1992	3	1995	1

Knoxville, Tennessee			
1990	25	1993	14
1991	35	1994	24
1992	35	1995	9

Irving, Texas			
1990	13	1993	8
1991	18	1994	14
1992	14	1995	2

Lakewood, Colorado			
1990	3	1993	6
1991	3	1994	5
1992	2	1995	2

Jackson, Mississippi			
1990	44	1993	83
1991	74	1994	91
1992	63	1995	53

Lancaster, California			
1990	4	1993	7
1991	14	1994	10
1992	10	1995	3

Lansing, Michigan

1990	11	1993	14
1991	12	1994	10
1992	7	1995	8

Laredo, Texas

1990	14	1993	21
1991	15	1994	24
1992	21	1995	5

Las Vegas, Nevada

1990	79	1993	91
1991	103	1994	105
1992	99	1995	46

Lexington, Kentucky

1990	20	1993	8
1991	13	1994	23
1992	18	1995	7

Lincoln, Nebraska

1990	3	1993	4
1991	0	1994	2
1992	7	1995	0

Little Rock, Arkansas

1990	33	1993	68
1991	46	1994	56
1992	56	1995	30

Livonia, Michigan

1990	1	1993	1
1991	0	1994	1
1992	0	1995	0

Long Beach, California

1990	106	1993	126
1991	94	1994	80
1992	104	1995	37

Los Angeles, California

1990	983	1993	1076
1991	1027	1994	845
1992	1094	1995	358

Louisville, Kentucky

1990	39	1993	37
1991	43	1994	52
1992	39	1995	18

Lowell, Massachusetts

1990	na	1993	6
1991	na	1994	9
1992	na	1995	0

Lubbock, Texas

1990	16	1993	17
1991	18	1994	20
1992	14	1995	7

Macon, Georgia

1990	21	1993	20
1991	32	1994	31
1992	36	1995	13

Madison, Wisconsin

1990	3	1993	2
1991	2	1994	4
1992	3	1995	1

Memphis, Tennessee			
1990	195	1993	198
1991	169	1994	159
1992	176	1995	83

Mesa, Arizona			
1990	9	1993	6
1991	15	1994	17
1992	9	1995	4

Mesquite, Texas			
1990	4	1993	5
1991	4	1994	4
1992	3	1995	0

Miami, Florida			
1990	129	1993	127
1991	134	1994	116
1992	128	1995	48

Milwaukee, Wisconsin			
1990	155	1993	157
1991	163	1994	139
1992	146	1995	54

Minneapolis, Minnesota			
1990	na	1993	58
1991	64	1994	62
1992	60	1995	na

Mobile, Alabama			
1990	41	1993	42
1991	40	1994	39
1992	35	1995	25

Modesto, California			
1990	8	1993	12
1991	7	1994	12
1992	17	1995	7

Montgomery, Alabama			
1990	34	1993	39
1991	36	1994	41
1992	32	1995	25

Moreno Valley, California			
1990	6	1993	12
1991	21	1994	11
1992	15	1995	6

Nashville, Tennessee			
1990	67	1993	87
1991	88	1994	73
1992	90	1995	46

Newark, New Jersey			
1990	112	1993	96
1991	88	1994	96
1992	87	1995	43

New Haven, Connecticut			
1990	31	1993	22
1991	34	1994	32
1992	30	1995	na

New Orleans, Louisiana			
1990	304	1993	395
1991	345	1994	424
1992	279	1995	189

Newport News, Virginia

1990	26	1993	22
1991	18	1994	22
1992	33	1995	13

New York, New York

1990	2245	1993	1946
1991	2154	1994	1561
1992	1995	1995	574

Norfolk, Virginia

1990	63	1993	62
1991	86	1994	61
1992	79	1995	25

Oakland, California

1990	146	1993	154
1991	149	1994	140
1992	165	1995	na

Oceanside, California

1990	11	1993	18
1991	13	1994	15
1992	16	1995	9

Oklahoma City, Oklahoma

1990	68	1993	80
1991	56	1994	65
1992	61	1995	198

Omaha, Nebraska

1990	11	1993	na
1991	35	1994	33
1992	na	1995	na

Ontario, California

1990	19	1993	19
1991	26	1994	25
1992	19	1995	11

Orange, California

1990	5	1993	3
1991	5	1994	8
1992	9	1995	5

Orlando, Florida

1990	30	1993	15
1991	na	1994	17
1992	13	1995	13

Overland Park, Kansas

1990	1	1993	na
1991	1	1994	na
1992	0	1995	na

Oxnard, California

1990	6	1993	16
1991	8	1994	8
1992	14	1995	4

Pasadena, California

1990	13	1993	27
1991	15	1994	16
1992	18	1995	8

Pasadena, Texas

1990	4	1993	10
1991	6	1994	9
1992	10	1995	10

Paterson, New Jersey			
1990	13	1993	23
1991	19	1994	15
1992	16	1995	6

Peoria, Illinois			
1990	4	1993	na
1991	18	1994	11
1992	13	1995	na

Philadelphia, Pennsylvania			
1990	503	1993	439
1991	440	1994	404
1992	425	1995	191

Phoenix, Arizona			
1990	128	1993	158
1991	128	1994	231
1992	136	1995	102

Pittsburgh, Pennsylvania			
1990	35	1993	80
1991	36	1994	64
1992	44	1995	26

Plano, Texas			
1990	4	1993	2
1991	3	1994	1
1992	1	1995	1

Pomona, California			
1990	34	1993	40
1991	25	1994	39
1992	39	1995	21

Portland, Oregon			
1990	33	1993	58
1991	53	1994	50
1992	46	1995	18

Portsmouth, Virginia			
1990	18	1993	33
1991	32	1994	23
1992	36	1995	13

Providence, Rhode Island			
1990	31	1993	22
1991	18	1994	20
1992	19	1995	10

Pueblo, Colorado			
1990	6	1993	9
1991	13	1994	8
1992	9	1995	3

Raleigh, North Carolina			
1990	24	1993	27
1991	25	1994	30
1992	19	1995	9

Rancho Cucamonga, CA			
1990	6	1993	4
1991	6	1994	5
1992	3	1995	5

Reno, Nevada			
1990	11	1993	16
1991	9	1994	21
1992	13	1995	8

Richmond, Virginia

1990	113	1993	112
1991	116	1994	160
1992	117	1995	55

Riverside, California

1990	22	1993	33
1991	39	1994	37
1992	23	1995	22

Rochester, New York

1990	40	1993	64
1991	64	1994	62
1992	49	1995	24

Rockford, Illinois

1990	na	1993	22
1991	13	1994	30
1992	12	1995	4

Sacramento, California

1990	43	1993	85
1991	66	1994	62
1992	45	1995	na

St. Louis, Missouri

1990	177	1993	267
1991	260	1994	248
1992	231	1995	107

St. Paul, Minnesota

1990	18	1993	22
1991	12	1994	29
1992	33	1995	na

St. Petersburg, Florida

1990	31	1993	19
1991	33	1994	23
1992	31	1995	16

Salem, Oregon

1990	6	1993	7
1991	2	1994	10
1992	7	1995	4

Salinas, California

1990	11	1993	15
1991	7	1994	24
1992	16	1995	6

Salt Lake City, Utah

1990	25	1993	19
1991	14	1994	20
1992	14	1995	15

San Antonio, Texas

1990	208	1993	220
1991	208	1994	194
1992	219	1995	78

San Bernardino, CA

1990	na	1993	82
1991	na	1994	71
1992	75	1995	28

San Diego, California

1990	135	1993	133
1991	167	1994	113
1992	146	1995	39

San Francisco, California

1990	101	1993	129
1991	95	1994	91
1992	117	1995	na

San Jose, California

1990	35	1993	41
1991	53	1994	33
1992	43	1995	18

Santa Ana, California

1990	43	1993	78
1991	59	1994	74
1992	58	1995	34

Santa Clarita, California

1990	1	1993	4
1991	2	1994	0
1992	4	1995	1

Santa Rosa, California

1990	1	1993	7
1991	6	1994	5
1992	2	1995	2

Savannah, Georgia

1990	33	1993	33
1991	59	1994	29
1992	23	1995	9

Scottsdale, Arizona

1990	0	1993	3
1991	8	1994	4
1992	4	1995	4

Seattle, Washington

1990	53	1993	67
1991	43	1994	69
1992	60	1995	23

Shreveport, Louisiana

1990	65	1993	76
1991	50	1994	63
1992	47	1995	24

Simi Valley, California

1990	1	1993	0
1991	6	1994	1
1992	2	1995	3

Sioux Falls, South Dakota

1990	4	1993	2
1991	2	1994	3
1992	0	1995	1

South Bend, Indiana

1990	na	1993	19
1991	na	1994	19
1992	18	1995	10

Spokane, Washington

1990	8	1993	13
1991	7	1994	7
1992	12	1995	6

Springfield, Illinois

1990	12	1993	na
1991	10	1994	18
1992	11	1995	5

Springfield, Massachusetts

1990	13	1993	20
1991	13	1994	16
1992	13	1995	11

Springfield, Missouri

1990	7	1993	7
1991	4	1994	3
1992	8	1995	1

Stamford, Connecticut

1990	10	1993	8
1991	10	1994	6
1992	7	1995	3

Sterling Heights, MI

1990	2	1993	0
1991	0	1994	1
1992	2	1995	na

Stockton, California

1990	51	1993	45
1991	55	1994	44
1992	53	1995	17

Sunnyvale, California

1990	2	1993	3
1991	3	1994	2
1992	2	1995	2

Syracuse, New York

1990	14	1993	18
1991	13	1994	16
1992	13	1995	6

Tacoma, Washington

1990	25	1993	31
1991	31	1994	33
1992	31	1995	7

Tallahassee, Florida

1990	na	1993	9
1991	14	1994	9
1992	15	1995	6

Tampa, Florida

1990	60	1993	43
1991	64	1994	62
1992	49	1995	22

Tempe, Arizona

1990	3	1993	4
1991	6	1994	9
1992	8	1995	7

Thousand Oaks, California

1990	2	1993	3
1991	1	1994	1
1992	1	1995	0

Toledo, Ohio

1990	37	1993	45
1991	36	1994	40
1992	43	1995	13

Topeka, Kansas

1990	11	1993	na
1991	16	1994	na
1992	8	1995	na

Torrance, California			
1990	2	1993	12
1991	2	1994	3
1992	2	1995	3

Washington, DC			
1990	472	1993	454
1991	482	1994	399
1992	443	1995	151

Tucson, Arizona			
1990	30	1993	44
1991	24	1994	37
1992	42	1995	na

Waterbury, Connecticut			
1990	5	1993	20
1991	9	1994	8
1992	12	1995	5

Tulsa, Oklahoma			
1990	57	1993	54
1991	42	1994	42
1992	33	1995	14

West Covina, California			
1990	8	1993	5
1991	11	1994	6
1992	4	1995	4

Vallejo, California			
1990	8	1993	10
1991	13	1994	30
1992	13	1995	6

Wichita, Kansas			
1990	18	1993	48
1991	24	1994	42
1992	30	1995	22

Virginia Beach, Virginia			
1990	16	1993	22
1991	27	1994	33
1992	23	1995	8

Winston-Salem, NC			
1990	24	1993	36
1991	23	1994	41
1992	33	1995	13

Waco, Texas			
1990	22	1993	29
1991	23	1994	25
1992	21	1995	6

Worcester, Massachusetts			
1990	na	1993	12
1991	na	1994	13
1992	13	1995	na

Warren, Michigan			
1990	19	1993	na
1991	2	1994	3
1992	5	1995	0

Yonkers, New York			
1990	18	1993	19
1991	9	1994	14
1992	13	1995	4

BODY COUNT: NINETY YEARS OF MURDER IN AMERICA

Murder Victims By Decade
1900 - 1989
Number of persons reported murdered by decade

1900 - 1909	8,426	1950 - 1959	77,528
1910 - 1919	39,158	1960 - 1969	111,000
1920 - 1929	81,451	1970 - 1979	201,017
1930 - 1939	103,917	1980 - 1989	217,937
1940 - 1949	79,620		

Reported Number Of Murders
1900 - 1989

1900	230	1910	2,161
1901	233	1911	2,978
1902	255	1912	2,938
1903	236	1913	3,521
1904	283	1914	3,776
1905	463	1915	3,633
1906	1,310	1916	4,237
1907	1,701	1917	4,864
1908	1,858	1918	5,113
1909	1,857	1919	5,973
1920	5,815	1930	10,331
1921	7,090	1931	10,862
1922	7,381	1932	10,722
1923	7,557	1933	12,124
1924	8,014	1934	12,055
1925	8,440	1935	10,587
1926	8,740	1936	10,232
1927	8,997	1937	9,811
1928	9,780	1938	8,799
1929	9,637	1939	8,394

1940	8,329	1950	7,942
1941	8,048	1951	7,495
1942	7,890	1952	8,054
1943	6,823	1953	7,640
1944	6,675	1954	7,735
1945	7,547	1955	7,418
1946	8,913	1956	7,629
1947	8,708	1957	7,641
1948	8,654	1958	7,815
1949	8.033	1959	8,159
1960	8,464	1970	16,848
1961	8,578	1971	18,787
1962	9,013	1972	19,638
1963	9,225	1973	20,465
1964	9,814	1974	21,465
1965	10,712	1975	21,310
1966	11,606	1976	19,554
1967	13,425	1977	19,968
1968	14,686	1978	20,432
1969	15,477	1979	22,550
1980	24,278		
1981	23,203		
1982	21,912		
1983	19,729		
1984	19,367		
1985	19,445		
1986	21,185		
1987	20,615		
1988	21,469		
1989	22,270		

Murder Victims By Sex/Year
1900 - 1989
Number of persons males/females reported murdered

	Males / Females			Males / Females	
1900	167	63	1910	1,670	491
1901	150	83	1911	2.385	593
1902	168	87	1912	2,305	633
1903	175	61	1913	2,818	703
1904	193	90	1914	3,000	776
1905	339	124	1915	2,829	804
1906	1,013	297	1916	3,419	818
1907	1,334	367	1917	3,904	960
1908	1,421	437	1918	4,107	1,006
1909	1,400	457	1919	4,820	1,153
1920	4,661	1,154	1930	8,233	2,098
1921	5,682	1,408	1931	8,761	2,101
1922	5,996	1,385	1932	8,646	2,076
1923	6,096	1,461	1933	9,847	2,250
1924	6,408	1,606	1934	9,850	2,205
1925	6,823	1,617	1935	8,554	2,033
1926	7,057	1,683	1936	8,134	2,098
1927	7,168	1,829	1937	7,731	2,080
1928	7,889	1,891	1938	6,935	1,864
1929	7,644	1,993	1939	6,657	1,737
1940	6,647	1,682	1950	6,089	1,853
1941	6,408	1,640	1951	5,669	1,826
1942	6,266	1,624	1952	6,202	1,852
1943	5,363	1,460	1953	5,828	1,812
1944	5,251	1,424	1954	5,886	1,849
1945	5,969	1,578	1955	5,630	1,788
1946	7,012	1,901	1956	5,705	1,924
1947	6,858	1,850	1957	5,739	1,902
1948	6,796	1,885	1958	5,804	2,011
1949	6,214	1,819	1959	6,068	2,091

1960	6,269	2,195		1970	13,278	3,570
1961	6,346	2,232		1971	14,812	3,975
1962	6,707	2,306		1972	15,642	3,996
1963	6,921	2,304		1973	15,840	4,625
1964	7,367	2,447		1974	16,747	4,718
1965	8,148	2,564		1975	16,553	7,757
1966	8,729	2,877		1976	15,142	4,412
1967	10,236	3,189		1977	15,355	4,613
1968	11,523	3,163		1978	15,838	4,594
1969	12,166	3,311		1979	17,628	4,922

1980	19,088	5,190
1981	18,253	4,950
1982	16,990	4,922
1983	15,177	4,552
1984	14,734	4,633
1985	14,738	4,707
1986	16,201	4,984
1987	15,497	5,118
1988	16,308	5,161
1989	17,225	5,045

Reported Murder Rates
1900 - 1989
Rate per each 100,000 persons reported murdered

Year	Rate	Year	Rate
1900	1.2	1910	4.6
1901	1.2	1911	5.5
1902	1.2	1912	5.4
1903	1.1	1913	6.1
1904	1.3	1914	6.2
1905	2.1	1915	5.9
1906	3.9	1916	6.3
1907	4.9	1917	6.9
1908	4.8	1918	6.5
1909	4.2	1919	7.2
1920	6.8	1930	8.8
1921	8.1	1931	9.2
1922	8.0	1932	9.0
1923	7.8	1933	9.7
1924	8.1	1934	9.5
1925	8.3	1935	8.3
1926	8.4	1936	8.0
1927	8.4	1937	7.6
1928	8.6	1938	6.8
1929	8.4	1939	6.4
1940	6.3	1950	5.3
1941	6.0	1951	4.9
1942	5.9	1952	5.2
1943	5.1	1953	4.8
1944	5.0	1954	4.8
1945	5.7	1955	4.5
1946	6.4	1956	4.6
1947	6.1	1957	4.5
1948	5.9	1958	4.5
1949	5.4	1959	4.6

1960	4.7		1970	8.3
1961	4.7		1971	8.5
1962	4.8		1972	8.9
1963	4.9		1973	9.3
1964	5.1		1974	9.7
1965	5.5		1975	9.6
1966	5.9		1976	9.0
1967	6.8		1977	9.1
1968	7.3		1978	9.2
1969	7.7		1979	10.0

1980	10.7
1981	10.3
1982	9.6
1983	8.6
1984	8.4
1985	8.3
1986	9.0
1987	8.7
1988	9.0
1989	9.2

The Chronology Of Headline Murders

It is an infinitely atrocious act to take a life.
                                                    - Leonardo DaVinci

If every murder in America, every infinitely atrocious act, made the headlines, there would be no other news to report. Headline murders are those crimes so outrageous and traumatic to the public conscience, either for their brutality, depravity, or insanity, that they have become a part of our common memory.

In the following *Chronology Of Headline Murders* we have selected from the past ninety-five years many of the murders that so shocked and scarred America's collective conscience that the mere mention of the name of a murder victim: Mary Phagan, Bobbie Franks, Kitty Genovese, the slightest reference to the place of the murder: Luby's Cafeteria, Gein's Farm, The Texas Tower, or the use of the name of a murderer: Charles Manson, David Berkowitz, Theodore Bundy, Richard Speck, Jeffrey Dahmer, instantly recalls to the mind of the listener the horror of the crime.

These headline murders, reported in their own time in horrific and lurid detail, are reported here in a plain and factual manner. The story of every headline murder that follows has been carefully and thoroughly researched. We have made every effort to wring sensationalism out of this murder chronology in order to separate fact from fiction, false terrors from real horror.

In these pages you will find real horror. *The Chronology Of Headline Murders* is peopled with murderous parents: Joel Steinberg and Susan Smith, murderous children: Erik and Lyle Menendez, murderous lovers: Harry Thaw and Betty Broderick, and murderous husbands and fathers: Jeffrey MacDonald and John List. You will find in *The Chronology Of Headline Murders* America's serial murderers: Boston's Albert DeSalvo, Chicago's John Wayne Gacy, Yuba City's Juan Corona, and America's mass murderers: San Diego's Oliver Huberty, Austin's Charles Whitman, Killeen's George Hennard, America's child murderers: Wayne Williams and Genene Jones, and America's political murderers: Lee Harvey Oswald, Sirhan Sirhan, and James Earl Ray. No imagination is required - the horror of their crimes is all too real.

Absent by editorial choice from this chronology, but no less important, are murders committed by or against Americans outside our borders: Vietnam's My Lai Massacre; Beirut, Lebanon's Marine Barrack Bombing; Lockerbie, Scotland's Pan Am Flight 103; Guyana's Jonestown Massacre.

The Chronology Of Headline Murders is neither a freak show of the pathetic nor a roll call of the psychotic. It is just a recitation of the facts of murder year in and year out.

The next time you open your newspaper, turn up your radio, or tune in to television there will be a murder reported. Will it become a headline murder? Only time will tell.

1900 - 1909

8,426 people (6,360 males and 2,066 females) were murdered.

On September 23, 1900, Texas multi-millionaire, William Marsh Rice, eighty-four, was murdered, poisoned, in his New York City home by two conspirators, his personal secretary, Charles Jones, twenty-five, and his lawyer, Albert Patrick, thirty-five. Patrick, who had forged Rice's signature to a will naming himself and Jones as Rice's beneficiaries, was arrested for the murder after Jones, in return for immunity from prosecution, confessed to their crime. Albert Patrick was found guilty of first degree murder on March 26, 1902 and sentenced to death. Financed by his brother-in-law's fortune, Patrick fought a ten-year legal battle against his conviction. In 1906 his death sentence was commuted to life imprisonment. In 1912 he won a full pardon.

On September 6, 1901 at the Pan-American Exposition in Buffalo, New York, Leon Czolgosz, twenty-eight, an anarchist, shot, at point-blank range, President William McKinley, fifty-eight. McKinley, the twenty-fifth President of the United States, died of his wounds on September 14. Czolgosz, put on trial on September 23, was found guilty the next day of first degree murder. Leon Czolgosz, whose last words were, "I am not sorry," was put to death in the electric chair in New York's Auburn Prison on October 29, 1901.

On August 13, 1902 near Bennington, Vermont, Mary Mabel Rogers, nineteen, murdered her husband, Marcus Rogers, in order to marry her lover, Maurice Knapp. Mrs. Rogers, on the pretext of a sexual tryst, had lured her husband to the banks of the Wallomsac River, where she knocked him out and threw him into the river. His body was found the next day. Mary Mabel Rogers was arrested, tried, and convicted of murder. On December 8, 1905, despite vehement nationwide protests by women's groups, she was hung.

On December 5, 1904 in Chicago, Illinois, Marie Walcker, forty-six, a spinster who had answered a lonely hearts ad, married Johann Hoch, forty-two. Unbeknownst to his new bride, Hoch, "The Chicago Bluebeard," had been marrying and murdering lonely women for their money for at least ten years - marrying as many as twenty-four, and murdering as many as twelve of his wives. A month after their wedding, Marie Walcker was dead, poisoned with arsenic. Hoch, after collecting Walcker's $500 life insurance money, fled to New York City, where (while romancing another woman) he was captured and returned to Chicago for trial. Convicted of the murder of Marie Walcker, Johann Hoch was hung on February 23, 1906.

On June 25, 1906, before hundreds of witnesses in New York City's Madison Square Garden Roof Theatre, Harry Thaw, thirty-four, heir to a forty million dollar fortune, shot and killed renowned architect, Stanford White, fifty-three, the ex-lover of Thaw's new bride, famed chorus girl Evelyn Nesbit, twenty-two, known as "The Floradora Girl." At his murder trial, Thaw's lawyers argued that their client, obsessed with White's sexual mistreatment of Nesbit (then called by the press "The Girl In The Red Velvet Swing"), was driven temporarily insane. A first trial, in 1907, ended with a hung jury. A second trial, in 1908, ended with a verdict of not guilty by reason of insanity. Thaw was sentenced to life in the New York State Asylum for the Criminally Insane. A third trial, in 1915, freed Thaw from the Asylum.

On July 11, 1906, Chester Gillette, twenty-two, murdered his pregnant girlfriend, Grace "Billie" Brown. Gillette was a well-educated, socially ambitious manager in his family's Cortland, New York dress factory. Grace Brown, eighteen, was a poor, illiterate farm girl, who had come to work in the Gillette factory. Chester Gillette and Grace Brown became lovers. Brown became pregnant and demanded that Gillette marry her. Gillette took Brown, supposedly on vacation, to a lake in New York's Adirondack Mountains. One day the two went out in a rowboat. Only Gillette returned. Brown's body was found the following day. Gillette under questioning claimed that Grace Brown, despondent over her unwanted pregnancy, had committed suicide. An autopsy found that Brown had been struck over the head. Gillette was charged with murder, tried, found guilty, and, on December 4, 1906, sentenced to die. On Monday, March 30, 1908, Chester Gillette was electrocuted for the 1906 murder of Grace "Billie" Brown. Writer Theodore Dreiser attended Chester Gillette's trial and wrote a fictional account based on the murder of Grace Brown, *An American Tragedy.*

On April 28, 1908 in La Porte, Indiana, the farmhouse of Belle Guiness was destroyed in a mysterious fire. The widow Guiness, living with her three children after the 1904 death of her second husband, had been seen about town with many men, who were attracted by her lonely hearts newspaper ads. Investigators searching the charred remains of the Guiness farmhouse found the buried bodies of fourteen unidentified men (whom it is believed had collectively given Belle Guiness as much as $30,000), the three Guiness children, (killed, one theory goes, because they had seen too much), and a headless female corpse found wearing Mrs. Guiness' jewelry (thought by many not to be serial killer Belle Guiness but a Chicago prostitute). The "Black Widow Murders" remain unsolved.

On October 3, 1909, multi-millionaire Thomas Hunton Swope of Kansas City, Missouri, eighty, while under the medical care of his niece's husband, Dr. Bennett Clarke Hyde, died under suspicious circumstances. Dr. Hyde, thirty-eight, married to Frances Swope, one of the co-heirs to the Swope fortune, supervised the medical care of four other members of the Swope family, all co-heirs, who also suddenly fell ill. One, Chrisman Swope, also died. An investigation found that the Swopes had been poisoned with a mixture of strychnine and cyanide. Dr. Bennett Hyde was tried for first degree murder and, on May 16, 1901, was found guilty. Dr. Hyde, financed by his wife Frances' inheritance, appealed, was tried three additional times, and, in 1917, was freed on a legal technicality.

1910 - 1919

39,194 people (31,257 males and 7,937 females) were murdered.

John Sparling, forty-six, lived with his wife Carrie, and their sons, Peter, Albert, and Cyril, on a farm near Bad Axe, Michigan. In June 1909, John Sparling fell suddenly ill and Carrie Sparling called in the family physician, Dr. John MacGregor. John Sparling soon died, leaving Carrie Sparling a rich widow. The three Sparling sons then died: Peter in June 1910, Albert in May 1911, and Cyril in August 1911, all under suspicious circumstances, and all, like their father, after having been treated by Dr. MacGregor and nursed by their mother. John MacGregor and Carrie Sparling were arrested on suspicion of murder in the four "Bad Axe" murders. Carrie Sparling was never tried. In 1912 Dr. MacGregor was found guilty of Cyril Sparling's murder by arsenic poisoning and sentenced to life imprisonment. In 1916 Dr. John MacGregor, inexplicably, received a full pardon.

On March 25, 1911, a fire swept through the workrooms of the Triangle Shirtwaist Company, a New York City sweatshop located on the ninth floor of a "fire-proof" Greenwich Village building. There were two stairways out. One was engulfed in flames. The other, to keep the workers at their places, was kept locked by the Company. One hundred and forty-six women workers, mostly Jewish and Italian immigrants, die. Max Blanck and Isaac Harris, owners of the Triangle Shirtwaist Company, were charged with one hundred and forty-six counts of first degree manslaughter for having kept the stairway door locked. On December 27, 1911, they were found not guilty.

On March 14, 1912 at the Carroll County Courthouse in Hinsville, Virginia, Judge Thornton Massie sentenced Floyd Allen to one year's imprisonment for assaulting a police officer. Upon hearing his sentence, Floyd Allen yelled at Judge Massie, "I ain't 'goin!", pulled out a gun, and began shooting. Allen's son, Claude, did the same. When the shooting ended, five people - the judge, the prosecutor, the sheriff, a jury member, and a witness - were all dead. Floyd Allen was found guilty of murder on May 18, 1912. His son, Claude, was found guilty of murder on July

12, 1912. Both Allens were executed on March 28, 1913 for the "Carol County Courthouse Massacre."

On April 27, 1913 in Atlanta, Georgia, Mary Phagan, fourteen, a worker at the The National Pencil Factory, was found raped and strangled to death in the factory's basement. The factory superintendent, Leo Frank, twenty-nine, a Jew from New York City, and the last person to admit seeing Mary Phagan alive, was accused of the murder. Leo Frank was tried on shoddy evidence, convicted of Mary Phagan's murder, and sentenced to death. The United States Supreme Court refused to overturn the conviction, despite the patent unfairness of the trial. Georgia Governor Slaton commuted Frank's death sentence to life imprisonment. On August 16, 1915, a lynch mob, fearful that Frank would receive a new trial, broke into the Midgeville, Georgia jail, seized Leo Frank, drove him to Mary Phagan's birthplace, and hanged him.

On July 30, 1915 New York City Police Lieutenant Charles Becker, forty-one, was executed in Sing Sing Prison for ordering the July 12, 1912 murder of gambler Herman Rosenthal. Rosenthal, cheated by the crooked Becker, had informed New York City District Attorney Charles Whitman that Lieutenant Becker was the leader of a criminal gang involved in prostitution, gambling, and extortion. Rosenthal agreed to testify against him. Becker sent his henchman to gun Rosenthal down. On May 22, 1914 Charles Becker was found guilty of murder and sentenced to die. A last minute appeal, to Charles Whitman, by that date New York State's Governor, failed, and Becker was executed.

Dr. Warren Waite, a dentist, married heiress Clara Peck on September 9, 1915. Her millionaire parents, Mr. and Mrs. John Peck of Grand Rapids, Michigan, both suddenly fell ill and died while visiting the newlywed couple in New York City, Mrs. Peck on January 20, 1916, Mr. Peck on March 12, 1916. Dr. Waite, who investigators discovered was keeping a mistress in an expensive suite in New York's Plaza Hotel, was arrested and confessed, after an unsuccessful suicide attempt, to murdering his parents-in-law, to get his hands on their money. He killed them with a deadly bacterial mixture of typhoid, anthrax, influenza, diptheria, and tuberculosis.   Warren Waite, age thirty, was executed at New York's Sing Sing Prison on May 1, 1917.

On March 26, 1916, Robert Stroud, twenty-nine, while serving twelve years in the Leavenworth Kansas Federal Prison for a 1909 manslaughter conviction, murdered a prison guard. Stroud was sentenced to death for the killing of a prison guard but President Wilson commuted his death sentence to life imprisonment in solitary confinement.   While in solitary in the 1920's, Robert Stroud began to raise and study birds. Stroud was sent, in 1942, to Alcatraz Island Federal Prison in San Francisco Bay, where he continued his studies and became known as "The Birdman of Alcatraz."   Robert Stroud, double murderer and world-renowned authority on birds, died on November 21, 1963.

1920 - 1929
81,451 people (65,424 males and 16,027 females)
were murdered.

On June 21, 1920, in Chicago, Illinois, Carl Wanderer, thirty-three, a highly decorated World War I veteran, murdered his wife, Ruth Johnson Wanderer, twenty, and a homeless man, Al Watson. Wanderer, in an attempt to get away with murder, had lured Watson, called by the press "The Ragged Stranger," to the murder scene. There he killed his wife and Watson, later telling police that he killed "The Ragged Stranger" in self-defense after Watson, during a botched robbery, had killed his beloved wife. An investigation uncovered his devious murder plot. Tried and convicted of the murders of Ruth Johnson Wanderer and Al Watson, Carl Wanderer was executed, by hanging, on March 19, 1921.

On September 4, 1921 at San Francisco's St. Francis Hotel, Hollywood comedy film star Roscoe "Fatty" Arbuckle (who weighed over three hundred pounds), thirty-four, allegedly brutally raped model Virginia Rappe, twenty-five. Rappe later died of internal injuries. Arbuckle, called by the press "The Fat Rapist," was tried three times for murder and, in April 1922, was found not guilty.

On September 16, 1922, in New Brunswick, New Jersey, the Reverend Edward Wheeler Hall, forty-one, Rector of St. John's Episcopal Church, and his mistress, Mrs. Eleanor Mills, thirty-four, the church's choir singer, were found in an orchard, lying in each other's arms, shot to death. Scattered around them were several years' worth of their love letters. The Reverend's wife, Mrs. Francis Stevens Hall, and her two brothers, William and Henry Stevens, were charged with the Hall-Mills murders. All were acquitted. The double murder of Edward Wheller Hall and Eleanor Mills remains unsolved.

On May 24, 1924 in Chicago, Illinois, thrill killers Nathan Leopold, eighteen, and Richard Loeb, seventeen, kidnapped and murdered fourteen-year-old Bobbie Franks. When arrested, both Leopold and Loeb confessed to the killing. Famed defense attorney Clarence Darrow was hired by their millionaire parents to keep them out of the electric chair. Tried and convicted of kidnapping and murder, Leopold and Loeb were sentenced to ninety-nine years for kidnapping and life imprisonment for murder. Richard Loeb was killed in prison in 1936. Nathan Leopold was paroled on March 13, 1958.

On February 20, 1926, in San Francisco, California, necrophiliac Earle Nelson, thirty, called by the press "The Gorilla Murderer," murdered and raped Clara Newman. Nelson, over the next year and a half, murdered and raped nineteen additional females in San Francisco, Santa Barbara, and Oakland, California; Portland, Oregon; Council Bluffs, Iowa; Kansas City, Missouri; Philadelphia, Pennsylvania; Buffalo, New York; Detroit, Michigan; Chicago, Illinois; and Winnipeg, Canada. Earle Nelson was arrested, tried, and convicted of the June 9, 1927 murder and rape of Emily Patterson in Winnipeg, Canada, and was executed there on January 12, 1928.

On March 20, 1927 in New York City, lovers Henry Judd Gray, thirty-four, and Ruth Brown Snyder, thirty-two, murdered, by bludgeoning him to death, Mrs. Snyder's husband of ten years, Albert, forty-two. Gray and Snyder confessed separately and blamed each other for the murder. Tried and convicted of first degree murder, Henry Judd Grey and Ruth Brown Snyder were executed, at Sing Sing Prison, New York, by electrocution, on January 12, 1928.

On August 27, 1927 at Charlestown, Massachusetts State Prison, Nicola Sacco and Bartolomeo Vanzetti, both immigrants and anarchists, having been found guilty on July 14, 1921 of the murders of Fredrick Permenter and Alessandro Berardelli (killed during a robbery on April 15, 1920, in Braintree, Massachusetts) were executed.

On June 2, 1928 in Westchester, New York, Albert Fish, fifty-eight, called by the press "The Cannibal," kidnapped, raped, murdered, and then ate pieces of the dead body of Grace Budd, twelve. Fish, suspected of multiple sex crimes and serial child murders committed over more than a quarter of a century, was arrested and tried for the murder of Grace Budd. Albert "The Cannibal" Fish was executed, at the age of sixty-six, in Sing Sing Prison on January 16, 1936.

On December 15, 1928 in Los Angeles, California, Edward Hickman, twenty-three, kidnapped twelve-year-old Marion Parker. Hickman strangled Parker and then, after payment of a $1,500 ransom, delivered her, dead and mutilated, to her father. Edward Hickman, failing twice to kill himself, was executed for the murder of Marion Parker at San Quentin Prison on October 19, 1928.

On February, 14, 1929, St. Valentine's Day, at the North Clark Street Garage in Chicago, Illinois, seven members of the "Bugs" Moran Gang - Adam Hyer, Frank and Peter Gusenberg, John May, Al Weinshank, James Clark, and Reinhardt Schwimmer - were lined up against a wall and shot to death by members of the rival Al Capone Gang. No one was ever tried for "The St. Valentine's Day Massacre."

1930 - 1939
103,917 people (83,375 males and 20,542 females)
were murdered.

On September 9, 1931 in Honolulu, Hawaii, Thalia Fortesque Massie, twenty, a Navy wife, claimed to have been beaten and gang-raped by five young, native Hawaiians. The five, arrested and released on bail, claimed that the sex was voluntary. Her husband, U.S. Navy Lieutenant Thomas Massie, thirty-one, ordered two sailors, Albert Jones and Edward Lord, to bring him one of the accused rapists, Joseph Kahawawai, for interrogation. When Kahawawai admitted in front of Thomas Massie and Thalia's mother, Mrs. Granville Fortesque, that he had had sex with Thalia Massie, Thomas Massie murdered him. All four - Massie, Fortesque, Jones, and Lord - were tried and convicted of second degree murder and sentenced to ten years. Hawaii's Governor commuted their sentences to one hour. Riots ensued.

Charles Augustus Lindbergh, Jr., twenty months old, now known as "The Lindbergh Baby," was the child of Charles "Lucky Lindy" Lindbergh, the first man to fly across the Atlantic Ocean, and his wife, Anne Morrow Lindbergh. On the night of Tuesday, March 1, 1932 Charles A. Lindbergh, Jr., was kidnapped from his parents' Hopewell, New Jersey home. A ransom note was left in the nursery. The ransom, paid in marked money, was handed over on April 2, 1932 in a Bronx, New York cemetery. The dead body of Charles A. Lindbergh, Jr., his skull fractured, was found on May 12, 1932 in a shallow grave near Hopewell. Arrested for kidnapping and murder, after he began to spend the marked ransom money, was Richard Bruno Hauptmann, thirty-one, a German immigrant. The "Trial of the Century," held in Flemington, New Jersey, lasted from January 2 to February 13, 1933. Hauptmann was found guilty of the first degree murder of Charles Augustus Lindbergh, Jr. and sentenced to death. On April 3, 1936 Bruno Richard Hauptmann, protesting his innocence to the last, was electrocuted for the murder of the Lindbergh Baby.

On October 17, 1932 in Phoenix, Arizona, Winnie Ruth Judd, twenty-three, murdered her two roommates, Agnes LeRoi and Helwig "Sammy" Samuelson. Judd then dismembered their

their bodies and stuffed them in a trunk, which she shipped by rail to Los Angeles, California, where they were discovered. Winnie Ruth Judd, called by the press "The Trunk Murderess," was tried, convicted, and sentenced to death for the double murders. She was released on December 22, 1971.

On February 15, 1933 in Miami, Florida, Joseph Zangara, thirty-one, attempted to assassinate President Franklin Roosevelt. Four shots were fired at the President's car. Chicago Mayor Anton Chermak, shot twice, was mortally wounded. Joseph Zangara was executed for the murder of Anton Chermak on March 21, 1933.

On November 9, 1933 in San Jose, California, Brooke Hart, twenty-two, son of a local department store owner, was kidnapped and murdered. Two men, Jack Holmes, twenty-nine, and Harold Thurmond, twenty-seven, were arrested and confessed to the kidnapping and subsequent murder of Brooke Hart. They admitted to having, on the night of the abduction, thrown Hart, bound and unconscious, off the San Mateo Bridge into San Francisco Bay. Alameda County District Attorney (and future U.S. Supreme Court Chief Justice) Earl Warren prepared to charge Holmes and Thurmond with murder. In San Jose on the night of November 26, 1933, a mob broke into the County Jail, seized Holmes and Thurmond, dragged the two into a downtown park, and hanged them. No one was ever prosecuted for the lynchings.

On May 23, 1934 outside of Gibsland, Louisiana, bank robbers Clyde Barrow, twenty-five, and Bonnie Parker, twenty-three, were ambushed and killed by police. "Bonnie and Clyde" had murdered thirteen people, including eight police officers. Clyde Barrow and Bonnie Parker were the subjects of the 1967 movie, *Bonnie and Clyde.*

On June 17, 1935 in Peoria, Illinois, Gerald Thompson, twenty-five, serial rapist of sixteen women between November 1934 and June 1935, murdered Mildred Hallmark, intended victim number seventeen, when she fought back. Gerald Thompson confessed to the murder of Mildred Hallmark and was sentenced to death. On

October 15, 1935 he was executed in the electric chair of Joliet State Prison.

On August 5, 1935 in Los Angeles, California, Robert James murdered his pregnant wife, Mary. Robert James got Mary James drunk and, when she passed out, placed her feet into a box filled with rattlesnakes. Robert James was arrested, tried, and convicted of the "Rattlesnake Murder." He was executed, by hanging, in San Quentin Prison on May 1, 1942.

On September 8, 1935 at the State House in Baton Rouge, Louisiana, United States Senator Huey P. Long, forty-two, known as "The Kingfish," was shot by Dr. Carl Austin Weiss, Jr., twenty-nine. Long's bodyguards killed Weiss in a hail of bullets. Long died of his wounds the next day. A fictional account of the murder of Huey Long by Carl Weiss is found in Robert Penn Warren's *All The King's Men.*

Early in 1936 in San Francisco, California, Ralph Selz, twenty-seven, called "The Laughing Killer," murdered his live-in girlfriend, Ada French Rice, fifty-eight. Selz, who led police to the grave of Rice and laughed as they dug out her corpse, confessed to the murder and was sentenced to life imprisonment.

On June 15, 1936 in Chicago, Illinois, Mildred Bolton, fifty, in an unwarranted jealous rage, murdered her husband, Joseph Bolton, Jr. Mildred Bolton, "The Insanely Jealous Wife," was tried for murder and sentenced to death. After her death sentence was commuted to life imprisonment, Mrs. Bolton committed suicide.

On September 24, 1938 at The Sociable Inn, a roadside bar outside Elmendorf, Texas, Joe Ball, forty-six, "The 'Gator Man," killed himself to escape capture by the Texas Rangers for the serial murders of as many as a dozen women whose dead bodies Ball had fed to the alligators he kept as pets.

1940 - 1949

79,620 people (62,757 males and 16,863 females)
were murdered.

On November 12, 1941 in Brooklyn, New York, mob hit man turned informer, Abe "Kid Twist" Reles, "fell" to his death from the sixth floor of Coney Island's Half Moon Hotel. Abe Reles, set to testify against his "Murder, Inc." confederates, Albert Anastasia (see the 1950's) and Benjamin "Bugsy" Siegal, (see below), was in protective police custody at the time of his death, with a $50,000 mob contract out for his murder. The death of Abe Reles remains unsolved.

On May 30, 1944 in Los Angeles, California, Louise Peete, sixty-one, paroled in 1939 after serving nineteen years for the murder of her lover, Jacob Denton, shot and killed Margaret Logan, the social worker under whose sponsorship she had been paroled and with whom she was living. Peete buried the body of Margaret Logan in her own backyard and continued, until arrested for murder, to live in the Logan house. Louise Peete was tried was for the first degree murder of Margaret Logan. Convicted, she was sentenced to death. On April 11, 1947 Louise Peete was executed in the gas chamber of San Quentin Prison.

On December 10, 1945 in Chicago, Illinois, William Heirens, "The Lipstick Killer," seventeen, a student at Chicago University, murdered and then mutilated thirty-three-year-old Frances Brown. Heirens, who had committed a similar mutilation murder the previous March, took Frances Brown's lipstick and wrote on the wall over her bed, "For Heaven's sake, catch me before I kill more. I cannot control myself!" Heirens' control failed him again on January 7, 1946, when he kidnapped and murdered Suzanne Degnan, six, whom he then cut to pieces and discarded in Chicago's sewers. Arrested June 26, 1946, William Heirens was tried, found guilty of three murders, and was sentenced to life imprisonment.

On January 15, 1947 in Los Angeles, California, the mutilated body of aspiring actress, twenty-two-year-old Elizabeth Ann Short, called by her friends "The Black Dahlia," was found in a vacant lot. The murder of "The Black Dahlia" remains unsolved.

On June 20, 1947, mobster/gambler Benjamin "Bugsy" Siegal, 41, was shot to death in his Beverly Hills, California home. Siegal's life and death was the subject of the movie *Bugsy*.

On December 8, 1947 in Highland Park, Michigan, Nina Housden, thirty-one, murdered her estranged husband, cut his body into pieces, and wrapped the pieces as Christmas presents. Nina Housden was tried, convicted, and sentenced to life imprisonment.

The "Lonely Hearts Killers," Raymond Fernandez and Martha Beck, were suspected in as many as twenty murders in the late 1940's. Fernandez, thirty-five, a self-described "Latin-lover," and his obese girlfriend Beck, thirty, posing as his sister, would romance lonely women and then murder them for their money. Arrested in January 1949 in Grand Rapids, Michigan (a state without a death penalty) for the murders of a lonely widow, twenty-eight-year-old Delphine Dowling (shot to death by Fernandez), and her two-year-old daughter, Rainelle (drowned by Beck), the murderous couple were extradited to New York (a state which did have a death penalty) for the December 1948 murder on Long Island, New York, of Mrs. Janet Fay, sixty-six, who had surrendered her heart and money to her new "husband" Fernandez and her life to his "sister" Beck. Raymond Fernandez and Martha Beck both pled not guilty to the murder by reason of insanity. They were both convicted, on August 22, 1949, of the first degree murder of Janet Fay and, on March 8, 1951, both were executed in the electric chair in Sing Sing Prison.

On September 6, 1949 in Camden, New Jersey, World War II veteran Howard Unruh, twenty-eight, went berserk and randomly murdered, in twelve minutes, thirteen people - five men, five women and three children. Mass murderer Howard Unhuh, who meekly surrendered to the police, later told a psychiatrist, "I'd have killed a thousand if I'd had bullets enough." Unruh was judged insane and sent to the New Jersey State Mental Hospital for life.

1950 - 1959
77,528 people (58,620 males and 18,908 females)
were murdered.

On November 17, 1950 in Minotola, New Jersey, Ernest Ingenito, twenty-four, estranged from his wife and children, went berserk and, in three hours, wounded his wife, Theresa Mazzoli Ingenito, and murdered his father-in-law and mother-in-law, Mike and Pearl Mazzoli, and five other members of the Mazzoli family. Ernest Ingenito, murderer of seven, was committed for life to the New Jersey State Hospital for the Insane.

On December 30, 1950 on Route 66 outside Tulsa, Oklahoma, a hitchhiker, William Cook, twenty-two, was picked up by Carl and Thelma Mosser, who, along with their three children (Ronald, seven, Gary, five, and Pamela, three), were on a family trip to New Mexico. Cook, hitchhiking after his release from five years in reform school, took the Mossers hostage at gunpoint, and forced them to drive to a deserted place near Joplin, Missouri where, on December 31, 1950, he murdered all five. On the run, Cook took hostage another driver, Robert Dewey, whom he killed in California. William Cook, arrested in Mexico, was extradited to California, tried, and convicted of Dewey's murder, and, on December 12, 1952, he was executed.

On March 9, 1953 in Burbank, California, Barbara Graham, thirty-two, a petty criminal and prostitute, murdered Mabel Monohan, sixty-three, an invalid whose home she was burglarizing. Barbara Graham, called by the press "Bloody Babs" for the brutality of the killing, was found guilty of first degree murder and sentenced to death. On June 3, 1955 Barbara Graham was executed in the gas chamber of San Quentin Prison. A fictionalized account of the story of Barbara Graham was told in the 1958 movie, *I Want To Live*.

On September 23, 1953 in Kansas City, Missouri, Robert "Bobby" Greenlease, Jr., six years old, was kidnapped from his pre-school. The kidnappers, after murdering Bobby Greenlease, buried his body in St. Joseph, Missouri, and then demanded, and were paid, a $600,000 ransom. Carl Austin Hall, thirty-four, a paroled thief, and Bonnie Brown Headly, forty-one, his prostitute girlfriend, were arrested for the kidnapping and subsequent murder. Hall and Headly were convicted, on November 19, 1953. They were executed in the gas chamber of the Missouri State Penitentiary on December 16, 1953.

On July 4, 1954 in Bay Village, a suburb of Cleveland, Ohio, Marilyn Shepard, thirty-one, then pregnant with her second child, was bludgeoned to death. Her husband, Dr. Samuel Shepard, thirty, was arrested, tried, and, on December 21, 1954, convicted of her murder. Dr. Shepard was sentenced to life imprisonment. In 1956 the United States Supreme Court, citing prejudicial news coverage which prevented a fair first trial, ordered that Dr. Shepard receive a second trial, which, in 1966, resulted in a verdict of not guilty.

On September 17, 1954 in Stinson Beach, California, Bart Caritativo, fifty-two, a Filipino houseboy, murdered his wealthy employer of many years, Camille Malmgren, and her ex-husband, Joseph Banks. Caritativo, who had forged Camille Malmgren's signature to a will leaving her entire estate to him, was tried for the double murder of Malmgren and Banks. He was found guilty and sentenced to die. Bart Caritativo was executed on October 24, 1958.

On November 1, 1955 Jack Gilbert Graham, twenty-three, murdered his mother, Mrs. Daisy King, fifty-four, and forty-three other people, by blowing up United Airlines Flight 629, from Denver, Colorado to Seattle, Washington, minutes after its takeoff from Denver's Stapleton Airport. He was convicted, on May 5, 1956, of placing and exploding a homemade bomb of twenty-six sticks of dynamite, wrapped as a Christmas present, on the plane, in order to collect his mother's $37,500 insurance policy. Jack Gilbert Graham was executed, on January 11, 1957, in the gas chamber of the Colorado State Penitentiary.

On March 4, 1957, in Mahwah, New Jersey, Edgar Smith, twenty-four, murdered Victoria Zielinski, fifteen. Smith, convicted of murder and sentenced to death, spent the next fourteen years fighting execution. While on New Jersey's Death

Row, Smith wrote two bestselling books protesting his innocence, *Brief Against Death* and *A Reasonable Doubt,* which eventually led to his 1971 release. Edgar Smith, arrested again for a violent crime against a young woman in 1976, was tried, convicted, and sentenced to life imprisonment. During the second trial, he confessed to the Zielenski murder.

Between June 26, 1957, the day he raped and murdered his first victim, Margaret Harold, near Annapolis, Maryland, and January 11, 1959, the day he murdered Carol and Mildred Jackson and their daughters, Susan, four, and Janet, eighteen months, near Fredericksburg, Virginia, sexual sadist and serial killer, Melvin David Rees, twenty-four, called "The Sex Beast," killed nine. These included the sadistic rape murders of Marie Shomette, sixteen, Ann Ryan, fourteen, Mary Elizabeth Fellers, eighteen, and Shelby Jean Venable, sixteen. Tried and convicted of the murder of the Jackson Family, Melvin David Rees was executed.

On August 1, 1957 in Los Angeles, California, Harvey Glatman, thirty-one, raped and then murdered, by strangulation, nineteen-year-old Judy Ann Dull. Glatman claimed two additional victims, Shirley Bridgeford, twenty-four, raped and murdered on March 9, 1958, and Ruth Mercado, twenty-four, raped and murdered on July 23, 1958. Harvey Glatman, who took photographs of all his victims, bound and gagged, before killing them, was executed, on August 18, 1959, in the gas chamber of San Quentin Prison.

On October 25, 1957 in New York City, Albert Anastasia, fifty-four, called "The Lord High Executioner of Organized Crime," was murdered, shot to death, in the barbershop of the Park Sheraton Hotel.

On November 16, 1957 in Plainfield, Wisconsin, farmer Edward Gein, fifty-one (the real-life basis for the Norman Bates character in the 1960 movie, *Psycho),* murdered and mutilated the last of his fifteen female victims, Bernice Worden. Edward Gein, found criminally insane, was sent to Wisconsin's Central State Mental Hospital where he died in 1984.

On December 1, 1957 in Lincoln, Nebraska, Charles Starkweather, nineteen, and his fourteen-year-old girlfriend, Caril Ann Fugate, murdered the first of their ten victims, gas station attendant Robert Colvert, twenty-one. On January 28, 1958, Starkweather killed Fugate's mother, stepfather, and her two-year-old baby sister. Six more murders followed. Charles Starkweather and Caril Ann Fugate were arrested, tried, and convicted of ten murders. Charles Starkweather was executed in the Nebraska State Penitentiary on June 25, 1959. Caril Ann Fugate, sentenced to life imprisonment, was released in 1977.

On April 4, 1958 in Beverly Hills, California, Cheryl Crane, fourteen, the daughter of Hollywood film star Lana Turner, stabbed to death her mother's abusive lover, mobster Johnny Stompanato, thirty-three. The death of Stompanato was ruled justifiable homicide. Cheryl Crane was never prosecuted.

On July 18, 1958 in Los Angeles, California, Dr. Raymond Finch, forty-two, and his live-in girlfriend, twenty-two-year-old Carole Tregoff, murdered the doctor's wife of seven years, Barbara Daugherty Finch, thirty-six, by shooting her in the back. On March 27, 1961, after two previous murder trials had failed to reach a verdict, Raymond Finch and Carole Tregoff were found guilty of second degree murder and sentenced to life imprisonment. Barbara Tregoff was released in 1969. Bernard Finch was released in 1971.

The Clutter Family, Herbert William Clutter, forty-eight, his wife, Bonnie Fox Clutter, forty-five, and their children, daughter Nancy, sixteen, and son Ken, fifteen, lived on a farm outside Holcomb, Kansas. On the night of Sunday, November 15, 1959, two petty criminals, Richard Eugene Hickock, twenty-eight and Perry Edward Smith, thirty-one, having heard a story that the Clutters had money in a hidden safe, broke into the home, tied up the family, and, failing to find any more than forty dollars, shotgunned the Clutter family to death. Hickock and Smith were arrested, tried, and found guilty of four counts of first degree murder and sentenced to die. On Wednesday, April 14, 1965, Richard Hickock and Perry Smith were hanged for the Clutter Family murders.

1960 - 1969
111,000 people (84,412 males and 26,588 females)
were murdered.

On June 14, 1962 in Boston, Massachusetts, "The Boston Strangler" raped and murdered the first of his thirteen female victims, Anna Slesers, fifty-five. The murders continued until January 4, 1964, with the rape and murder of the last victim, Mary Sullivan, nineteen. Paroled sex offender Albert DeSalvo, thirty-one, arrested and convicted of a September 1964 rape, confessed, while in custody, to the "Boston Strangler" murders of thirteen women between the ages of nineteen and eighty-five, but he was never charged with the murders. DeSalvo was sentenced to life imprisonment for rape and sent to Walpole State Prison, where, on November 26, 1973, he was murdered.

On August 28, 1962 in San Jose, California, "The Acid Doctor," Hungarian-born Dr. Geza de Kaplany, thirty-six, tortured to death his wife, Hanja, twenty-five, making surgical incisions in her body and then pouring in sulphuric, hydrochloric, and nitric acid. Geza de Kaplany, charged with his wife's murder, initially pled not guilty by reason of insanity. After seeing the gruesome autopsy photos of his acid-burned wife, he changed this plea to guilty, and, on March 1, 1963, Dr. de Kaplany was sentenced to life imprisonment. He was paroled in 1976.

On June 12, 1963 in Jackson, Mississippi, the NAACP's Medgar Evers, thirty-seven, was murdered. White supremacist Byron De la Beckwith was, in 1994, found guilty of the murder and was sentenced to life imprisonment.

On August 28, 1963 in New York City, roommates Janice Wylie, twenty-one, and Emily Hoffert, twenty-three, were molested, mutilated, and murdered. Richard Robles, twenty, a heroin addict, was tried and convicted of the double Wylie-Hoffert murders and was sentenced to life imprisonment.

On October 10, 1963 in New York City, Mark Fein, thirty-two, a wealthy businessman, murdered his bookmaker, Rubin Markowitz, over a $7,200 gambling debt. Fein, on November 25, 1964, was found guilty of second degree murder and sentenced to thirty years imprisonment.

On November 22, 1963 in Dallas, Texas, President John F. Kennedy, forty-six, was murdered, shot to death. While attempting to arrest murder suspect Lee Harvey Oswald, twenty-four, Dallas Police Officer J.D. Tippitt was shot to death. Oswald was murdered while in police custody on November 24, 1963 by Dallas nightclub owner, Jack Ruby, fifty-two. Ruby was tried, convicted, and sentenced to death for the murder of Lee Harvey Oswald. Jack Ruby died on January 3, 1967, while still in prison awaiting execution.

On March 13, 1964 in Kew Gardens, Queens, New York, Kitty Genovese, twenty-eight, was murdered on the street, repeatedly stabbed, as thirty-eight witnesses listened to her screams for help for thirty-five minutes - no one called the police. Winston Mosely, twenty-nine, confessed to the "Urban Apathy Murder" and was sentenced to life imprisonment.

On May 31, 1964 in Tucson, Arizona, Charles Schmid, Jr., twenty-two, raped and murdered Allen Rowe, fifteen. On August 16, 1964, Schmid, called "The Pied Piper of Tucson," lured two additional girls, Gretchen Fritz, seventeen, and her sister, Wendy, thirteen, to their deaths. Charles Schmid, Jr., was found guilty of three murders and, after the death penalty was abolished in Arizona, was sentenced to two life terms plus fifty years.

On June 21, 1964 outside Philadelphia, Mississippi, three young civil rights workers, Michael Schwerner, twenty-four, Andrew Goodman, twenty, and James Chaney, twenty-one, were murdered by the Ku Klux Klan. Seven Klan members received sentences of from three to ten years imprisonment.

On June 30, 1964 in Key Biscayne, Florida, Texas oil and banking multi-millionaire, Jacques Mossler, sixty-nine, was murdered, stabbed, and bludgeoned to death. His wife, Candace

"Candy" Mossler, forty-five, and her nephew, Melvin Powers, twenty-four (with whom it is alleged she was having an incestuous love affair), were charged with and tried for murder. On March 6, 1966, Candy Mossler and Melvin Powers were acquitted. The murder of Jacques Mossler remains unsolved.

On February 21, 1965, New York City's Harlem's Malcolm X, thirty-nine, former Black Muslim leader, was shot to death by three Black Muslims - Talmadge Hayer, Norman Butler, and Thomas Johnson. The three were convicted of the murder.

On July 14, 1965 in Queens, New York, Alice Marie Crimmins, twenty-six, estranged from her husband, reported the disappearance of her two young children, Edmund, Jr., called "Eddie," five, and Marie, called "Missy," four. The Crimmins children were both found murdered. Alice Crimmins was tried and convicted of the first degree murder of Edward and the first degree manslaughter of Missy, and was sentenced to life imprisonment. She was paroled in 1977.

On August 28, 1965 in Long Boat Key, Sarasota County, Florida, Dr. Carl Coppolino, thirty-four, already under suspicion for the 1963 suffocation murder of William Farber, his lover Marjorie's husband, murdered, by injection of a hard-to-trace poison, his wife, Carmela Musetto Coppolino, who refused to give him a divorce. Dr. Coppolino was tried and acquitted of the murder of William Farber, but convicted and sentenced to life imprisonment for the murder of his wife. Dr. Carl Coppolino, who wrote *The Crime That Never Was*, was paroled in 1979.

On July 13, 1966 in Chicago, Illinois, petty criminal Richard Speck, twenty-five, murdered eight student nurses - Valentina Passion, twenty-three, Pamela Wilkening, twenty, Patricia Matusek, twenty, Suzanne Farris, twenty-one, Mary Ann Jordan, twenty, Marlita Gargullo, twenty-two, Gloria Davy, twenty-two, and Nine Schmale, twenty-four - in their dormitory at the South Chicago Community Hospital. Identified in court by the sole survivor of the massacre, Corazon Amuro, twenty-four, Richard Speck was convicted of the mass murder. He was sentenced, on June 6, 1967, to death. After the death penalty was abolished, Richard Speck was resentenced to life imprisonment. He died in prison of a heart attack in 1991.

On August 1, 1966 in Austin, Texas, ex-Marine marksman, Charles Whitman, twenty-five, after killing his wife, Kathy, and his mother, climbed, heavily armed, to the top of the twenty-seven-story Texas Tower on the University of Texas in Austin campus. He began to shoot down the people below. The shooting continued for ninety minutes. By the time Austin Police killed Charles Whitman, he had wounded thirty and murdered sixteen.

On November 12, 1966 in Mesa, Arizona, mass murderer Robert Smith, eighteen, made seven people - five women and two children - lie down on the floor of the Rose-Mar Beauty College, and coldbloodedly executed each one. Smith, who told police that he "just wanted to be someone," was sentenced to life imprisonment.

On December 17, 1966 in Salt Lake City, Utah, Walter Kellbach, twenty-eight, and Myron Lance, twenty-five, kidnapped, sexually assaulted, and then murdered Stephen Shea, eighteen. Kellbach and Lance murdered five more victims - Michael Holtz, Grant Strong, James Sizemore, Beverly Mace, and Fred Lille - before their arrest on December 21, 1966. Walter Kellbach and Myron Lance were convicted of the murders and received life sentences.

Between July 10, 1967, the day he raped and murdered his first female victim, Eastern Michigan University co-ed, May Fleszar, and July 23, 1969, the day he raped and murdered his last female victim, Karen Sue Beckemann, eighteen, John Norman Collins, twenty-two, "The Michigan Co-ed Killer," killed seven young females in Ypsilanti and Ann Arbor, Michigan. John Norman Collins, tried and convicted of the murder of Karen Sue Beckemann, was sentenced to life imprisonment.

Between August 19 and 24, 1967, two teenage thrill killers, Thomas Braun and Leonard Maine, both eighteen, murdered Deanna Buse, twenty-two, in Washington State, Samuel Ledgerwood, in Oregon, and Timothy Luce, seventeen, in California. Tried and convicted of murder in Washington State, Thomas Braun was sentenced to death. Leonard Maine was sentenced to life imprisonment.

On April 4, 1968 at the Lorraine Motel in Memphis, Tennessee, civil rights leader, Dr. Martin Luther King, Jr., thirty-nine, was shot to death as he stood on the second floor balcony. James Earl Ray, forty, confessed to the murder, pled guilty (later recanting his confession), and, on March 10, 1969, he was sentenced to ninety-nine years imprisonment.

On June 5, 1968 at the Ambassador Hotel in Los Angeles, California, United States Senator Robert F. Kennedy, forty-two, was murdered. The assassin, Sirhan Bishara Sirhan, twenty-two, a Palestinian, killed Robert Kennedy on the first anniversary of the 1967 Arab-Israeli "Six Day War," over the Senator's support for Israel. Sirhan, tried and found guilty of first degree murder, was sentenced, on April 29, 1969, to death. After the death penalty was abolished, Sirhan Sirhan was sentenced to life imprisonment.

On December 20, 1968 in suburban San Francisco, California, a serial killer calling himself "The Zodiac," murdered his first two victims, David Faraday, seventeen, and Bettilou Jansen, sixteen. Three more "Zodiac" murders occurred before the killing stopped. No one was ever charged in the "Zodiac" serial murders.

On August 9, 1969 in Los Angeles, California, five people - Sharon Tate Polanski, Abigail Folger, Jay Sebring, Voytek Frykowski, and Steven Parent - were found savagely murdered in the Hollywood Hills. The next night two other Los Angelinos - Leno and Rosemary LaBianca - were similarly murdered. The words HELTER SKELTER were found at both murder scenes, written in the victims' blood. Arrested for ordering the Tate-

LaBianca murders was Charles Manson, thirty-five, the leader of The Manson Family, a hippie cult living in California's Death Valley. Arrested for carrying out Manson's orders were four Family members - Charles Watson, Susan Atkins, Patricia Krenwinkel, and Leslie Van Houten. After the longest murder trial in American history, over nine months, Charles Manson was, on March 29, 1971, found guilty on seven counts of first degree murder and sentenced to die. California abolished the death penalty in 1972 and all death sentences were commuted to life. Manson, Watson, Atkins, Krenwinkel, and Van Houten remain in prison to this day.

On December 17, 1969 at the Altamont Speedway in Altamont, California, Meredith Hunter, eighteen, attending a Rolling Stones/Grateful Dead "Woodstock West" Concert, was murdered, allegedly by the Hell's Angels. The murder of Meredith Hunter, seen in the film, *Gimme Shelter*, remains unsolved.

On December 30, 1969 in Clarksville, Pennsylvania, Joseph Albert "Jock" Yablonski, a dissident official in the United Mine Workers Union, his wife, Margaret, and his daughter, Charlotte, were all murdered on the orders of union boss Tony Boyle. Boyle and three henchmen hired to murder Yablonski were arrested, tried, and convicted of the Yablonski murders. Tony Boyle, who survived a suicide attempt, was sentenced, in 1974, to life imprisonment.

1970 - 1979
201,017 people (156,835 males and 44,182 females)
were murdered.

On February 17, 1970 at Fort Bragg, North Carolina, the family of Green Beret Captain Jeffrey MacDonald, his pregnant wife Colette, twenty-six, and daughters Kimberly, five, and Kristen Jean, two, were brutally murdered. Captain MacDonald, twenty-six, who claimed that four "drug-crazed hippies" murdered his family, was, in 1975, convicted of the "Fatal Vision" killings and sentenced to life imprisonment.

On Monday, October 19, 1970 in Santa Cruz County, California, John Linley Frazier, twenty-four, ritualistically murdered five people - Dr. Victor Ohta, his wife, Virginia, their two children, Taggart and Derrick, and the doctor's secretary, Mrs. Dorothy Cadwallader. John Frazier was tried and convicted of five counts of first degree murder and sentenced to life imprisonment.

Between May 19 and June 4, 1971, near the farming community of Yuba City, California, the bodies of twenty-five men, all transients or migrant farm workers between the ages of forty and sixty-eight, were unearthed in mass graves. All twenty-five male victims had been stabbed, mutilated, and raped. Juan Corona, thirty-eight, a local farm labor contractor, was tried and convicted of the serial sex murders and was sentenced to twenty-five consecutive life sentences.

On November 9, 1971 in Westfield, New Jersey, John List murdered his mother, Alma, eighty-five, his wife, Helen, forty-six, and his children, Patricia, sixteen, John, Jr., fifteen, and Fredrick, thirteen. List was captured in 1988, tried for the murders of his family, and sentenced to five consecutive life terms.

Between May 7, 1972, the day he murdered his first two victims, college co-eds Anita Luchese and Mary Anne Pesce, in Santa Cruz, California, and April 20, 1973, the day he murdered his last two victims, his mother, Clarnell Kemper, and Sally Hallett, his next door neighbor, serial sex killer Edmund Emil Kemper III, twenty-five, called "The California Co-ed

Killer," murdered a total of eight women. Kemper, who had been released in 1969 from a California State Mental Hospital for the August 1963 murders (when he was fourteen) of his paternal grandparents, Edward and Maude Kemper, was found guilty on eight counts on first degree murder and sentenced to life imprisonment.

Between October 13, 1972, the day he murdered Lawrence White, his first victim, and February 13, 1974, the day he murdered Fred Perez, his last victim, released mental patient Herbert William Mullin, twenty-five, murdered thirteen people in Northern California's Santa Cruz Mountains. Herbert Mullin was convicted, on August 20, 1973, of two counts of first degree murder and eight counts of second degree murder. He was sentenced to life imprisonment.

On April 10, 1973 in New York City, Theresa Jordan, thirty-nine, was found, raped and murdered, in her room at the Park Plaza Hotel. Eight more rape-murders of middle-aged and elderly women occurred at or near the Park Plaza in the next eighteen months, until Calvin Jackson, twenty-six, a hotel employee, confessed to the September 12, 1974 rape-murder of Pauline Spanierman, fifty-nine. Calvin Jackson, "The Park Plaza Killer," received two life terms, one for rape, one for murder, for each of his nine victims.

On August 8, 1973 in Houston, Texas, Dean Alan Corill, thirty-three, a serial sex murderer called "The Candy Man," was shot to death by his teenaged henchman, Wayne Henley, eighteen. Dean Corill, according to Henley's confession, was a sadistic homosexual who, with the sometime assistance of Henley, and David Brooks, had between 1970 and 1973 tortured and murdered twenty-seven young boys, mostly runaways, to whose mutilated remains he led police. Wayne Henley admitted to procuring, for money and drugs, many young victims for Corill, and participating himself in six of the torture-murders. Fearing that Dean Corill was planning to kill him, Henley shot Corill six times and then called the police. Wayne Henley was sentenced to six ninety-nine year prison terms. David Brooks was sentenced to life imprisonment.

On October 20, 1973 in San Francisco, California, four members of a Black Muslim hate-cult, "The Death Angels" - Manuel Moore, thirty-one, J.C. Simon, twenty-nine, Larry Green, twenty-four, and Jessie Lee Cooks, thirty - murdered husband and wife, Richard, thirty, and Quita Hague, twenty-eight. "The Death Angels" murdered twelve additional victims in the racially-motivated "Zebra Murders." Moore, Simon, Green, and Cooks were convicted of murder and sentenced to life imprisonment.

Between January 31, 1974, the day he raped and murdered his first female victim, Lynda Ann Healy, twenty-one, near Seattle, Washington, and February 15, 1978, the day he raped and murdered his last female victim, Kimberly Leach, twelve, in Pensacola, Florida, serial sex murderer Theodore Bundy, forty-two, "The Vampire Killer," claimed he killed thirty young women in seven states. Ted Bundy, tried and convicted of the 1978 rape murder of Kimberly Leach and the double Florida State University "Chi Omega" rape-murders, was executed at the Florida State Penitentiary on January 24, 1989.

On November 13, 1974 in Amityville, New York, Ronald DeFeo, Jr., twenty-three, murdered his father, mother, two sisters and two brothers in the "Amityville Horror" murders. Ronald DeFeo was tried, convicted, and sentenced to 150 years in prison.

On Easter Sunday, 1975, at a family gathering in Hamilton, Ohio, James Ruppert, forty-one, murdered eleven members of his family, three adults and eight children, ranging in age from his sixty-five-year-old mother to his four-year-old nephew. Tried twice for the "Easter Sunday Massacre," Ruppert was found guilty of two murders, those of his mother, Charity, and brother, James, and not guilty by reason of insanity of the nine other killings. James Ruppert was sentenced, on July 23, 1982, to two consecutive terms of life imprisonment.

On July 19, 1976 in Orem, Utah, Gary Gilmore, thirty-seven, a life-long petty criminal then on parole, murdered Max Jensen, twenty-four, in a gas station robbery. The next day, July 20th, Gilmore killed Bennie Bushnell, twenty-five, in a motel robbery in Provo, Utah. The two robberies netted Gilmore $250. Convicted for the murders of Jensen and Bushnell, Gary Gilmore was sentenced to death. Gilmore, in an unprecedented action which created a national sensation, insisted he had a "right to die," refused to appeal his death sentence, and demanded an immediate execution. On January 17, 1977, in the glare of national publicity, Gary Gilmore, the first person put to death in America in ten years, was executed by firing squad.

Between July 29, 1976, the day he murdered his first victim, Donna Lauria, eighteen, in the Bronx, New York, and July 31, 1977, the day he murdered his last victim, Stacy Moskowitz, twenty, in Queens, New York, David Richard Berkowitz, twenty-three, a psychotic who called himself "The Son-of-Sam," and whom the New York City Police called "The .44-Caliber Killer," murdered six people - five females and one male between the ages of eighteen and twenty-six. Captured on August 10, 1977, serial murderer David Berkowitz pled guilty, on July 12, 1978, to all six "Son-of-Sam" murders and was sentenced to six consecutive three-hundred-and-sixty-five-year terms.

On February 14, 1977 in New Rochelle, New York, Frederick Cowan, thirty-three, a neo-Nazi fired from his job after publicly exhibiting his white supremacist attitudes, returned to his former workplace, the Neptune Worldwide Moving Company, to murder his Jewish supervisor and black co-workers. Cowan, dressed in military fatigues, was armed with four pistols and a semi-automatic assault rifle. In forty-five minutes, Frederick Cowan killed four of his co-workers, all people of color, and white New Rochelle Police Officer Allen McLeod, thirty-two, before committing suicide.

Between October 18, 1977, the day they raped and murdered their first victim, Yolanda Washington, nineteen, and January 11, 1979, the day they murdered their last victim, Cindy Lee

Hudspeth, twenty, "The Hillside Stranglers," Angelo Buono, Jr., forty-three, and Kenneth Bianchi, twenty-eight, raped, tortured, and murdered ten women, all between the ages of twelve and twenty-one, in the Hollywood Hills surrounding Los Angeles, California. Angelo Buono, Jr. was convicted of nine of the "Hillside Strangler Murders" and sentenced, on July 9, 1984, to life imprisonment. Kenneth Bianchi, who had testified against Buono, had already pled guilty to the January 13, 1979 murders of two young women in Bellingham, Washington and was sentenced to life imprisonment.

On July 5, 1978 in San Diego, California, Robert Alton Harris, twenty-five, previously convicted of manslaughter, kidnapped two young boys, John Mayeski and Michael Baker, as they left a Jack-in-the-Box Restaurant. Harris took Mayeski and Baker to a deserted reservoir, where he murdered them both and then ate their lunch. Robert Alton Harris was convicted of murder and was executed in 1992.

On July 23, 1978 in Salt Lake City, Utah, multi-millionaire Franklin Bradshaw, seventy-six, was murdered, shot to death, by his grandson, Marc Schreuder, seventeen, on orders of his mother, Frances Bradshaw Schreuder, forty, who feared that her father would disinherit them. Marc Schreuder, found guilty of second degree murder, and sentenced to five years to life imprisonment, testified against his mother, Frances Schreuder, who was found guilty of first degree murder, and was sentenced to life imprisonment.

On November 27, 1978 in San Francisco, California, former City Supervisor Dan White, thirty-two, entered City Hall and shot to death Mayor George Moscone and openly gay City Supervisor Harvey Milk, forty-eight. White's "Twinkie Defense" (a claim that his junk food addiction had warped his judgment) obtained him, on May 21, 1979, a verdict of voluntary manslaughter in the killings of Moscone and Milk. A riot over the verdict erupted in the gay community. Dan White, murderer of two, was sentenced to eight years imprisonment. He was released in 1984 and committed suicide in 1985.

On December 11, 1978 in Des Plaines, Illinois, a Chicago suburb, John Wayne Gacy, thirty-six, a homosexual with a previous conviction for sodomizing under-age boys, raped and murdered, by slow strangulation, Robert Priest, fifteen, the last of his thirty-three young male victims. Gacy, who had murdered his first victim in 1975, had buried twenty-nine bodies under the crawlspace of his suburban Chicago home. When the crawlspace was filled, Gacy threw four victims into the Des Plaines River. Arrested four days after Priest's murder, John Wayne Gacy was tried on thirty-three counts of first degree murder and, on March 12, 1980, was convicted of all counts and sentenced to life imprisonment.

Between July 28, 1979, the day his first two young, African American male victims, Edward Smith, fourteen, and Alfred Evans, thirteen, were found dead in Atlanta, Georgia, and May 24, 1981, the day his last African American male victim, Nathaniel Cater, twenty-seven, was found dead, serial killer Wayne Bertram Williams, twenty-four, killed as many as twenty-eight. Tried and convicted of two "Atlanta Child Murders," Wayne Williams was sentenced to two consecutive life sentences.

Between August 1979, the day he murdered his first victim, Edda Kane, forty-four, in Marin County, California, and May 1, 1980, the day he murdered his last victim, Heather Scaggs, twenty, in San Jose, California, paroled sex offender David Carpenter, fifty, the "Trailside Killer," killed a total of seven. He was convicted of murder in 1984 and was sentenced to the gas chamber.

1980 - 1989
213,473 people (164,211 males and 49,262 females)
were murdered.

On March 10, 1980 in Westchester County, New York, Jean Harris, fifty-six, headmistress of the exclusive Madeira School, murdered her ex-lover, Dr. Herman Tarnower, sixty-nine, best-selling author of the *Scarsdale Medical Diet*, after he left her for a younger woman. Jean Harris was found guilty of the murder of "The Scarsdale Diet Doctor" and was sentenced to fifteen years to life in prison. In 1992, she was granted clemency and released.

On August 14, 1980 in Los Angeles, California, model Dorothy Stratten, twenty, Playboy Magazine's Playmate of the Year, was murdered by her estranged husband, Paul Snider, who then committed suicide. A fictional account of the murder of Dorothy Stratten is given in the 1983 movie *Star 80.*

On December 8, 1980 in New York City, former Beatle John Lennon, forty, was murdered outside his Central Park home by an obsessed fan, Mark David Chapman, twenty-five. Chapman pled guilty to murder and was sentenced to twenty years to life imprisonment.

On July 18, 1981 in New York City, paroled murderer Jack Henry Abbott, thirty-seven, author of the book, *In the Belly of the Beast*, a memoir of his twenty-three years in prison, murdered Richard Adan, twenty-two, in a bar fight. Abbott was found guilty of murder and was sentenced to life imprisonment.

On March 6, 1982 in suburban Boston, Massachusetts, Tufts Medical School Professor William Henry James Douglas, forty-one, murdered Robin Benedict, twenty-one, a prostitute with whom he had become obsessed. William Douglas pled guilty to manslaughter in the "Professor and the Prostitute" murder and was sentenced to twenty years imprisonment.

Between July 1982 and March 1984, along Seattle, Washington's notorious "Sea-Tac Strip," a serial murderer, "The Green River Killer," named after the polluted stream where the victims were dumped, murdered forty-nine young women. All forty-nine "Green River" killings remain unsolved.

On September 17, 1982 near San Antonio, Texas, Genene Jones, thirty-four, a licensed pediatric nurse, murdered, by injection of poison, fourteen-month-old Chelsea McClellan. Nurse Jones, called by the press "The Baby Killer," is thought by police to have been responsible, over a two-year period, for poisoning as many as sixty and the subsequent deaths of as many as thirty additional infants. Genene Jones was found guilty of the murder of Chelsea McClellan and was sentenced to life imprisonment.

On September 29, 1982 in Chicago, Illinois, the "Tylenol Killer," who had laced bottles of Extra-Strength Tylenol with cyanide, murdered Mary Kellerman, twelve, of Elk Grove Village, Illinois, the first victim of seven over-the-counter drug-tampering deaths in the Chicago area. The "Tylenol Killings" remain unsolved.

On February 19, 1983 in Seattle, Washington's Chinatown, three Hong Kong immigrants, "Bennie" Ng, "Willie" Ng and "Tony" Mak, murdered fourteen people during a robbery of the Wah Mee Gambling Club. The sole survivor of the "Chinatown Massacre" identified the three gunmen, who were tried and convicted of the mass murders. Mak was sentenced to death. "Bennie" Ng was sentenced to life imprisonment. "Willie" Ng was sentenced to seven consecutive life terms.

On June 6, 1984 in Beverly Hills, California, Joe Hunt, twenty-seven, founder of the Billionaire Boys Club, a "get rich quick" group of twenty-somethings, murdered Ron Levin, forty-two, who had swindled "The Boys" out of their investment. Hunt was convicted of Levin's murder and sentenced to life imprisonment.

On July 18, 1984 in San Ysidro, California, James Oliver Huberty, forty-two, heavily armed and dressed in battle fatigues, murdered twenty-one people in a MacDonald's restaurant. Huberty was killed by police, bringing the "MacDonald's Massacre" to an end.

Between March and August 1985, in Los Angeles, California, serial killer Richard Ramirez, twenty-four, called "The Night Stalker," murdered thirteen people. In 1989 Ramirez was convicted of all thirteen murders and was sentenced to death.

On October 15, 1985 in Salt Lake City, Utah, con artist Mark Hofman, involved in a forged documents swindle, murdered Steven Christiansen, thirty-one, and Katherine Sheets, fifty. Hofmann pled guilty to reduced charges and was sentenced to five years to life.

On August 26, 1986, in New York City's Central Park, Jennifer Levin, eighteen, was killed by her boyfriend, Robert Chambers, nineteen, in what the press named "The Preppie Murder." Robert Chambers confessed to killing Jennifer Leven during "rough sex" and, in a plea bargain, pled guilty to manslaughter. He was sentenced to five to fifteen years imprisonment.

On November 2, 1987 in New York City's Greenwich Village, Lisa Steinberg, six, physically abused by her drug-addicted, adoptive father, Joel Steinberg, was beaten into a coma and died three days later. Joel Steinberg was tried and convicted of charges of first degree manslaughter and sentenced to up to twenty-five years imprisonment.

Between March 1988 and December 1989, Arthur John Shawcross, forty, "The Rochester Strangler," on parole after having served fifteen years for two 1971 child rape-murders, raped and murdered eleven young women in Rochester, New York. Arthur John Shawcross, convicted serial rapist-murderer of two children and eleven women, is currently serving a two-hundred-and-fifty year prison sentence.

Between November 11 and 14, 1988, in Sacramento, California, the bodies of seven elderly people were found buried in the backyard of Dorothea Puente, fifty-nine, an ex-convict, who ran a boarding house for elderly or disabled people, and who continued to receive and cash the victims' Social Security checks. Puente was arrested, tried, and convicted of three murders, and was sentenced to life without parole.

On January 17, 1989 in Stockton, California, Patrick Purdy, twenty-four, murdered five children in the schoolyard of the Cleveland Elementary School, firing one hundred and ten rounds from an AK-47 semi-automatic rifle, before killing himself. The "Stockton Schoolyard Massacre" led to passage of the Federal Assault Weapons Ban.

On July 18, 1989 in Los Angeles, California, actress Rebecca Schaeffer, twenty-one, co-star of the television sit-com, *My Sister Sam*, was murdered by obsessed fan, Robert John Bardo, nineteen. Bardo was convicted of first degree murder and was sentenced to life.

On August 20, 1989 in Beverly Hills, California, Lyle Menendez, twenty-two, and his brother, Eric, nineteen, murdered their millionaire parents, Jose and Kitty Menendez. A first murder trial resulted in a hung jury. A second murder trial ended in verdicts of guilty of first degree murder.

On August 23, 1989 in Brooklyn, New York's Bensonhurst section, Yusef Hawkins, sixteen, an African American, was murdered by a white street gang. Joseph Fama, nineteen, was convicted of second degree murder and was sentenced to thirty-two and two-thirds years imprisonment.

On October 23, 1989 in Boston, Massachusetts, a white suburban couple, thirty-three-year-old Carol DiMaiti Stuart, then eight months pregnant, and her husband, thirty-year-old Charles M. Stuart, Jr., were shot in an apparent armed robbery in a poor black neighborhood. Carol Stuart died that night. Her child, Christopher (delivered by emergency Caesarian section), died on November 9th. Charles Stuart, who had survived his injuries and blamed a black assailant, was uncovered as the actual killer of his wife and child. Stuart, his murder scheme exposed, jumped to his death off a bridge over Boston Harbor.

Between November 30, 1989, the day she murdered her first victim, Richard Mallory, fifty-one, near Ormond Beach, Florida, and November 19, 1990, the day she murdered her last victim, Walter Antonio, sixty, near Merritt Island, Florida, serial murderer Aileen Carol Wuornos, thirty-three, killed seven men.

Wuornos was found guilty of the first degree murder of Richard Mallory and was sentenced to death.

1990 - 1995

119,723 people were murdered from 1990 through 1994.
An estimated 21,400 people were murdered in 1995.

On March 25, 1990 in the Bronx, New York, Julio Gonzalez, thirty-seven, set fire to his ex-girlfriend's workplace, the Happy Land Social Club, killing eighty-seven people. He was convicted of one hundred and seventy-four counts of murder and was sentenced to concurrent sentences of twenty-five years to life on each count.

On May 5, 1990 in Derry, New Hampshire, Gregory Smart, twenty-four, was murdered in a plot concocted by his wife, high school teacher Pamela Smart. She was found guilty in the murder and was sentenced to life.

On May 16, 1990 in Santa Monica, California, Christian Brando, thirty-two, the son of actor Marlon Brando, murdered Dag Drollet, twenty-six, the boyfriend of his pregnant half-sister, Cheyenne. Christian Brando pled guilty to voluntary manslaughter and was sentenced to ten years imprisonment. His sister committed suicide in 1995.

On September 2, 1990 in New York City, Brian Watkins, twenty-two, a tourist from Utah, was murdered, stabbed to death, on a Manhattan subway platform, while defending his parents during a robbery. Eight teenagers were arrested. One, Yull Gary Morales, nineteen, was charged with murder.

On November 5, 1990 in New York City, Rabbi Meir Kahane, fifty-eight, leader of the militant Jewish Defense League, was murdered, shot to death. An Arab-American, El Sayyid Nosair, thirty-four, was tried and acquitted of the murder.

On November 19, 1990 in Boston, Massachusetts, Kimberly Rae Harbour, twenty-six, was raped and murdered, stabbed over one hundred times, by a gang of teenagers in the "Halloween Horror" murder.

On March 16, 1991 in Los Angeles, California, Latasha Harlins, a fifteen-year-old African American girl, was murdered, shot in the back, by Soon Ja Du, a Korean immigrant grocer, after a fight over an unpaid-for bottle of orange juice. Du was convicted of voluntary manslaughter, fined $500, and given four hundred hours of community service.

On March 18, 1991 in Detroit, Michigan, Anthony Riggs, twenty-two, a soldier just returned from Gulf War service, was murdered by his wife, Tonie Cato Riggs, and his brother-in-law, Michael Cato, for his insurance money. Both were found guilty of first degree murder.

On July 23, 1991 in Milwaukee, Wisconsin, Jeffrey Dahmer was arrested for the murder and dismemberment of fifteen people. Jeffrey Dahmer was found guilty on all fifteen counts and, on February 17, 1992, was sentenced to nine hundred and fifty-seven years imprisonment. On November 28, 1994, he was murdered in prison.

On Wednesday, October 16, 1991 in Killeen, Texas, George Hennard, thirty-five, murdered twenty-three people before killing himself in the Luby's Cafeteria Massacre.

On October 17, 1992 in Baton Rouge, Louisiana, Yoshihiro Hattori, sixteen, a Japanese exchange student who spoke little English, was shot to death by a frightened homeowner, Rodney Peairs, when he failed to heed the warning, "Freeze!" Peairs was acquitted of murder charges.

On November 15, 1992 in Detroit, Michigan, Malice Green, an African American, was beaten to death by two white policemen, Larry Nevers and Walter Budzyn. Both were convicted and sentenced to long prison terms.

On February 26, 1993 in New York City, Muslim fundamentalist terrorists, at the alleged direction of blind cleric, Sheik Omar Abel Rahman, bombed the World Trade Center, killing six and injuring over a thousand. Four men were convicted and each was sentenced to two hundred and forty years.

On July 1, 1993 in San Francisco, California, Gian Luigi Ferri, fifty-five, murdered eight people in a high-rise office tower before killing himslf.

On July 23, 1993 near Fayetteville, North Carolina, James Jordan, fifty-six, the father of basketball star Michael Jordan, was murdered by two teenagers, Larry Demery and Daniel Green. Demery and Green were both convicted and were sentenced to life imprisonment.

On October 1, 1993 in Petaluma, California, Polly Klass, twelve, was kidnapped and murdered. Paroled sex offender Richard Allen Davis was convicted of first degree murder.

On December 7, 1993 on Long Island, New York, Colin Ferguson, thirty-five, murdered six rush hour commuters on a Long Island Rail Road train. He was sentenced to life imprisonment.

On June 12, 1994 in Brentwood, California, Nicole Brown Simpson, thirty-five, and Ronald Lyle Goldman, twenty-five, were murdered, slashed to death. Tried and acquitted for the double murder was former football star, O.J. Simpson.

On July 29, 1994 in Pensacola, Florida, John Bayard Britton, sixty-nine, a local abortion doctor, and clinic escort John Parrett, seventy-four, were murdered by Paul Hill, an anti-abortion activist. Hill, forty, was convicted and sentenced to die in the electric chair.

On October 25, 1994 at a lake outside of Union, South Carolina, Susan Smith, twenty-three, murdered, by drowning, her two sons, Michael, three, and Alex, fourteen months. She was sentenced to life imprisonment.

On December 30, 1994 in Brookline, Massachusetts, anti-abortion activist John Salvi, twenty-two, murdered Shannon Lowney, twenty-five, and Lee Ann Nichols, thirty-eight, at two abortion clinics. John Salvi was convicted of the two murders and was sentenced to life.

On March 31, 1995 in Corpus Christi, Texas, Tejano singer Selena Quintanila Perez, twenty-three, was murdered. Former fan club president Yolanda Saldivar was convicted of her murder and was sentenced to life imprisonment.

On April 19, 1995 in Oklahoma City, Oklahoma, one hundred and sixty-seven people, including nineteen children, were murdered in the bombing of the Alfred Murrah Federal Building. Two men, Terry Nichols, forty, and Timothy McVeigh, twenty-seven, were charged with the worst mass murder in American history.

On November 14, 1995 outside Richmond, Kentucky, Glen Rogers, thirty-three, suspected in the serial murders of four young women carried out between September 29 and November 9, 1995 in California, Louisiana, Florida, and Mississippi, was arrested.

On November 16, 1995 near Los Angeles, California, former L.A. Raider's cheerleader Linda Sobek, twenty-seven, was murdered. Photographer Charles Rathbun, thirty-seven, confessed to accidentally killing her, and then pled not guilty.

On November 17, 1995 in Addison, Illinois, Deborah Evans, twenty-eight, then nine months pregnant, was murdered when her unborn child was cut from her womb, allegedly by a couple, Fedel Caffey and Jacqueline Williams, who, unable to conceive a child of their own, decided to steal one. The couple also allegedly murdered Evans' eleven-year-old daughter, Samantha and eight-year-old son, Joshua. The baby, Elijah Evans, survived.

On November 23, 1995 in Brooklyn, New York, Elisa Izquierdo, six, physically abused all her life, was allegedly beaten to death by her mother, Awilda Lopez, who, in a drug-induced hallucination believed Elisa was possessed by the devil. Lopez was charged with murder.

On November 26, 1995 in New York City, subway token clerk Harry Kaufman, fifty, was burned to death in an arson attack by three teenagers. Police believed the attack was inspired by the 1995 movie, *Money Train.*

Murder Ink

Everyone is a potential murderer.

- Clarence Darrow

Murder Ink is an annotated bibliography of hundreds of well-written, thoroughly researched, non-fiction, "true murder" books.

This is a "people's reading list" designed specifically for the lay reader. We have purposely excluded all legal, statistical, sociological, criminological, or psychological works on murder. No scholarly treatises. No police manuals. No doctoral dissertations. All these works, while valuable, are characterized as being being written by experts to be read by experts. We have searched and researched all the available true crime literature for the very best in plain-English murder reporting.

Many of these books are classics in the files of murder reporting. Three in particular come to mind:

> Truman Capote's *In Cold Blood,* the story of the 1959 four-victim "Clutter Family Murders," committed by Richard Hickock and Perry Smith in rural Kansas.

> Vincent Bugliosi's *Helter Skelter,* the story of the 1969 seven-victim "Tate-La Bianca Murders," committed on the orders of Charles Manson in Los Angeles.

> Norman Mailer's *The Executioner's Song,* the story of double murderer Gary Gilmore's public campaign to have the state of Utah put him to death.

What these three books have in common is that they went beyond the mundane recitation of 'Who, What, When, Where and How' to the essential question: 'Why?'

Murder Ink is made up of books that ask and answer 'Why?' Why these victims? Why these murderers?

In several instances *Murder Ink* has collected multiple titles on the same subject: The story of serial killer Theodore Bundy is told in four separate works, including Ann Rule's *The Stranger Beside Me*, and Richard Larsen's *The Deliberate Stranger*. Each work has been selected for inclusion because it stands on its own and together with the others combines to cover and uncover the complete story.

In other instances *Murder Ink* has collected first-person accounts of murder: child killer Edgar Smith's *Brief Against Death*, double murderer Jack Henry Abbott's *In the Belly of the Beast*, "thrill killer" Leopold Nathan's *Life Plus 99 Years*.

All the books in *Murder Ink* are listed by *Author* (Alexander, Shana) and indexed by *Title* (Very Much A Lady), and in selected cases are indexed by *Murderer* (Harris, Jean), and *Victim* (Tarnower, Herman). To assist the reader, writer, or researcher in locating material, we have also added to the index any *Popular Names* or *Catch Phrases* (Scarsale Diet Doctor) that have attached themselves to murders.

All of these books, and many others, are available in or through your public library. Check your library's card or on-line catalog under: "Murder." When in doubt, ask a librarian.

Murder Ink: A Reader's Guide

Abrahamsen, Daniel. *Confessions of the Son of Sam.*
New York: Columbia University Press, 1985.
The 1976-77 six-victim "Son Of Sam Murders" committed
by serial killer David Berkowitz in New York City.
See also:
Klauner. *Son Of Sam.*

Alexander, Shana. *Nutcracker.*
New York: Doubleday, 1985.
The 1978 murder of Salt Lake City multi-millionaire
Franklin Bradshaw, plotted by his daughter, Frances
Bradshaw Schreuder, and committed his grandson, Marc
Schreuder.
See also:
Coleman. *At Mother's Request.*

Alexander, Shana. *Very Much A Lady.*
Boston: Little, Brown, 1983.
The 1980 murder of "Scarsdale Diet Doctor" Herman
Tarnower by his ex-mistress, Jean Harris.
See also:
Harris. *Stranger In Two Worlds.*
Trilling. *The Death Of The Scarsdale Diet Doctor.*

Allen, William. *Starkweather.*
Boston: Houghton Mifflin, 1976.
The 1957 ten-victim rampage of serial killer Charles
Starkweather in Lincoln, Nebraska.
See also:
Reinhardt. *The Murderous Trail Of Charles Starkweather.*

Angelella, Michael. *Trail Of Blood.*
New York: Bobbs-Merrill, 1979.
The 1928 murder of twelve-year-old Grace Budd by sexual
serial killer Albert "The Cannibal" Fish in Westchester,
New York.

See also:
Schecter. *Deranged.*

Armbrister, Trevor. *Act Of Vengeance.*
New York: Saturday Review Press, 1975.
The 1970 triple-victim "Yablonski Family Murders" in
Clarksville, Pennsylvania.
See also:
Brown. *A Man Named Tony.*

Bain, David Howard. *Aftershocks.*
New York: Methuen, 1980.
The 1977 "Post-Traumatic Stress Syndrome Murder" of Le
My Hahn, a seventeen-year-old Vietnamese refugee, by ex-
Marine Louis Kahan in Queens, New York.

Baldwin, James. *The Evidence Of Things Not Seen.*
New York: Holt, 1985.
The 1979-1981 twenty-eight-victim "Atlanta Child Murders"
committed by serial child killer Wayne Williams.
See also:
Dettlinger. *The List.*

Barker, Rodney. *The Broken Circle.*
New York: Simon & Schuster, 1992.
The 1974 hate-crime murders of three Navajos in
Farmington, New Mexico.

Barthel, Joan. *A Death In California.*
New York: Congdon, 1981.
The 1973 murder trial and acquittal of Beverly Hills
socialite Hope Masters for the murder her fiance.

Baumann, Ed. *Step Into My Parlor.*
  Chicago: Bounus, 1991.
    The story of Milwaukee's serial killer of fifteen, Jeffrey
    Dahmer.
      See also:
        Dahmer. *A Father's Story.*
        Davis. *Milwaukee Murders.*
        Dvorchak. *Milwaukee Massacre.*
        Jaeger. *Massacre In Milwaukee.*
        Schwartz. *The Man Who Could Not Kill Enough.*

Beck, Janet Parker. *Too Good To Be True.*
  Fall Hills, NJ: New Horizons Press, 1991.
    The 1985 murder of Denise Redlick by her ex-fiance in the
    Santa Clara Valley, California.

Bembenek, Lawrencia. *Woman On Trial.*
  New York: Harper Collins, 1992.
    The first-person account by Lawrencia "Bambi" Bembenek,
    ex-police officer, ex-Playboy bunny, convicted of the 1981
    murder of her husband's ex-wife.
      See also:
        Radish. *Run, Bambi, Run.*

Benford, Timothy. *Righteous Carnage.*
  New York: Scribners, 1991.
    The 1971 five-victim "List Family Murders" committed by
    mass murderer John List in Westfield, New Jersey.
      See also:
        Ryzuk. *Thou Shalt Not Kill.*

Bern, Noel. *Lindbergh: The Crime.*
  New York: AMP, 1994.
    The 1932 kidnap-murder of Charles Augustus Lindbergh, Jr.,
    "The Lindbergh Baby," committed by Richard Bruno
    Hauptmann in Hopewell, New Jersey.

See also:
   Fisher. *The Lindbergh Case.*
   Kennedy. *The Airman And The Carpenter.*
   Waller. *Kidnap.*

Bishop, Jim. *The Day Kennedy Was Shot.*
   New York: Funk & Wagnalls, 1968.
      The 1963 assassination of President John F. Kennedy in
      Dallas, Texas.
      See also:
         Lane. *Rush To Judgment.*
         Manchester. *The Death Of A President.*
         United States. *The Warren Commission's Report.*

Black, D. *Murder At The Met.*
   New York: Dial, 1984.
      The 1980 "Phantom Of The Opera Murder" at New York
      City's Metropolitan Opera House.

Blackburn, Daniel J. *Human Harvest.*
   New York: Knightsbridge Publishing Company, 1990.
      The story of Sacramento's serial killer of seven elderly
      persons under her care, Dorothea Puente.
      See also:
         Norton. *Disturbed Ground.*

Bledsoe, J. *Blood Games.*
   New York: Dutton, 1991.
      The 1988 "Dungeons & Dragons Murder" of Leith von Stein
      in Washington, North Carolina.
      See also:
         McGinniss. *Cruel Doubt.*

Bogdanovich, Peter. *The Killing Of The Unicorn.*
   New York: Morrow, 1984.
      The 1980 murder of Dorothy Stratten, Playboy Magazine's
      Playmate of the Year, by her estranged husband, Paul
      Snider.

Bommersbach, J. *The Trunk Murderess.*
　New York: Simon & Schuster, 1992.
　　The 1931 double-victim "Trunk Murders" committed by
　　Winnie Ruth Judd in Phoenix, Arizona.
　　　See also:
　　　Dobkins. *Winnie Ruth Judd: The Trunk Murders.*

Bosco, Joseph. *Blood Will Tell.*
　New York: Morrow, 1993.
　　The 1984 murder of Janet Cannon Myers by her husband
　　and his best friend in suburban New Orleans, Louisiana.

Boswell, Charles. *The Girl in Lover's Lane.*
　Greenwich, CT: Fawcett, 1962.
　　The 1922 double murders of the Reverend Edward Wheeler
　　Hall and his mistress Eleanor Mills in New Brunswick, New
　　Jersey.
　　　See also:
　　　Kunstler. *The Hall-Mills Murder Case.*

Braudy, Susan. *This Crazy Thing Called Love.*
　New York: Knopf, 1992.
　　The 1955 "Shooting Of The Century" of millionaire William
　　Woodward, Jr., in Oyster Bay, Long Island.

Breitman, George. *The Assassination Of Malcolm X.*
　New York: Pathfinder Press, 1976.
　　The 1965 murder of Black Muslim leader Malcolm X in
　　New York City's Harlem.
　　　See also:
　　　Friedly. *Malcolm X: The Assassination.*

Brown, Stuart. *A Man Named Tony.*
　New York: Norton, 1976.
　　The 1970 triple-victim "Yablonski Family Murders" in
　　Clarksville, Pennsylvania.
　　　See also:
　　　Armbrister. *Act of Vengeance*

Brownell, Joseph. *Adirondack Tragedy.*
  Interlaken, NY: Heart Of The Lakes, 1986.
    The 1906 murder of Grace "Billie" Brown by Chester
    Gillette in New York's Adirondack Mountains.

Buchanan, Edna. *Carr: Five Years Of Rape And Murder.*
  New York: Dutton, 1979.
    The story of serial rapist-murderer Robert Fredrick Carr III.

Bugliosi, Vincent. *Helter Skelter.*
  New York: Norton, 1974.
    The 1969 seven-victim "Tate-LaBianca Murders" committed
    on the orders of Charles Manson in Los Angeles, California.

Cagin, Seth. *We Are Not Afraid.*
  New York: Bantam Books, 1991.
    The 1964 murders of three civil rights workers, Andrew
    Goodman, Michael Schwerner, and James Chaney, outside of
    Philadelphia, Mississippi by members of the Ku Klux Klan.

Cahill, Tim. *Buried Dreams.*
  New York: Bantam, 1986.
    The story of Chicago's serial murderer of thirty-three,
    John Wayne Gacy.
      See also:
        Linedecker. *The Man Who Killed Boys.*
        Sullivan. *Killer Clown.*

Cantlupe, Joe. *Badge Of Betrayal.*
  New York: Avon, 1991.
    The 1986 "CHIPS Murder" of Cara Knott by California
    Highway Patrolman Alan Peyer in San Diego, California.

Capote, Truman. *In Cold Blood.*
  New York: Random House, 1965.
    The 1959 four-victim "Clutter Family Murders" committed
    by Richard Hickock and Perry Smith in Holcomb, Kansas.

Carlo, Philip. *The Night Stalker.*
New York: Kensington Books, 1996.
The 1985 thirteen-victim "Nightstalker Murders," committed
by serial murderer Richard Ramirez in Los Angeles.
See also:
Linedecker *Night Stalker.*

Carpenter, Teresa. *Missing Beauty.*
New York: Norton, 1988.
The 1983 murder of Robin Benedict by Tufts University
Professor William Douglas in Boston, Massachusetts.
See also:
Wolf. *The Professor And The Prostitute.*

Cauffiel, Lowell. *Forever And Five Days.*
New York: Zebra, 1992.
The 1988 "Alpine Manor Murders" of five elderly nursing
home residents in Grand Rapids, Michigan, committed by
nurses Catherine Wood and Gwendolyn Graham.

Cheney, Margaret. *The Coed Killer.*
New York: Walker, 1976
The story of Santa Cruz, California's serial murderer of
eight, Edmund Emil Kemper.

Coleman, Jonathan. *At Mother's Request.*
New York: Atheneum, 1985.
The 1978 murder of Salt Lake City multi-millionaire
Franklin Bradshaw, plotted by his daughter, Frances
Bradshaw Schreuder, and committed his grandson, Marc
Schreuder.
See also:
Alexander. *Nutcracker.*

Cook, Thomas. *Blood Echoes.*
New York: Dutton, 1992.
The 1973 mass murder of the six members of the Alday
Family in Seminole County, Georgia.

See also:
　　Howard. *Brothers In Blood.*

Cooper, Cynthia, and Sam Shepard. *Mockery Of Justice.*
　New York: Northeastern University Press, 1995.
　　The story, co-written by their son, of Doctor Sam Shepard,
　　convicted of the 1954 murder of his wife, Marilyn, in
　　Bay Village, Ohio.

Cope, Carol Soret. *In The Fast Lane.*
　New York: Simon & Schuster, 1993.
　　The 1986 "Miami Vice" murder of Stan Cohen in Miami,
　　Florida.

Coppolino, Carl A. *The Crime That Never Was.*
　Tampa, FL: Justice Press, 1980.
　　The 1965 murder of Carmela Coppolino in Sarasota, Florida
　　as told by the man convicted of the crime, her husband, Carl.

Corcoran, James. *Bitter Harvest.*
　New York: Viking, 1990.
　　The 1983 "Posse Comitatus Massacre" of three federal
　　agents in Medina, Ohio.

Crey, Ed. *Burden of Proof.*
　New York: Macmillan, 1973.
　　The story of Yuba City, California's serial murderer of
　　twenty-five, Juan Vallejo Corona.
　　See also:
　　　Kidder. *The Road To Yuba City.*
　　　Villasenor. *Jury.*

Dahmer, Lionel. *A Father's Story.*
　New York: Morrow, 1994.
　　The story of Milwaukee's serial murderer of fifteen,
　　Jeffrey Dahmer.

See also:
  Baumann. *Step Into My Parlor.*
  Davis. *Milwaukee Murders.*
  Dvorchak. *Milwaukee Massacre.*
  Jaeger. *Massacre In Milwaukee.*
  Schwartz. *The Man Who Could Not Kill Enough.*

Darden, Christopher A. *In Contempt.*
  New York: Regan Books, 1996.
  The 1994 murders of Nicole Brown Simpson and Ronald
  Lyle Goldman in Brentwood, California and the murder trial
  and acquittal of O.J. Simpson.
  See also:
    Dershowitz. *Reasonable Doubts.*
    Shapiro. *The Search for Justice.*

Davis, Don. *Bad Blood.*
  New York: St. Martin's, 1994.
  The story of the 1989 double murder of Jose and Kitty
  Menendez by their children Lyle and Eric in Beverly Hills,
  California.
  See also:
    Soble. *Blood Brothers.*

Davis, Don. *Milwaukee Murders.*
  New York: St. Martin's, 1991.
  The story of Milwaukee's serial murderer of fifteen,
  Jeffrey Dahmer.
  See also:
    Baumann. *Step Into My Parlor.*
    Dahmer. *A Father's Story.*
    Dvorchak. *Milwaukee Massacre.*
    Jaeger. *Massacre In Milwaukee.*
    Schwartz. *The Man Who Could Not Kill Enough.*

Deakin, James. *A Grave For Bobby.*
  New York: Morrow, 1990.
    The 1953 kidnap-murder of Robert "Bobby" Greenlease, Jr.,
    in Kansas City, Missouri.

Dershowitz, Alan M. *Reasonable Doubts.*
  New York: Simon & Schuster, 1996.
    The 1994 murders of Nicole Brown Simpson and Ronald
    Lyle Goldman in Brentwood, California and the murder trial
    and acquittal of O.J. Simpson.
      See also:
        Darden. *In Contempt.*
        Shapiro. *The Search For Justice.*

Dershowitz, Alan. *Reversal Of Fortune.*
  New York: Random House, 1986.
    The 1980 attempted murder of Martha "Sunny" von Bulow
    and the trials of her husband Klaus in Newport, Rhode
    Island.
      See also:
        Wright. *The von Bulow Affair.*

DeSantos, John. *For The Color Of His Skin.*
  New York: Pharos, 1991.
    The 1989 hate-murder of Yusef Hawkins in the
    Howard Beach section of Brooklyn, New York.
      See also:
        Hynes. *Incident At Howard Beach.*

Dettlinger, Chet, and Jeff Prugh. *The List.*
  Atlanta: Philmay Enterprises, 1983.
    The 1979-1981 twenty-eight-victim "Atlanta Child Murders"
    committed by serial killer Wayne Williams.
      See also:
        Baldwin. *The Evidence Of Things Not Seen.*

Deutsch, Harmann B. *The Huey Long Murder Case.*
Garden City, NY: Doubleday, 1963.
  The 1935 murder of United States Senator Huey Long in
  Baton Rouge, Louisiana by Dr. Carl Austin Weiss, Jr.

Dillman, John. *The French Quarter Killers.*
New York: Macmillan, 1987.
  The 1976 execution-style murders in New Orleans,
  Louisiana, of two people in the Federal Witness Protection
  Program.

Dobkins, J. Dwight. *Winnie Ruth Judd: The Trunk Murders.*
New York: Grossett & Dunlap, 1973.
  The 1931 double-victim "Trunk Murders" committed by
  Winnie Ruth Judd in Phoenix, Arizona.
    See also :
      Bommersbach. *The Trunk Murderess.*

Douglas, Geoffrey. *Dead Opposite.*
New York: Henry Holt, 1995.
  The 1991 murder of Yale University student Christian
  Prince in New Haven, Connecticut.

Duncan, Lois. *Who Killed My Daughter?*
New York: Delacorte, 1992.
  The 1989 murder of Kaitlyn Duncan in Albuquerque, New
  Mexico, as told by her mother.

Dvorchak, Robert. *Milwaukee Massacre.*
New York: Dell, 1991.
  The story of Milwaukee's convicted serial killer of
  fifteen, Jeffrey Dahmer.
    See also:
      Baumann. *Step Into My Parlor.*
      Dahmer. *A Father's Story.*
      Davis. *Milwaukee Murders.*
      Jaeger. *Massacre In Milwaukee.*
      Schwartz. *The Man Who Could Not Kill Enough.*

Dwyer, Jim. *Two Seconds Under The World.*
  New York: Crown Publishers, 1994.
    The 1993 bombing of New York City's World Trade Center.

Earley, Pete. *Circumstantial Evidence.*
  New York: Bantam, 1995.
    The 1986 murder of Ronda Morrison in Monroeville,
    Alabama.

Earley, Pete. *Prophet Of Death.*
  New York: Morrow, 1991.
    The 1989 "Mormon Cult" ritual-execution murders of the
    five-member Avery Family, committed by Jeffrey Don
    Lundgren, founder of the Reorganized Church of the Latter
    Day Saints in Kirtland, Ohio.
      See also:
      Sasse. *The Kirtland Massacre.*

Edmonds, Andy. *Hot Toddy.*
  New York: Morrow, 1989.
    The 1935 murder of Hollywood film star Thelma
    "Hot Toddy" Todd.

Egginton, Joyce. *Day Of Fury.*
  New York: Morrow, 1991.
    The 1988 murder-suicide at the Hubbard Woods Elementary
    School in Winnetka, Illinois.

Elkind, Peter. *The Death Shift.*
  New York: Viking, 1989.
    The 1982 "Texas Baby Murder" of fourteen-month-old
    Chelsea McClellan by serial baby killer, Nurse Genene Jones.
      See also:
      Reed. *Deadly Medicine.*

Englade, Ken. *Beyond Reason.*
  New York: St. Martin's, 1990.
  The 1985 murder of Derek and Nancy Hayson by their
  daughter Elizabeth and her boyfriend in suburban
  Lynchburg, Virginia.

Englade, Ken. *To Hatred Turned.*
  New York: St. Martin's, 1990.
  The 1983 murder of her husband's mistress, Rozanne
  Guiliunas, arranged by Joy Aylor in Dallas, Texas.

Farr, Louise. *The Sunset Murders.*
  New York: Pocketbooks, 1992.
  The "Sunset Strip" serial murders of six, committed by Carol
  Bundy and Douglas Clark in Los Angeles, California.

Farrell, Harry. *Swift Justice.*
  New York: St. Martin's, 1992.
  The 1933 kidnap-murder of Brooke Hart and the lynch mob
  murders of suspects Jack Holmes and Harold Thurmond in
  San Jose, California.

Finch, Philip. *Fatal Flaw.*
  New York: Villard, 1992.
  The Christmas 1975 "Winter Garden Murders" of four
  people in Winter Garden, Florida.

Finstad, Suzanne. *Ulterior Motives.*
  New York: Morrow, 1987.
  The 1983 murder of Texas multimillionaire Henry Kyle in
  Los Angeles, California.

Fisher, Jim. *The Lindbergh Case.*
  New York: Atlantic Monthly Press, 1994.
  The 1932 kidnap-murder of Charles Augustus Lindbergh,
  Jr., "The Lindbergh Baby," committed by Richard Bruno
  Hauptmann in Hopewell, New Jersey.

See also:
Bern. *Lindbergh: The Crime.*
Kennedy. *The Airman And The Carpenter.*
Waller. *Kidnap.*

Fogo, Fred. *"I Read the News Today".*
Lanham, MD: Rowman & Littlefield Publishers, 1994.
The 1980 murder of ex-Beatle John Lennon by obsessed fan Mark David Chapman in New York City.
See also:
Jones. *"Let Me Take You Down."*

Fraenkel, Osmond K. *The Sacco-Vanzetti Case.*
New York: Knopf, 1931.
The controversial trial and execution, for a 1920 double murder in Braintree, Massachusetts, of immigrant anarchists Nicola Sacco and Bartolomeo Vanzetti.
See also:
Russell. *Sacco & Vanzetti.*
Young. *Postmortem.*

France, David. *Bag Of Toys.*
New York: Warner, 1992.
The 1985 sadomasochistic "Death Mask Murder" of Eigil Vesti in New York City.

Franch, Thomas. *Unanswered Cries.*
New York: St. Martin's, 1991.
The 1984 rape and murder of Karen Gregory in Gulfport, Florida.

Frank, Gerald. *An American Death.*
Garden City, NY: Doubleday, 1972.
The 1968 murder of Dr. Martin Luther King, Jr., by James Earl Ray in Memphis, Tennessee.

See also:
McMillan. *The Making Of An Assassin.*
Pepper. *Orders To Kill.*
Ray. *Who Killed Martin Luther King?*

Frank, Gerald. *The Boston Strangler.*
New York: New American Library, 1967.
The story of the thirteen-victim "Boston Strangler Murders"
committed by Albert De Salvo.

Franklin, Eileen, and William Wright. *Sins Of The Father.*
New York: Crown, 1991.
The 1969 "Recovered Memory Murder" of eight-year-old
Susan Nason in Foster City, California, committed by George
Franklin, whose daughter, Eileen, recovered the memory of
the murder of her best friend twenty years later.
See also:
MacLean. *Once Upon A Time.*

Freedberg, Sydney. *Murder In The Temple Of Love.*
New York: Pantheon, 1994.
The story of hate-cult leader Yahweh Ben Yahweh and the
Nation Of Yahweh's "Death Angel Murders" in Miami,
Florida.

Freeman, Lucy. *Before I Kill Again.*
New York: Pocket Books, 1955.
The story of Chicago's "Lipstick Killer," serial murderer of
three, William Heirens.

Frey, Robert Seitz. *The Silent And The Damned.*
Lanham, MD: Madison Books, 1988.
The 1913 murder of Mary Phagan in Atlanta and the
lynching of the man wrongly convicted of her murder, Leo
Frank.
See also:
Golden. *A Little Girl is Dead.*

Friedland, Martin L. *The Death Of Old Man Rice.*
New York: New York University Press, 1994.
The 1900 murder of Texas multi-millionaire William Marsh
Rice in New York City by Albert Patrick and Charles Jones.

Friedly, Michael. *Malcolm X: The Assassination.*
New York: Carroll & Graf, 1992.
The 1965 murder of Black Muslim leader Malcolm X in
New York City.
See also:
Breitman. *The Assassination Of Malcolm X.*

Gaddis, Thomas E. *Birdman Of Alcatraz.*
New York: Random House, 1955.
The story of double murderer Robert Stroud.

Gallagher, Mike. *Lovers Of Deceit.*
New York: Doubleday, 1993.
The 1989 "Fatal Attraction Murder" of Betty Jeanne
Solomon by Carolyn Warmus in Westchester County, New
York.

Gelb, Alan. *Most Likely To Succeed.*
New York: Dutton, 1990.
The 1986 murder of three members of the Gates Family in
East Chatham, New York.

Gibson, Edie, and Ray Turner. *Blind Justice.*
New York: St. Martin's, 1991.
The 1982 murder of Dianne Masters in Chicago, Illinois.

Gilmore, John. *Severed: The Black Dahlia Murder.*
Los Angeles: Zanja Press, 1994.
The story of the still unsolved 1947 "Black Dahlia Murder"
of Elizabeth Short in Los Angeles, California.

Gilmore, Mikal. *Shot In The Heart.*
New York: Doubleday, 1993.
The life and death of Utah double murderer Gary Gilmore.
See also:
Mailer. *The Executioners Song.*

Ginsburg, Philip. *Poisoned Blood.*
New York: Scribners, 1987.
The 1975 murder of Frank Hillery by his wife Marie in
Anniston, Alabama.

Ginsburg, Philip. *The Shadow Of Death.*
New York: Scribners, 1993.
The story of the serial killer called the "Connecticut River
Valley Ripper," murderer of at least six women since 1984.

Girox, Robert. *A Deed Of Death.*
New York: Knopf, 1990.
The 1922 murder of Hollywood film director William
Desmond Taylor.
See also:
Kirkpatrick. *A Cast Of Killers.*

Golden, Harry. *A Little Girl Is Dead.*
Dallas: World, 1965.
The 1913 murder of Mary Phagan in Atlanta and the
lynching of the man wrongly convicted of her murder, Leo
Frank.
See also:
Frey. *The Silent and the Damned.*

Gollmar, Robert. *Ed Gein.*
Delavan, WI: Hallberg, 1981.
The story of Plainfield, Wisconsin's serial murderer Edward
Gein, upon whom the movie *Psycho* is based.
See also:
Schecter. *Deviant.*

Good, Jeffrey, and Susan Goreck. *Poison Mind.*
New York: Morrow, 1995.
The 1988 "Mensa Murder" of Peggy Carr by high I.Q. group
Mensa member George Trepal in Alturas, Florida.

Goodman, Jonathan. *The Slaying Of Joseph Bowne Elwell.*
New York: St. Martin's, 1987.
The 1920 murder of famed bridge player Joseph Bowne
Elwell in New York City.

Gray, Albert. *Poisoned Dreams.*
New York: Dutton, 1993.
The 1991 murder of department store heiress Nancy Dillard
in Dallas, Texas.

Graysmith, Robert. *The Murder Of Bob Crane.*
New York: Crown, 1993.
The 1978 "Hogan's Heroes Murder" of TV sit-com star Bob
Crane in Scottsdale, Arizona.

Graysmith, Robert. *The Sleeping Lady.*
New York: Dutton, 1990.
The story of San Francisco's "Trailside Killer," serial
murderer of seven, David Carpenter,

Graysmith, Robert. *Zodiac.*
New York: St. Martin's, 1986.
The story of San Francisco's five-victim "Zodiac Murders."

Green, Ben. *The "Soldier Of Fortune" Murders.*
New York: Delacorte, 1992.
The story of the three killer-for-hire murderers arranged
through classified ads in "Soldier Of Fortune" magazine.

Greenya, John. *Blood Relations.*
New York: Harcourt, 1987.
The 1985 murder of tobacco heiress Margaret Benson,
committed by her son Steven in Naples, Florida.

See also:
Mewshaw. *Money To Burn.*

Gross, Kenneth. *The Alice Crimmins Case.*
New York: Knopf, 1975.
The 1965 murders of Eddie and Missy Crimmins, five and
four, by their mother Alice in New York City.

Haden-Guest, Anthony. *Bad Dreams.*
New York: Macmillan, 1991.
The 1978 murder of Jack Tupper by Buddy Jacobson on
New York City's Upper East Side.

Hammer, Richard. *Beyond Obsession.*
New York: Morrow, 1992.
The 1987 murder of Joyce Aparo in Bernardston,
Massachusetts.

Hammer, Richard. *The CBS Murders.*
New York: Morrow, 1987.
The 1982 six-victim "CBS Murders" in New York City.

Harris, Ellen Francis. *Dying To Get Married.*
New York: Carol, 1991.
The 1986 "Sexual Bondage Murder" of Julie Miller Bulloch,
committed by her husband Dennis in St. Louis, Missouri.

Harris, Jean. *Stranger In Two Worlds.*
New York: Macmillan, 1986.
The story of the 1980 murder of Scarsdale Diet Doctor
Herman Tarnower by his ex-mistress Jean Harris.
See also:
Alexander. *Very Much A Lady.*
Trilling. *The Death Of The Scarsdale Diet Doctor.*

Hawkes, Ellen. *Feminism On Trial.*
New York: Morrow, 1986.
The 1983 trial of Ginny Foat, a leader in the National
Organization for Women, acquitted of the "NOW Murder" in
New Orleans, Louisiana.

Headley, Lake, and William Hoffman. *Loud And Clear.*
New York: Holt, 1990.
The 1976 murder of award-winning investigative reporter
Don Bolles in Phoenix, Arizona.

Heilbroner, David. *Death Benefit.*
New York: Harmony, 1993.
The 1987 murder of Deana Hubbard Wild in Big Sur,
California.

Herzog, Arthur. *The Woodchipper Murder.*
New York: Henry Holt, 1989.
The 1986 "Woodchipper Murder" of Helle Crafts,
committed by her husband in Newton, Connecticut.

Higdon, Hal. *The Crime Of The Century.*
New York: Putnam, 1975.
The 1924 kidnap-murder of Bobby Franks by "Thrill
Killers" Nathan Leopold and Richard Loeb.
See also:
Leopold, Nathan. *Life Plus 99 Years.*

Horton, Sue. *The Billionaire Boys Club.*
New York: St. Martin's, 1989.
The 1984 Los Angeles/Redwood City, California double
murders committed by or on the orders of Billionaire Boys
Club founder Joe Hunt.
See also:
Sullivan. *The Price Of Experience.*

Howard, Clark. *Brothers In Blood.*
  New York: St. Martin's, 1983.
    The 1973 mass murder of the six members of the Alday
    Family in Seminole County, Georgia.
      See also:
        Cook, Thomas. *Blood Echoes.*

Howard, Clark. *Zebra.*
  New York: Berkeley, 1979.
    The story of the San Francisco's 1973-74 "Zebra Murders"
    committed by the Black Muslim hate cult, the "Death
    Angels."

Humes, Edward. *Buried Secrets.*
  New York: Dutton, 1991.
    The 1989 "Human Sacrifice Murder" of American student
    Mark Kilroy by a Matamoros, Mexico satanic cult.
      See also:
        Kilroy. *Sacrifice.*

Humes, Edward. *Mississippi Mud.*
  New York: Simon & Schuster, 1994.
    The 1987 "Dixie Mafia Murder" of Vincent and Margaret
    Sherry in Biloxi, Mississippi.

Hynes, Charles and Bob Drury. *Incident At Howard Beach.*
  New York: Putnam, 1990.
    The 1989 hate-murder of Yusef Hawkins in the
    Howard Beach section of Brooklyn, New York.
      See also:
        DeSantos. *For The Color Of His Skin.*

Irving, Clifford. *Daddy's Girl.*
  New York: Summit, 1988.
    The 1982 murder of James and Virginia Campbell in
    Houston, Texas.

Jaeger, Richard and William Balousek. *Massacre In Milwaukee.*
 Oregon, WI: Waubesa Press, 1991.
 The story of Milwaukee, Wisconsin's serial murderer of
 fifteen, Jeffrey Dahmer.
  See also:
   Baumann. *Step Into My Parlor.*
   Dahmer. *A Father's Story.*
   Davis. *Milwaukee Murders.*
   Dvorchak. *Milwaukee Massacre.*
   Schwartz. *The Man Who Could Not Kill Enough.*

Johnson, Joyce. *What Lisa Knew.*
 New York: Putnam, 1990.
 The 1987 child abuse murder of seven-year-old Lisa
 Steinberg by her adoptive father Joel in New York City's
 Greenwich Village.

Jones, Ann. *Everyday Death.*
 New York: Holt, 1985.
 The 1978 murder trial of Bernadette Powell, convicted of
 killing her abusive ex-husband in Ithaca, New York.

Jones, Jack. *Let Me Take You Down.*
 New York: Villard, 1992.
 The 1980 murder of ex-Beatle John Lennon by obsessed fan
 Mark David Chapman in New York City.
  See also:
   Fogo. *"I Read the News Today".*

Kaiser, Robert Blair. *"R.F.K. Must Die!"*
 New York: Dutton, 1970.
 The 1968 murder of U.S. Senator Robert F. Kennedy by
 Sirhan Sirhan in Los Angeles, California.
  See also:
   Melanson. *The Robert F. Kennedy Assassination.*
   Moldea. *The Killing of Robert F. Kennedy.*
   Morrow. *The Senator Must Die.*

Kaplan, John, and Jon Waltz. *The Trial Of Jack Ruby.*
New York: Macmillan, 1965.
  The story of the 1963 murder of suspected Presidential
  assassin Lee Harvey Oswald by nightclub owner Jack Ruby
  in Dallas, Texas.
    See also:
      Ruby. *Dallas Justice.*

Karpf, Jason, and Elinor Karpf. *Anatomy Of A Massacre.*
Waco, TX: WRS Publishing, 1994.
  The 1991 "Luby's Cafeteria Massacre" of twenty-three by
  George Hennard in Killeen, Texas.

Katz, Robert. *Naked By The Window.*
New York: Atlantic Monthly Press, 1990.
  The 1985 plunge to her death of sculptor Ana Mendieta in
  New York City's Greenwich Village.

Kendall, Elizabeth. *The Phantom Prince.*
Seattle: Madrona, 1981.
  The story of serial murderer of thirty, Theodore Bundy.
    See also:
      Larsen. *The Deliberate Stranger.*
      Michaud. *The Only Living Witness.*
      Rule. *The Stranger Beside Me.*
      Winn. *Ted Bundy: The Killer Next Door.*

Kennedy, Ludovic. *The Airman And The Carpenter.*
New York: Viking, 1985.
  The 1932 kidnap-murder of Charles Augustus Lindbergh,
  Jr., "The Lindbergh Baby," committed by Richard Bruno
  Hauptmann in Hopewell, New Jersey
    See also:
      Bern. *Lindbergh: The Crime.*
      Fisher. *The Lindbergh Case.*
      Waller. *Kidnap.*

Kent, David. *Forty Whacks.*
  Emmaus, PA: Yankee Books, 1992.
    The 1892 axe murders of Andrew and Abby Borden in Fall
    River, Massachusetts and the trial and acquittal of their
    daughter Lizzie.
      See also:
        Spiering,. *Lizzie.*

Keyes, Edward. *The Michigan Murders.*
  New York: Readers Digest, 1976.
    The story of Ann Arbor/Ypsilanti Michigan's "Co-ed Killer,"
    serial murderer of seven, Norman Collins.

Kidder, Tracy. *The Road To Yuba City.*
  New York: Doubleday, 1974.
    The story of Yuba City, California's serial murderer of
    twenty-five, Juan Vallejo Corona.
      See also:
        Crey. *Burden Of Proof.*
        Villasenor. *Jury.*

Kilroy, Jim, and Bob Stewart. *Sacrifice.*
  Dallas: World, 1990.
    The 1989 "Human Sacrifice Murder" of American student
    Mark Kilroy by a Matamoros, Mexico satanic cult.
      See also:
        Humes. *Buried Secrets.*

Kirkpatrick, Sidney. *A Cast Of Killers.*
  New York: Dutton, 1986.
    The 1922 murder of Hollywood film director
    William Desmond Taylor.
      See also:
        Girox. *A Deed Of Death.*

Klauner, Lawrence. *Son Of Sam.*
  New York: McGraw-Hill, 1981.
  The 1976-77 six-victim "Son Of Sam Murders," committed
  by serial killer David Berkowitz in New York City.
    See also:
      Abrahamsen. *Confessions Of The Son Of Sam.*

Kleiman, Dena. *A Deadly Silence.*
  New York: Atlantic Monthly Press, New York, 1988.
  The 1986 murder-for-hire of James Pierson arranged by his
  sexually-abused, sixteen-year-old daughter Cheryl on Long
  Island, New York.

Kohn, Howard. *Who Killed Karen Silkwood?*
  New York: Summit, 1981.
  The 1974 murder of nuclear industry whistler-blower Karen
  Silkwood on Highway 74 outside of Oklahoma City,
  Oklahoma.

Kunstler, William. *The Hall-Mills Murder Case.*
  New Brunswick, NJ: Rutgers University Press, 1964.
  The 1922 double murders of the Reverend Edward Wheeler
  Hall and his mistress Eleanor Mills in New Brunswick, New
  Jersey.
    See also:
      Boswell. *The Girl In Lover's Lane.*

Lane, Mark. *Rush To Judgment.*
  New York: Thundermouth, 1966.
  The 1963 assassination of President John F. Kennedy.
    See also:
      Bishop. *The Day Kennedy Was Shot.*
      Manchester, William. *The Death Of A President.*
      United States. *The Warren Commission's Report.*

Langford, Gerald. *The Murder Of Stanford White.*
  New York: Bobbs-Merrill, 1962.
    The 1906 murder in New York City's Madison Square
    Garden of architect Stanford White by millionaire Harry
    Thaw over "The Girl In The Red Velvet Swing," showgirl
    Evelyn Nesbit.
      See also:
        Mooney. *Evelyn Nesbit And Stanford White.*

Langlos, Ruth, and Dennis Niemiec. *Murder, No Doubt.*
  Fall Hills, NJ: New Horizon, 1993.
    The 1976 murder of Dr. Jack Langlos in Los Angeles,
    California, as told by his wife.

Larsen, Richard. *The Deliberate Stranger.*
  Englewood Cliffs, NJ: Prentice-Hall, 1980.
    The story of the serial murderer of thirty, Theodore Bundy.
      See also:
        Kendall. *The Phantom Prince.*
        Michaud. *The Only Living Witness.*
        Rule. *The Stranger Beside Me.*
        Winn. *Ted Bundy: The Killer Next Door.*

Lefkowitz, Bernard, and Kenneth Gross. *The Victims.*
  New York: Putnam, 1969.
    The 1963 murders of Janice Wylie and Emily Hoffert in
    New York City.
      See also:
        Wylie, Max. *Gift Of Janice.*

Leopold, Nathan. *Life Plus 99 Years.*
  Garden City, NY: Doubleday, 1958.
    The 1924 kidnap-murder of Bobby Franks in Chicago by
    "Thrill Killers" Nathan Leopold and Richard Loeb.
      See also:
        Higdon. *The Crime Of The Century.*

Levy, Steven. *The Unicorn's Secret.*
New York: Prentice-Hall, 1988.
The 1977 murder of Holly Maddux committed by Ira
Einhorn in Philadelphia, Pennsylvania.

Lindsey, Robert. *A Gathering Of Saints.*
New York: Simon & Schuster, 1988.
The story of the 1985 double "Mormon Forgery Murders"
committed by Mark Hofmann in in Salt Lake City, Utah.
See also:
Naifeh. *The Mormon Murders.*
Sillitoe. *Salamander.*

Linedecker, Clifford. *The Man Who Killed Boys.*
New York: St. Martin's, 1980.
The story of Chicago's serial murderer of thirty-three,
John Wayne Gacy.
See also:
Cahill. *Buried Dreams.*
Sullivan. *Killer Clown.*

Linedecker, Clifford. *Night Stalker.*
New York: St. Martin's, 1991.
The 1985 thirteen-victim "Nightstalker Murders," committed
by serial murderer Richard Ramirez in Los Angeles.
See also:
Carlo. *The Night Stalker.*

Logan, Andy. *Against The Evidence.*
New York: McCall Publishing, 1970.
The 1915 murder of gambler Herman Rosenthal by corrupt
New York City Police Lieutenant Charles Becker.

Lunde, Donald, and Morgan Jefferson. *The Die Song.*
New York: Norton, 1980.
The story of Santa Cruz, California's serial killer of
thirteen, Herbert William Mullin.

MacLean, Harry. *In Broad Daylight.*
New York: Harper & Row, 1988.
The 1981 "Vigilante Murder" of small town bully Ken Rex McElroy, killed in broad daylight and before multiple witnesses in Skidmore, Missouri.

MacLean, Harry. *Once Upon A Time.*
New York: Harper Collins, 1993.
The 1969 "Recovered Memory Murder" of eight-year-old Susan Nason in Foster City, California, committed by George Franklin, whose daughter, Eileen, recovered the memory of the murder of her best friend twenty years later.
See also:
Franklin. *Sins Of The Father.*

Mailer, Norman. *The Executioner's Song.*
Boston: Little, Brown, 1979.
The life and death of Utah's double murderer Gary Gilmore.
See also:
Gilmore. *Shot In The Heart.*

Manchester, William. *The Death Of A President.*
New York: Harper & Row, 1967.
The 1963 assassination of President John F. Kennedy in Dallas, Texas.
See also:
Bishop. *The Day Kennedy Was Shot.*
Lane. *Rush To Judgment.*
United States. *The Warren Commission's Report.*

Mass, Peter. *In A Child's Name.*
New York: Simon & Schuster, 1990.
The 1984 murder of Teresa Benigno Taylor in New Jersey.

Massengill, Reed. *Portrait Of A Racist.*
New York: St. Martin's, 1994.
The 1963 murder of civil rights leader Medgar Evers by Byron de la Beckwith in Jackson, Mississippi.

See also.
Nossiter. *Of Long Memory.*
Vollers. *Ghosts of Mississippi.*

McAlary, Mike. *Cop Shot.*
New York: Putnam, 1990.
The 1988 murder by crack cocaine drug dealers of New
York City Police Officer Edward Byrne.

McCumber, David. *X-Rated.*
New York: Simon & Schuster, 1992.
The 1991 "Porno Kings Murder" of Artie Mitchell by his
brother James in San Francisco, California.

McDougal, Dennis. *In The Best Of Families.*
New York: Warner, 1994.
The 1983 rape-murder of Marguerite Miller by her son
Michael in Palos Verdes Estates, California.

McGinniss, Joe. *Blind Faith.*
New York: Putnam, 1989.
The 1984 murder of Maria Marshall by her husband Robert
at a New Jersey Turnpike rest stop.

McGinniss, Joe. *Cruel Doubt.*
New York: Simon & Schuster, 1991.
The 1988 "Dungeons & Dragons Murder" of Leith von Stein
in Washington, North Carolina.
See also:
Bledsoe. *Blood Games.*

McGinniss, Joe. *Fatal Vision.*
New York: Putnam, 1983.
The 1970 triple murders of his wife Colette and daughters
Kimberly and Kristen by Green Beret, Dr. Jeffrey
McDonald, at Fort Bragg, North Carolina.

McMillan, George. *The Making Of An Assassin.*
  Boston: Little Brown, 1976.
    The story of James Earl Ray, convicted of the 1968
    murder of Dr. Martin Luther King, Jr. in Memphis,
    Tennessee.
      See also:
        Frank. *An American Death.*
        Pepper. *Orders To Kill.*
        Ray. *Who Killed Martin Luther King?*

McNulty, Faith. *The Burning Bed.*
  New York: Harcourt Brace, 1980.
    The 1977 "Burning Bed Murder" of Mickey Hughes by his
    abused and battered wife Francine.

Melanson, Philip. *The Robert F. Kennedy Assassination.*
  New York: Shapolsky, 1991.
    The 1968 murder of Senator Robert F. Kennedy by Sirhan
    Sirhan in Los Angeles, California.
      See also:
        Kaiser. *"R.F.K. Must Die!"*
        Moldea. *The Killing of Robert F. Kennedy.*
        Morrow. *The Senator Must Die.*

Mewshaw, Michael. *Money To Burn.*
  New York: Atheneum, 1987.
    The 1985 murder of Margaret Benson, heir to the Benson &
    Hedges cigarette fortune, by her son Steven in Naples,
    Florida.
      See also:
        Greenya. *Blood Relations.*

Meyer, Peter. *Death Of Innocence.*
  New York: Putman, 1985.
    The 1981 rape-murder of twelve-year-old Melissa Walbridge
    in Essex Junction, Vermont.

Meyer, Peter. *The Yale Murder.*
New York: Empire, 1982.
The 1977 murder of twenty-year-old Bonnie Garland by her
twenty-four-year-old boyfriend Richard Herrin while they
were both students at Yale University.

Michaud, Stephen. *The Only Living Witness.*
New York: Simon & Schuster, 1983.
The story of the serial murderer of thirty, Theodore Bundy.
See also:
Kendall. *The Phantom Prince.*
Larsen. *The Deliberate Stranger.*
Rule. *The Stranger Beside Me.*
Winn. *Ted Bundy: The Killer Next Door.*

Milner, E.R. *The Lives and Times of Bonnie and Clyde.*
Carbondale, IL: Southern Illinois University Press, 1996.
The story of the thirteen-victim rampage of bank robbers
Bonnie Parker and Clyde Barrow.

Mitchell, Paige. *Act Of Love.*
New York: Knopf, 1976.
The 1973 "Mercy Murder" of terminally ill George
Zygmanik by his brother Lester at the Jersey Shore Medical
Center in Asbury Park, New Jersey.

Moldea, Dan. *The Killing of Robert F. Kennedy.*
New York: Norton, 1995.
The 1968 murder of Senator Robert F. Kennedy by Sirhan
Sirhan in Los Angeles, California.
See also:
Kaiser. *"R.F.K. Must Die!"*
Melanson. *The Robert F. Kennedy Assassination.*
Morrow. *The Senator Must Die.*

Mones, Paul. *Stalking Justice.*
New York: Pocketbooks, 1995.
The story of Arlington, Virginia's "Southside Strangler" and
the role of DNA fingerprinting in his capture.

Mooney, Michael. *Evelyn Nesbit and Stanford White.*
New York: Morrow, 1976.
The 1906 murder in New York City's Madison Square
Garden of architect Stanford White by millionaire Harry
Thaw over "The Girl In The Red Velvet Swing," showgirl
Evelyn Nesbit.
See also:
Langford. *The Murder Of Stanford White.*

Morrow, Robert. *The Senator Must Die.*
Santa Monica, CA: Roundtable, 1988.
The 1968 murder of Senator Robert F. Kennedy by Sirhan
Sirhan in Los Angeles, California.
See also:
Kaiser. *"R.F.K. Must Die!"*
Melanson. *The Robert F. Kennedy Assassination.*
Moldea. *The Killing Of Robert F. Kennedy.*

Moser, Don, and Jerry Cohen. *The Pied Piper Of Tucson.*
New York: American Library, 1967.
The 1964 three-victim rape-murder rampage of Charles
Schmid, Jr., "The Pied Piper" of Tucson, Arizona.

Naifeh, Steven. *The Mormon Murders.*
New York: Weidenfeld & Nicolson. 1988.
The story of the 1985 double "Mormon Forgery Murders"
committed by Mark Hofmann in in Salt Lake City, Utah.
See also:
Lindsey. *A Gathering Of Saints.*
Sillitoe. *Salamander.*

Norris, Joel. *Arthur Shawcross.*
New York: Pinnacle, 1992.
The 1988-89 eleven-victim "Rochester Strangler" murders
committed by serial killer Arthur John Shawcross in
Rochester, New York.
See also:
Olsen. *The Misbegotten Son.*

Norton, Carla. *Disturbed Ground.*
New York: Morrow, 1994.
The story of Sacramento, California's serial murderer of
seven elderly persons under her care, Dorothea Puente.
See also:
Blackburn. *Human Harvest.*

Nossiter, Adam. *Of Long Memory.*
Reading, MA: Addison-Wesley, 1994.
The 1963 murder of civil rights leader Medgar Evers by
Byron de la Beckwith in Jackson, Mississippi.
See also:
Massengill. *Portrait Of A Racist.*
Vollers. *Ghosts of Mississippi.*

O'Brien, Darcy. *Murder In Little Egypt.*
New York: Morrow, 1989.
The 1984 murder of Sean Cavaness by his father, Dr. John
Dale Cavaness, in Eldorado, Illinois.

O'Brien, Darcy. *Two of a Kind: The Hillside Stranglers.*
New York: New American Library, 1985.
The 1977-79 ten-victim "Hillside Strangler Murders" in Los
Angeles, committed by serial murders Angelo Buono and
Kenneth Bianchi.
See also:
Schwartz. *The Hillside Strangler.*

Olsen, Jack. *Give A Boy A Gun.*
  New York: Delacorte, 1985.
   The 1981 "Mountain Man Murders" of two Idaho Fish &
   Game wardens by Claude Dallas, Jr.

Olsen, Jack. *The Man With The Candy.*
  New York: Simon & Schuster, 1974.
   The story of Houston's "Candy Man," serial murderer of
   twenty-seven, Dean Alan Coril.

Olsen, Jack. *The Misbegotten Son.*
  New York: Delacorte, 1993.
   The 1988-89 eleven-victim "Rochester Strangler" murders
   committed by serial killer Arthur John Shawcross in
   Rochester, New York.
    See also:
    Norris. *Arthur Shawcross.*

Pepper, William. *Orders To Kill.*
  New York: Carroll & Graf, 1995.
   The 1968 murder of Dr. Martin Luther King, Jr. in
   Memphis, Tennessee.
    See also:
    Frank. *An American Death.*
    Ray. *Who Killed Martin Luther King?*

Perry, Hamilton Darby. *Libby Holman.*
  Boston: Little Brown, 1983.
   The 1932 murder of tobacco heir Zachary Smith Reynolds
   in Winston-Salem, North Carolina.

Radish, Kris. *Run, Bambi, Run.*
  New York: Carol, 1992.
   The first-person account by Lawrencia "Bambi" Bembenek,
   ex-police officer, ex-Playboy bunny, convicted of the 1981
   murder of her husband's ex-wife.
    See also:
    Bembenek. *Woman On Trial.*

Ray, James Earl. *Who Killed Martin Luther King?*
Washington, DC: National Press Books, 1992.
  The first-person story of James Earl Ray, convicted of the
  1968 murder of Martin Luther King, Jr. in Memphis,
  Tennessee.
    See also:
      Frank. *An American Death.*
      McMillan. *The Making Of An Assassin.*
      Pepper. *Orders To Kill.*

Reed, Dan, and Kelly Moore. *Deadly Medicine.*
New York: St. Martin's, 1988.
  The 1982 "Texas Baby Murder" of fourteen-month-old
  Chelsea McClellan by serial baby killer, Nurse Genene Jones.
    See also:
      Elkind. *The Death Shift.*

Reinhardt, James. *The Murderous Trail Of Charles
Starkweather.*
  Atlanta: Thomas, 1960.
    The 1957 ten-victim rampage of serial killer Charles
    Starkweather in Lincoln, Nebraska.
      See also:
        Allen. *Starkweather.*

Reuben, William A. *The Mark Fein Case.*
New York: Dial Press, 1967.
The 1963 murder of bookmaker Rubin Markowitz by
wealthy businessman Mark Fein in New York City.

Ruby, Jack, and Melvin Belli. *Dallas Justice.*
New York: McKay, 1964.
  The story of the 1963 murder of suspected Presidential
  assassin Lee Harvey Oswald in Dallas, Texas as told by his
  murderer, Jack Ruby.
    See also:
      Kaplan. *The Trial Of Jack Ruby.*

Rule, Ann. *If You Really Loved Me.*
New York: Simon & Schuster, 1991.
The 1985 murder of Linda Marie Brown in Garden Grove, California.

Rule, Ann. *The Stranger Beside Me.*
New York: Norton, 1980.
The story of the serial murderer of thirty, Theodore Bundy.
See also:
Kendall. *The Phantom Prince.*
Larsen. *The Deliberate Stranger.*
Michaud. *The Only Living Witness.*
Winn. *Ted Bundy: The Killer Next Door.*

Russell, Francis. *Sacco & Vanzetti.*
New York: Harper, 1986.
The controversial trial and execution, for a 1920 double murder in Braintree, Massachusetts, of immigrant anarchists Nicola Sacco and Bartolomeo Vanzetti.
See also:
Fraenkel. *The Sacco-Vanzetti Case.*
Young. *Postmortem.*

Ryzuk, Mary S. *Thou Shalt Not Kill.*
New York: Warner Books, 1990.
The 1971 five-victim "List Family Murders" committed by mass murderer John List in Westfield, New Jersey.
See also:
Benford. *Righteous Carnage.*

Salerno, Steve. *Deadly Blessing.*
New York: Morrow, 1987.
The 1981 murder of Price Daniel, Jr. in Liberty, Texas.

Samit, Michele. *No Sanctuary.*
New York: Carol, 1993.
The 1990 murder of Anita Green by her husband Melvin
over her adulterous affair with their Rabbi in the San
Fernando Valley, California.

Sandiford, Kay, and Alan Burgess. *Shattered Night.*
New York: Warner, 1984.
The 1980 murder of Frank Sandiford by his abused and
battered wife Kay in Houston, Texas.

Sarlyan, Aram. *Rancho Mirage.*
New York: Barricade, 1993.
The 1981 "Sex Slave Murder" of Robert Sand by his wife
Andrea in Palm Springs, California.

Sasse, Cynthia, and Peggy Widder. *The Kirtland Massacre.*
New York: Fine, 1991.
The 1990 ritual-execution murders of the five-member
Avery Family by the followers of Jeffrey Lundgren's
Reorganized Church of the Latter Day Saints in Kirtland,
Ohio.
See also:
Earley. *Prophet Of Death.*

Scammell, Henry. *Mortal Remains.*
New York: Harper Collins, 1991.
The 1978 satanic ritual murders of three young girls in Fall
River, Massachusetts.

Schecter, Harold. *Deranged.*
New York: Pocket Books, 1990.
The 1928 murder of twelve-year-old Grace Budd by sexual
serial murderer Albert "The Cannibal" Fish in Westchester,
New York.
See also:
Angelella. *Trail of Blood.*

Schecter, Harold. *Deviant.*
New York: Pocketbooks, 1989.
The story of Plainfield, Wisconsin's serial murder of fifteen,
Edward Gein.
See also:
Gollmar. *Edward Gein.*

Schultze, Jim. *Preacher's Girl.*
New York: Morrow, 1993.
The 1986 murder of her lover committed by Blanch Taylor
Moore, a pastor's wife, in Burlington, North Carolina.

Schwartz, Anne. *The Man Who Could Not Kill Enough.*
New York: Carol, 1992.
The story of Milwaukee, Wisconsin's serial killer of fifteen,
Jeffrey Dahmer.
See also:
Baumann. *Step Into My Parlor.*
Dahmer. *A Father's Story.*
Davis. *Milwaukee Murders.*
Dvorchak. *Milwaukee Massacre.*
Jaeger. *Massacre In Milwaukee.*

Schwartz, Ted. *The Hillside Strangler.*
Garden City, NY: Doubleday, 1981.
The 1977-79 ten-victim "Hillside Strangler Murders" in Los
Angeles, committed by serial murders Angelo Buono and
Kenneth Bianchi.
See also:
O'Brien. *Two of a Kind: The Hillside Stranglers.*

Schwartz-Nobel, Loretta. *Engaged To Murder.*
New York: Viking, 1987.
The 1979 triple-victim "Main Line Murders" in
Philadelphia.
See also:
Wambaugh. *Echoes In The Darkness.*

Schwartz-Nobel, Loretta. *Forsaking All Others.*
  New York: Villard, 1993.
    The 1989 "Till Death Us Do Part Murders" of Dan
    Broderick and his new wife Linda, committed by his ex-wife
    Betty Broderick in San Diego, California.
    See also:
      Stumbo. *Until The Twelfth Of Never.*

Shapiro, Robert L. *The Search For Justice.*
  New York: Warner Books, 1996.
    The 1994 murders of Nicole Brown Simpson and Ronald
    Lyle Goldman in Brentwood, California and the murder trial
    and acquittal of O.J. Simpson.
    See also:
      Darden. *In Contempt.*
      Dershowitz. *Reasonable Doubts.*

Sharkey, Joe. *Above Suspicion.*
  New York: Simon & Schuster, 1993.
    The 1989 murder of his pregnant girlfriend by FBI Special
    Agent Mark Putnam in Pikeville, Kentucky.

Sharkey, Joe. *Deadly Greed.*
  New York: Prentice-Hall, 1991.
    The 1989 "911" double murder of his pregnant wife Carol
    and unborn son Christopher committed by Charles Stuart, Jr.
    in Boston, Massachusetts.

Siegal, Barry. *A Death In White Bear Lake.*
  New York: Bantam, 1990.
    The 1965 murder of three-year-old Craig Jurgens by his
    abusive adoptive mother Lois Jurgens in White Bear Lake,
    Minnesota.

Siegal, Beatrice. *Murder On The Highway.*
  New York: Fourwinds Press, 1993.
    The 1965 murder of civil rights worker Viola Liuzzo on
    Route 80 outside of Selma, Alabama.

Sikora, Frank. *Until Justice Rolls Down.*
   Tuscaloosa, AL: University of Alabama Press, 1991.
   The 1963 murder of four black schoolgirls in the bombing
   of the Sixteenth Street Baptist Church in Birmingham,
   Alabama.

Sillitoe, Linda, and Allen Roberts. *Salamander.*
   Salt Lake City, Utah: Signature, 1988.
   The story of the 1985 double "Mormon Forgery Murders"
   committed by Mark Hofmann in in Salt Lake City, Utah.
      See also:
         Lindsey. *A Gathering Of Saints.*
         Naifeh. *The Mormon Murders.*

Smead, Howard. *Blood Justice.*
   New York: Oxford University Press, 1986.
   The 1959 lynching, in Poplarville, Mississippi, of Mack
   Charles Parker, a black man accused of raping a white
   woman.

Smith, Carlton, and Thomas Guillen. *The Search For The Green
River Killer.*
   New York: Penguin, 1991.
   The 1982-84 unsolved forty-nine-victim "Green River
   Killings" in Seattle, Washington.

Smith, David, with Carol Calef. *Beyond All Reason.*
   New York: Kensington Books, 1995.
   The 1994 murders of her children, Michael, three, and Alex,
   fourteen months, by Susan Smith in Union, South Carolina,
   as told by her husband.

Smith, Edgar. *A Brief Against Death.*
   New York: Knopf, 1968.
   The first-person story of convicted child murderer Edgar
   Smith's life on New Jersey's Death Row.

Soble, Ron, and John Johnson. *Blood Brothers.*
New York: Penguin, 1994.
The 1998 murders of Jose and Kitty Menendez by their sons
Erik and Lyle in Beverly Hills, California.
See also:
Davis. *Bad Blood.*

Spiering, Frank. *Lizzie.*
New York: Random House, 1984.
The 1892 axe murders of Andrew and Abby Borden in Fall
River, Massachusetts and the trial and acquittal of their
daughter, Lizzie.
See also:
Kent. *Forty Whacks.*

Stumbo, Bella. *Until The Twelfth Of Never.*
New York: Pocketbooks, 1993.
The 1989 "Till Death Us Do Part Murders" of Dan
Broderick and his new wife Linda, committed by his ex-wife
Betty Broderick in San Diego, California.
See also:
Schwartz-Nobel. *Forsaking All Others.*

Sullivan, Gerard, and Harvey Aronson. *High Hopes.*
New York: Coward, 1981.
The 1974 "Amityville Horror Murders" of six members
of the DeFeo Family, committed by Ronald DeFeo, Jr. at the
family home in Amityville, Long Island.

Sullivan, Randall. *The Price Of Experience.*
New York: Atlantic Monthly Press, 1996.
The 1984 Los Angeles/Redwood City, California double
murders committed by or on the orders of Billionaire Boys
Club founder Joe Hunt.
See also:
Horton. *The Billionaire Boys Club.*

Sullivan, Terry, and Peter Maiken. *Killer Clown.*
  New York: Grosset & Dunlap, 1983.
    The story of Chicago's serial murderer of thirty-three, John
    Wayne Gacy.
      See also:
        Cahill. *Buried Dreams.*
        Linedecker. *The Man Who Killed Boys.*

Swindle, Howard. *Deliberate Indifference.*
  New York: Viking, 1993.
    The 1987 murder of Loyal Garner, a black man beaten to
    death by white police officers in Sabine County, Texas.

Tanenbaum, Robert and Philip Rosenberg. *Badge Of The
  Assassin.*
    New York: Dutton, 1979.
      The 1971 murders of two New York City policemen by
      the Black Liberation Army in Harlem, New York.

Trilling, Diana. *The Death Of The Scarsdale Diet Doctor.*
  New York: Harcourt Brace, 1981.
    The story of the 1980 murder of Scarsdale Diet Doctor
    Herman Tarnower by his ex-mistress Jean Harris.
      See also:
        Alexander. *Very Much A Lady.*
        Harris. *Stranger In Two Worlds.*

United States. *The Warren Commission's Report On The
  Assassination Of President John F. Kennedy.*
    Washington, DC: U.S. GPO, 1964.
      The 1963 assassination of President John F. Kennedy in
      Dallas, Texas.
        See also:
          Bishop. *The Day Kennedy Was Shot.*
          Lane. *Rush To Judgment.*
          Manchester. *The Death Of A President.*

van Hoffmann, Eric. *A Venom In The Blood.*
  New York: Fine, 1990.
    The story of the 1978-1980 ten-victim kidnap-rape-murder
    spree committed by husband and wife killers, Gerald and
    Charlene Gallego.

Villasenor, Victor. *Jury: The People v. Juan Corona.*
  Boston: Little, Brown, 1977.
    The story of Yuba City, California's serial murderer of
    twenty-five, Juan Vallejo Corona.
    See also:
      Crey. *Burden of Proof*
      Kidder. *The Road To Yuba City.*

Vollers, Maryanne. *Ghosts of Mississippi.*
  Boston: Little, Brown, 1995.
    The 1963 murder of civil rights leader Medgar Evers by
    Byron de la Beckwith in Jackson, Mississippi.
    See also:
      Massengill. *Portrait Of A Racist.*
      Nossiter. *Of Long Memory.*

Waller, George. *Kidnap.*
  New York: Dial Press, 1961.
    The 1932 kidnap-murder of Charles Augustus Lindbergh,
    Jr., "The Lindbergh Baby," committed by Richard Bruno
    Hauptmann in Hopewell, New Jersey.
    See also:
      Bern. *Lindbergh: The Crime.*
      Fisher. *The Lindbergh Case.*
      Kennedy. *The Airman And The Carpenter.*

Wambaugh, Joseph. *Echoes In The Darkness.*
  New York: Morrow, 1989.
    The 1979 triple-victim "Main Line Murders" in
    Philadelphia.
    See also:
      Schwartz-Nobel. *Engaged To Murder.*

Wambaugh, Joseph. *The Onion Field.*
  New York: Delacorte, 1973.
    The 1963 "Onion Field Murder" of Los Angeles
    Policeman Ian Campbell.

Watkins, Ronald. *Birthright.*
  New York: Morrow, 1992.
    The 1990 "U-Haul Murder" of Eva Berg Shoen, heiress to
    the U-Haul family fortune, in Telluride, Colorado.

Watkins, Ronald. *Evil Intentions.*
  New York: Morrow, 1992.
    The 1981 abduction and murder of Suzanne Rossetti in
    Arizona's Superstition Mountains.

Weiss, Mike. *Double Play.*
  Wesley, MA: Addison-Wesley, 1984.
    The 1978 "City Hall Murders" of Mayor George Moscone
    and Supervisor Harvey Milk by ex-Supervisor Dan White in
    San Francisco, California.

Weller, Sheila. *Marrying The Hangman.*
  New York: Random House, 1991.
    The 1987 murder of Diane Pikul by her husband Joseph on
    Long Island, New York.

Wesley, John. *The Man Who Shot McKinley.*
  South Brunswick, NJ: A.S. Barnes, 1970.
    The 1901 murder of President William McKinley by Leon
    Czolgosz in Buffalo, New York.

Wick, Steve. *Bad Company.*
  New York: Harcourt, 1990.
    The 1983 "Cotton Club Murder" of Roy Radin in Los
    Angeles, California.

Wilkinson, Alec. *A Violent Act.*
  New York: Knopf, 1993.
    The 1986 triple murders committed by Mike Wayne Jackson
    in Indianapolis, Indiana.

Winn, Stephen. *Ted Bundy: The Killer Next Door.*
  New York: Bantam, 1980.
    The story of the serial murderer of thirty, Theodore Bundy.
    See also:
      Kendall. *The Phantom Prince.*
      Larsen. *The Deliberate Stranger.*
      Michaud. *The Only Living Witness.*
      Rule. *The Stranger Beside Me.*

Wolf, Marvin and Larry Attebery. *Family Blood.*
  New York: Harper Collins, 1993.
    The 1985 "Yom Kippur Murders" of Gerald and Vera
    Woodman in Los Angeles, California.

Wolfe, Linda. *The Professor and the Prostitute.*
  Boston: Houghton Mifflin, 1986.
    The 1983 murder of Robin Benedict by Tufts University
    Professor William Douglas in Boston, Massachusetts.
    See also:
      Carpenter. *Missing Beauty.*

Wolfe, Linda. *Wasted.*
  New York: Simon & Schuster, 1989.
    The 1986 "Preppie Murder" of Jennifer Levin committed
    by Robert Chambers in New York City's Central Park.

Wright, Theon. *Rape in Paradise.*
  New York: Hawthorn Books, 1966.
    The 1931 murder of Joseph Kahawawai by Thomas Massie
    over the alleged rape of his wife, Thalia, in Honolulu,
    Hawaii.

Wright, William. *The von Bulow Affair.*
  New York: Delacorte, 1983.
    The 1980 attempted murder of Martha "Sunny" von Bulow
    and the trials of her husband Klaus in Newport, Rhode
    Island.
    See also:
      Dershowitz. *Reversal Of Fortune.*

Wylie, Max. *Gift of Janice.*
  Garden City, NY: Doubleday, 1964.
    The 1963 murders of Janice Wylie and Emily Hoffert in
    New York City.
    See also:
      Lefkowitz. *The Victims.*

Young, William. *Postmortem.*
  Amherst, MA: University of Massachusetts Press, 1985.
    The controversial trial and execution, for a 1920 double
    murder in Braintree, Massachusetts, of immigrant anarchists
    Nicola Sacco and Bartolomeo Vanzetti.
    See also:
      Fraenkel. *The Sacco-Vanzetti Case.*
      Russell. *Sacco & Vanzetti.*

Index To Murder Ink

Benson, Margaret *see* Greenya. Mewshaw.
Berkowitz, David. *see* Abrahamsen. Klauner.
Beyond All Reason. Smith
Beyond Obsession. Hammer.
Beyond Reason. Englade.
Bianchi, Kenneth *see* O'Brien. Schwartz.
The Billionaire Boys Club. Horton.
Birdman of Alcatraz Gaddis.
Birthright. Watkins.
Bitter Harvest. Corcoran.
The "Black Dahlia" Murder *see* Gilmore.
Blind Faith. McGinniss.
Blind Justice. Gibson.
Blood Brothers. Soble.
Blood Games. Bledsoe.
Blood Echoes. Cook.
Blood Justice. Smead.
Blood Relations. Greenya.
Blood Will Tell. Bosco.
Bonnie & Clyde *see* Milner.
Borden, Lizzie *see* Kent. Spiering.
The Boston Strangler. Frank.
The Broken Circle. Barker.
Brothers In Blood. Howard.
Brown, "Billie" *see* Brownell.
Bundy, Theodore *see* Kendall. Larsen. Michaud. Rule. Winn.
Buono, Angelo *see* O'Brien. Schwartz.
Burden of Proof. Crey.
Buried Dreams. Cahill.
Buried Secrets. Humes.
The Burning Bed. McNulty.

The "Candy Man" *see* Olsen.
Carr: Five Years Of Rape and Murder. Buchanan.
The CBS Murders. Hammer.
Chapman, Mark David *see* Fogo. Jones.
Circumstantial Evidence. Earley.
The "CHIPS Murder". Cantlupe.

Of Long Memory. Nossiter.
Once Upon A Time. MacLean.
The Onion Field. Wambaugh.
The Only Living Witness. Michaud.
Orders To Kill. Pepper.
Oswald, Lee Harvey *see* Bishop. Lane. Manchester. United
 States.

Phagan, Mary *see* Frey. Golden.
"Phantom Of The Opera Murder" *see* Black.
The Phantom Prince. Kendall.
The Pied Piper Of Tucson. Moser.
Poison Mind. Good.
Poisoned Blood. Ginsburg,.
Poisoned Dreams. Gray.
The "Porno Kings Murder" *see* McCumber.
Portrait Of A Racist. Massengill.
"Posse Comitatus Massacre" *see* Corcoran.
Postmortem. Young.
"Post-Traumatic Stress Syndrome Murder" *see* Bain
Preacher's Girl. Schultze.
The "Preppie Murder" *see* Wolfe.
The Price Of Experience. Sullivan.
The Professor and the Prostitute. Wolfe.
Prophet Of Death. Earley.
Puente, Dorothea *see* Blackburn. Norton.

Ramirez, Richard *see* Carlo. Linedecker.
Rancho Mirage. Sarlyan.
Rape in Paradise. Wright.
Ray, James, Earl *see* Frank. McMillan. Pepper. Ray.
Reasonable Doubts. Dershowitz.
The "Recovered Memory Murder" *see* Franklin. MacLean.
Reversal Of Fortune. Dershowitz.
"R.F.K. Must Die!" Kaiser.
Rice, William Marsh *see* Friedland.
Righteous Carnage. Benford.
The Road To Yuba City. Kidder.

THE RAPE REFERENCE
A Resource For People At Risk

Nearly 150,000 rapes are *reported* every year in America. As few as 625,000 to as many as 2,000,000 rapes may go *unreported.* 99.9% of rape victims are women and children. Rape is an ugly fact of life. **The Rape Reference** is about the facts of rape.

The Rape Reference is made up of five complementary parts - *America's Rape Laws:* Selected excerpts from current criminal rape laws of all fifty states carefully edited into plain non-legal English for the general adult reader; *Rape Statistics:* The "who, what, when, where" statistics of sexual assault. Over two decades of authoritative collected rape facts and figures gathered from the victims of sexual violence; *Rape Readings:* Many expert and first person writings on all forms of sexual coercion. Hundreds of books selected for those most at risk, covering every aspect of rape, written not in technical "expert-to-expert" jargon but in plain "person-to-person" English; *The Rape Glossary:* Plain everyday English definitions of the medical-legal words and phrases associated with rape; and *America's Rape Hot Lines:* Rape counseling and crisis intervention telephone hot lines serving nearly three hundred cities and towns, urban, suburban, and rural, in every state.

The information contained in **The Rape Reference** is drawn from hundreds of individual authoritative sources and is designed by the editors, a law librarian and a textbook editor, to be your all-in-one easy-to-use resource on rape and sexual violence.

EXCELLENT BOOKS ORDER FORM

(Please xerox this form so it will be available to other readers.)

Please send

Copy(ies)

_____ of THE MURDER REFERENCE @ $16.95 each
_____ of THE RAPE REFERENCE @ $16.95 each
_____ of LANDMARK DECISIONS @ $14.95 each
_____ of LANDMARK DECISIONS II @ $15.95 each
_____ of LANDMARK DECISIONS III @ $15.95 each
_____ of LANDMARK DECISIONS IV @ $15.95 each
_____ of LANDMARK DECISIONS V @ $16.95 each
_____ of ABORTION DECISIONS: THE 1970's @ $15.95 each
_____ of ABORTION DECISIONS: THE 1980's @ $15.95 each
_____ of ABORTION DECISIONS: THE 1990's @ $15.95 each
_____ of CIVIL RIGHTS DECISIONS: 19th CENTURY @ $16.95 ea.
_____ of CIVIL RIGHTS DECISIONS: 20th CENTURY @ $16.95 ea.
_____ of FREEDOM OF SPEECH DECISIONS @ $16.95 each
_____ of FREEDOM OF THE PRESS DECISIONS @ $16.95 each
_____ of FREEDOM OF RELIGION DECISIONS @ $16.95 each
_____ of THE ADA HANDBOOK @ $15.95 each

Name: _____

Address: _____

City: _____ **State:** _____ **Zip:** _____

Add $1 per book for shipping and handling
California residents add sales tax

OUR GUARANTEE: Any Excellent Book may be returned at
any time for any reason and a full refund will be made.

Mail your check or money order to: Excellent Books,
Post Office Box 927105, San Diego, California 92192-7105
or call/fax (619) 457-4895